POEMS

Wadsworth Handbook and Anthology

C. F. MAIN
Rutgers University

PETER J. SENG
Connecticut College

SECOND EDITION

POEMS

Wadsworth Handbook and Anthology

WADSWORTH PUBLISHING COMPANY, INC.
Belmont, California

COPYRIGHTS AND ACKNOWLEDGMENTS

GEORGE ALLEN & UNWIN LTD.—for "Dread," from *The Collected Works of J. M. Synge.*

BALLANTINE BOOKS, INC.—for "Hippopotamothalamion," by John Hall Wheelock, first appeared in *New Poems by American Poets # 2*, copyright 1957 by Ballantine Books, Inc.

JONATHAN CAPE LTD.—for "Naming of Parts," from *A Map of Verona* by Henry Reed; for "Out, Out," "Dust of Snow," "Stopping by Woods," "Desert Places," "The Road Not Taken," "Neither Out Far Nor In Deep," "Once by the Pacific," "The Onset," and "Come In," from *The Complete Poems of Robert Frost.*

CHATTO AND WINDUS LTD.—for "The Horse Chestnut Tree," from *Undercliff* by Richard Eberhart; for "On Shooting Particles beyond the World," "On a Squirrel Crossing the Road in Autumn, in New England," and "The Human Being Is a Lonely Creature," from *Collected Poems* by Richard Eberhart; for "Two Realities," from *Venus and a Comedy* by Aldous Huxley; and for "Arms and the Boy," from *Poems of Wilfred Owen.*

CHILMARK PRESS—for "Cock at Sea," from *Grooves in the Wind*, copyright C. A. Trypanis 1964.

COMMENTARY—for "The Line of an American Poet," by Reed Whittemore, reprinted from *Commentary*, March 1954, copyright American Jewish Committee. Also by permission of the author.

CONSTABLE AND COMPANY LTD.—for "Leda and the Swan," by Oliver St. John Gogarty. Also by courtesy of Mr. Oliver D. Gogarty; for "I Have a Rendezvous with Death," by Alan Seeger.

THE CRESSET PRESS LTD.—for "The Watch," from *Collected Poems* by Frances Cornford.

CRITERION BOOKS, INC.—for "To Any Member of My Generation," and "To My Mother," from *Collected Poems of George Barker, 1930–1955*, copyright 1957 by George Barker, published by Criterion Books, Inc., 1958.

J. M. DENT & SONS LTD.—for "The Donkey," from *The Wild Knight* by G. K. Chesterton; and for "In my craft or sullen art," and "Do not go gentle into that good night," by Dylan Thomas. All these poems by permission of J. M. Dent & Sons, London.

DOUBLEDAY & COMPANY, INC.—for "The Waking," from *The Waking: Poems 1933–1953* by Theodore Roethke, copyright 1953 by Theodore Roethke; for "In a Prominent Bar in Secaucus One Day," from *Nude Descending a Staircase* by X. J. Kennedy. Both these poems reprinted by permission of Doubleday & Company, Inc.

E. P. DUTTON & CO., INC.—for "The Donkey," from *The Wild Knight and Other Poems* by G. K. Chesterton, published by E. P. Dutton & Co., Inc., and reprinted with their permission.

NORMA MILLAY ELLIS—for "God's World," copyright 1913, 1941 by Edna St. Vincent Millay, from *Renascence and Other Poems* by Edna St. Vincent Millay, Harper & Brothers. By permission of Norma Millay Ellis.

PAUL ENGLE—for "Twilight." Copyright by Paul Engle.

EYRE AND SPOTTISWOODE LTD.—for "Captain Carpenter," from *Selected Poems* by John Crowe Ransom.

FABER & FABER LTD.—for "Musée des Beaux Arts," "O Where Are You Going," and "The Fall of Rome," from *Collected Shorter Poems, 1930–1944* by W. H. Auden; for "To Any Member of My Generation," and "To My Mother," from *Collected Poems* by George Barker; for "Nobody loses all the time," "Next to of course god," and "What if a much of a which of a wind," from *Selected Poems* by E. E. Cummings; for "Gerontion," and "Prelude I," by T. S. Eliot; for "Still, Citizen Sparrow," "The Death of a Toad," and "Piazza di Spagna, Early Morning," from *Poems 1943–56* by Richard Wilbur; for "Cock at Sea," from *The Cocks of Hades* by C. A. Trypanis; and for "The Monster," from *My Sad Captains* by Thom Gunn.

FARRAR, STRAUS & GIROUX, INC.—for "Plot Improbable, Character Unsympathetic." Reprinted from *The Scarecrow Christ* by Elder Olson, by permission of Farrar, Straus, & Giroux, Inc. Copyright 1954 by Elder Olson.

PREFACE

To Students:

Perhaps you are convinced that you don't like poetry. If you are, we, the authors of this textbook, will not quarrel with you. We are much less concerned with an indefinable essence known as "poetry" than with specific poems. We suspect that regardless of your general attitude toward "poetry," you do enjoy or have enjoyed at some time in your life certain individual poems: perhaps only nursery rhymes, the words of popular songs, or unprintable limericks—but *poems*. For most people liking depends on understanding. If you will study this book as carefully as you study your other college texts, you will understand more poems than you do now, and you will like them.

But does one study poems merely in order to like them? Yes and no. The study of literature, or of any of the humanities, gives pleasure and profit simultaneously, and without the former there is little of the latter. Certainly one useful by-product of studying poems is increased comprehension of all reading matter, including scientific textbooks. That reason alone should make the study seem worthwhile to some students. Furthermore, in addition to increasing one's general competence in language, poems provide a kind of knowledge unobtainable elsewhere, in college or out. This kind of knowledge is best described as "experiential," because it is not so much contained in a poem as in a reader's experience of a poem.

The aim of the book, then, is to show you how a poem imparts an experience. It does so by means of words, images, figures, symbols, rhythms, sounds, and tone. Although the book takes up these elements in separate chapters, it would be a mistake to regard them as separable in a poem. The next to the last chapter, therefore, treats the whole poem, which is something more significant than the sum of its parts.

The final chapter considers what makes a poem good or bad. The poems that we regard as bad, by the way, are not confined entirely to this chapter. Each chapter provides poems for study, and terms (printed in **bold face**) useful in literary discussion. The terms will help you say something more interesting about a poem and less revealing about yourself than "I don't like it."

Some of the poems and some of the critical notions in this book you may already be familiar with from your earlier studies. You may discover that further study will increase your understanding and, hence, your enjoyment of poems you already know. But you will also find in this book many new and fresh poems to challenge your growing taste and understanding, and you should not hesitate to turn from the old to the new.

Chapter 1 means what it says when it advises you to use your dictionary. We have not provided annotation for words found in the standard college dictionaries. Access to a translation of the Bible is also presupposed; references are in this form: Genesis xix:32, meaning the nineteenth chapter of Genesis, verse 32.

To Instructors:

This revised edition of *Poems* is intended to be as flexible as possible. Although the order follows the arrangement used in the first edition, that order is not indispensable for instructors who are used to teaching the understanding and criticism of poems in another way. The various chapters (or parts of chapters) may be assigned as the instructor sees fit: adequate cross-referencing and a separate Index of Terms permit a different ordering of material.

Depending on their students' backgrounds, some instructors may want to omit certain topics as too specialized or analytical, or repetitious of earlier work. Thus the discussion of Petrarchan conceits, for example, or the chapters entitled "The Poet's Use of Other Figures" and "The Rhythm and Meter of a Poem" may be passed over lightly or omitted entirely if it seems right to do so. The various critical topics taken up in this book are not so tightly interlocked that omissions will defeat other material chosen for study.

The authors have tried to make this book a useful text for advanced as well as introductory classes. Experience has shown that some advanced students can be left on their own to master the basic critical notions, thus freeing the instructor to devote class time to more extended analyses of individual poems. It will be readily apparent that neither the critical discussions in the text nor the questions in the exercises exhaust the poems to which they are directed. Rather, those discussions and questions are focused first on the particular critical notion under discussion, and only later are intended to provoke more general analysis. The poems in each chapter have been chosen for the clarity with which they illustrate a given critical concept, but they will usually be found rich enough to provide material for general analysis or class discussion as well.

The poems included in this book were selected, first, for their intrinsic merits as poems or for their usefulness as examples. Many of them are the standard poems which, for excellence or teachability, could not be omitted from any handbook or anthology. Others, not usually anthologized in texts of this sort, are nonetheless thoroughly representative of the best work of their authors. These poems have been singled out for their freshness or for the special appeal they may have for students who are resistant or hostile to the idea of studying poems.

While this book may be used as a self-teaching or self-reviewing text by advanced students, it also aims to provide material for class discussions, drills, and exercises, and for short or longer papers. Topics for short papers will readily be found in the various exercises (e.g., 1, 4, 6, 8, 9, 11, 12, 14, 16, 21, 24, 27, 33, 40, 46, 51, 53, 55, 56, 58, 59, and 61). Numerous subjects for long papers are provided by the groups of poems in the section titled "Poems for Comparison," as well as by the longer or more difficult individual poems included in that section.

This revision includes about 350 poems dating from the sixteenth century down to the present time. About three fourths of the total number of poems included are divided almost equally between two periods, the sixteenth to eighteenth centuries, and the nineteenth century (which includes American as well as English poems). The remaining one quarter of the poems are modern, including numerous new ones in this revised edition. The texts of poems prior to 1700 have had their spelling and punctuation reformed to modern usage; poems since that time are exactly reproduced from the best authoritative editions.

For helpful criticism in revising this book we are indebted to numerous instructors in the United States, Canada, Australia, and other countries of the British Commonwealth, who have used it in their classes and have sent us their practical suggestions and criticisms. And we are especially grateful to that more formidable group of critics, the students who have studied from the book, and who, more or less unwittingly, have provided us with the experience that has made a meaningful revision possible.

C. F. M.

P. J. S.

CONTENTS

xii CONTENTS

6. THE POET'S USE OF SYMBOL AND ALLEGORY, *133*

7. THE RHYTHM AND METER OF A POEM, *158*

8. THE SOUND OF A POEM, *185*

9. THE TONE OF A POEM, 210

10. THE WHOLE POEM, 239

PART TWO: POEMS FOR COMPARISON

PART
ONE

POEMS

FOR

DISCUSSION

1

THE WORDS
OF A POEM

Like any other writer, a poet makes arrangements of words. His medium is language, as the painter's medium is paint. Poems are his products—his secretions, someone has called them. No one of these products is the identical twin of any other. Yet regardless of the differences between individual poems, all poems are obviously alike in being made of words. For this reason a profitable discussion of a poem should begin (it may end almost anywhere) with its language.

PROSE AND POETRY

A good poet selects, arranges, and rearranges his words until he arrives at the one way in which they say what he wants them to say. If asked why he writes a poem rather than a prose work, he may answer that a poem best expresses what he feels and thinks. He may say that prose cannot convey an experience in the same way as a poem can, because it is not so accurate, pleasing, satisfying. He may even say that poems express meaning more powerfully because they persuade a man's feelings at the same time as they make statements to his mind. Finally, he could say that some things fizzle in prose, but go off like rockets in a poem.

Call It a Good Marriage

Call it a good marriage—
For no one ever questioned
Her warmth, his masculinity,
Their interlocking views;
Except one stray graphologist   5
Who frowned in speculation
At her h's and her s's,
His p's and w's.

Though few would still subscribe
To the monogamic axiom   10
That strife below the hip-bones
Need not estrange the heart,
Call it a good marriage:
More drew those two together,
Despite a lack of children,   15
Than pulled them apart.

Call it a good marriage:
They never fought in public,
They acted circumspectly
And faced the world with pride;   20
Thus the hazards of their love-bed
Were none of our damned business—
Till as jurymen we sat on
Two deaths by suicide.

ROBERT GRAVES

A prose account of this incident would be very different from the poem. A newspaper reporter, for instance, would avoid speculation about the couple's personal life. He would stick to the observable facts. Moreover, he would begin his story—not end it—with the information in the last two lines. He would omit everything else in the poem

except, perhaps, the fact in line 15, and this he would report at the end
of his story as "The couple had no children" or "There are no next of
kin." A psychiatrist, on the other hand, would largely ignore the
double suicide in concentrating on the events that may have led to it.
The possibility of "strife below the hip-bones" would claim a great deal
of attention in his case study. If interviews with friends of the couple
revealed the information contained in lines 18–20, he would probably
note it down as "repression." And he might be just slightly interested
in the fact that the couple once consulted a graphologist; even if they
did it as a "joke," he would detect in their action possible early symptoms of an insecure marriage.

Comments on the tragedy by friends and neighbors would come
closer to the human reality than a journalist's story or a psychiatrist's
case study. Most of what they would have to say would be summed up
in the poet's repetitious line, "Call it a good marriage." Besides, they
had known the couple socially, and it was perfectly evident that the
husband's and the wife's personalities were mutually complementary.
What would shock the friends and neighbors would be the complete
discrepancy between the known manner of their married life and the
tragic manner of their deaths.

Thus three different prose accounts of the same event would each tell
only part of the story. The journalist would be interested in the part
that was news, the suicide pact; the psychiatrist would concentrate on
symptoms of neurosis or emotional disturbance in the marriage;
friends would be baffled by the disparity between what they knew of
the couple and the double suicide. It is the poet who attempts to
present the total situation with all its tensions and contradictions. He
arranges his information so that we first see the marriage from the
outside, then are led more personally into it, and are finally brought to
the heart of the matter. In each stanza he repeats the opening line of
the poem, and with each repetition it seems progressively less accurate.
He tells us of the couple's *interlocking views* (line 4) as though a
union of minds were enough for a happy marriage. The only skeptic is
a *graphologist,* and a *stray* one at that, who is bothered by the way the
husband and wife shape a few of their letters. As a sophisticated modern, the poet is scornful of the *monogamic axiom* (line 10) that sex is
unimportant in marriage; and though *a lack of children* (line 15)
might suggest some incompatibility on this score, he easily dismisses
the notion in view of the couple's overwhelming evidences of closeness.

Besides, as he frankly admits, it is *none of our damned business* (line 22) until the public act of suicide demands an official explanation by a coroner's jury.

Thus the poet's arrangement of the story reveals not the incongruity but the congruity of the ending. He reinforces the contrast between the appearance and the reality of the marriage by contrasts between the words and phrases he chooses: *warmth, masculinity* vs. *interlocking views; strife below the hip-bones* vs. *monogamic axiom; fought in public* vs. *acted circumspectly.* He uses the opening line as a refrain: it was what everyone was always saying. He rhymes the fourth and eighth lines of each stanza, marking and giving finality to a unit of thought. Finally, although his language is very close to ordinary conversational prose, he does use a three-beat meter, which subtly plays on our feelings by setting up a rhythmic pattern and then fulfilling it.

Like some writers of prose, a poet occasionally conveys information, but in doing so he is only beginning his work. Beyond giving information, a poet uses words and sounds that will appeal to the reader's or hearer's feelings; he uses language that is meant to reverberate in the imagination and memory. Finally, a poet is not like a camera, looking at the world around him merely to record its outward surfaces; his view is rather that of the human eye, which sees not only the outer forms of things but also their inner significances.

EXERCISE 1

The difference between two ways of looking at an event can be studied by comparing a poem about a rural tragedy with an imaginary newspaper account of the same event.

"Out, Out—"

The buzz-saw snarled and rattled in the yard
And made dust and dropped stove-length sticks of wood,
Sweet-scented stuff when the breeze drew across it.
And from there those that lifted eyes could count
Five mountain ranges one behind the other   5
Under the sunset far into Vermont.
And the saw snarled and rattled, snarled and rattled,
As it ran light, or had to bear a load.
And nothing happened: day was all but done.

Call it a day, I wish they might have said   10
To please the boy by giving him the half hour
That a boy counts so much when saved from work.
His sister stood beside them in her apron
To tell them "Supper." At the word, the saw,
As if to prove saws knew what supper meant,   15
Leaped out at the boy's hand, or seemed to leap—
He must have given the hand. However it was,
Neither refused the meeting. But the hand!
The boy's first outcry was a rueful laugh,
As he swung toward them holding up the hand   20
Half in appeal, but half as if to keep
The life from spilling. Then the boy saw all—
Since he was old enough to know, big boy
Doing a man's work, though a child at heart—
He saw all spoiled. "Don't let him cut my hand off—   25
The doctor, when he comes. Don't let him, sister!"
So. But the hand was gone already.
The doctor put him in the dark of ether.
He lay and puffed his lips out with his breath.
And then—the watcher at his pulse took fright.   30
No one believed. They listened at his heart.
Little—less—nothing!—and that ended it.
No more to build on there. And they, since they
Were not the one dead, turned to their affairs.

ROBERT FROST

Lancaster, Nov. 18—John R. Adams, 15, son of Mr. and Mrs. James Adams, Route 3, Riverton, died last Saturday evening as a result of injuries he received while operating a power saw on his parents' farm.

The accident happened late Saturday afternoon while young Adams, his brother Stephen, 12, and his father were sawing logs. Apparently the boy was momentarily distracted while feeding a piece of wood into the blade, which caught his hand and amputated it.

The youth's sister, Maud, 17, was witness to the accident. She said that her mother had sent her to call her father and brothers to supper. The accident occurred, she said, just as she called out to them.

Mr. Adams immediately drove to nearby Riverton for a doctor. He finally located Dr. E. L. White and drove him back to the farm.

Dr. White said that when he arrived the boy was already in shock from loss of blood, and that it was impossible to save him. The cause of death was listed by the coroner as accidental.

Funeral services on Tuesday were held in Riverton Congregational Church, and interment was in Good Hope Cemetery.

1. Many details in the poem could not properly be included in a newspaper story because they are inferences and opinions rather than facts. What are these details? Why does the poem omit certain details that the newspaper account includes?

2. What lines, phrases, and words in the poem hint at the catastrophe to come? Why do you suppose the poet includes the information in lines 4–6 in the poem? Why does he repeat the substance of line 1 in line 7?

3. The appearance of the boy's sister (line 13) is extremely abrupt. Why? Why is *supper* (line 14) in quotation marks?

4. The accident is shocking, but it is not so plainly detailed as to be gruesome. How and why does Frost avoid gruesome details?

5. Lines 27–33 consist of eight short, factual sentences. What is their effect after the more complicated sentences earlier in the poem?

6. Do the last two lines indicate that the family do not care about the boy? How else can one account for their seeming callousness?

7. Why is the title in quotation marks? Does it remind you of anything?

THE INDISPENSABLE DICTIONARY

A reader of a prose work can sometimes skip over unfamiliar words without disaster: a magazine article will still make sense; the plot of a novel will still be clear. But in a poem every word is important. The loss of a single word may make a poem incomprehensible or distort its meaning. The very words skipped in a poem are likely to be its operative words, the ones on which the meaning especially depends.

Hap

If but some vengeful god would call to me
From up the sky, and laugh: "Thou suffering thing,
Know that thy sorrow is my ecstasy,
That thy love's loss is my hate's profiting!"

Then would I bear it, clench myself, and die,   5
Steeled by the sense of ire unmerited;
Half-eased in that a Powerfuller than I
Had willed and meted me the tears I shed.

But not so. How arrives it joy lies slain,
And why unblooms the best hope ever sown?   10
—Crass Casualty obstructs the sun and rain,
And dicing Time for gladness casts a moan. . . .
These purblind Doomsters had as readily strown
Blisses about my pilgrimage as pain.

THOMAS HARDY

Only a reader with a large vocabulary will know all the words in this poem without using his dictionary. Suppose, however, that a reader were so foolhardy as to try to understand the poem without help. At the outset he might absurdly assume that the title is a short form of *happy;* the words *laugh* (line 2) and *joy* (line 9) would seem to support that definition. But obviously the "I" in the poem is not happy, for he says that "joy lies slain" (line 9). To whom, then, does the title apply? It must, surely, apply to the god (line 1) who causes sorrow (line 3). By this time the reader is wallowing in confusion. What he will do with the rest of the poem is better imagined than described, but it seems likely that he will reach some such conclusion as this: "God is happy because man is unhappy." A few minutes with a dictionary would show him how mistaken he is.

EXERCISE 2

In the following poems underline every word whose meaning you are not positive of. Before consulting your dictionary, give each of the underlined words the best tentative definition that you can devise. Then, when you have compared your tentative definitions with those in the dictionary, be prepared to explain how you would have misunderstood the poems if you had relied on your own uncorrected impulses to explain their words.

The Maldive Shark

About the Shark, phlegmatical one,
Pale sot of the Maldive sea,
The sleek little pilot-fish, azure and slim,
How alert in attendance be.

From his saw-pit of mouth, from his charnel of maw   5
They have nothing of harm to dread,
But liquidly glide on his ghastly flank
Or before his Gorgonian head;
Or lurk in the port of serrated teeth
In white triple tiers of glittering gates,   10
And there find a haven when peril's abroad,
An asylum in jaws of the Fates!
They are friends; and friendly they guide him to prey,
Yet never partake of the treat—
Eyes and brains to the dotard lethargic and dull,   15
Pale ravener of horrible meat.

HERMAN MELVILLE

Aubade

O, Lady, awake! The azure moon
    Is rippling in the verdant skies,
The owl is warbling his soft tune,
    Awaiting but thy snowy eyes.
The joys of future years are past,   5
    Tomorrow's hopes are fled away;
Still let us love and even at last
    We shall be happy yesterday.

The early beam of rosy night
    Drives off the ebon moon afar,   10
Whilst through the murmur of the light
    The huntsman winds his mad guitar.
Then, Lady, wake! My brigantine
    Pants, neighs, and prances to be free;
Tell the creation I am thine,   15
    To some rich desert fly with me.

ANONYMOUS
(*Nineteenth Century*)

Grief

I tell you, hopeless grief is passionless—
That only men incredulous of despair,
Half-taught in anguish, through the midnight air,
Beat upward to God's throne in loud access
Of shrieking and reproach. Full desertness   5
In souls, as countries, lieth silent-bare
Under the blanching, vertical eye-glare
Of the absolute Heavens. Deep-hearted man, express
Grief for thy Dead in silence like to death;
Most like a monumental statue set   10
In everlasting watch and moveless woe
Till itself crumble to the dust beneath.
Touch it: the marble eyelids are not wet—
If it could weep, it could arise and go.

ELIZABETH BARRETT BROWNING

DENOTATION AND CONNOTATION

Understanding a poem presupposes knowing the connotation as well as the denotation of its words. **Denotation** is the dictionary meaning of a word. **Connotation** is the shade of meaning words have acquired through association and use. A dictionary defines the word *galleon* as "a sailing vessel of the fifteenth and following centuries, often having three or four decks, and used for commerce." This is the denotation of *galleon*. Among its connotations are "romance," "adventure," "piracy"; it brings to mind the Spanish Main, cutlasses, buccaneers, and pieces of eight. These connotations are part of the total meaning of the word.

In each of these columns the words have the same denotation but different connotations.

Canis familiaris	dame	murder	obese
canine quadruped	miss	slay	bloated
cur	wench	execute	portly
doggy	doll	kill	plump

The words in the first column, for instance, all denote "dog." Yet they carry very different connotations. The first word is associated with zoologists rather than with owners of pets; it would be appropriate in a scientific context. The second might be used by a pretentious or facetious person. The difference in the connotations of the last two can be illustrated by the remarks that two people might make to describe the same event. One might say, "There's a cur in the backyard"; the other, "There's a doggy in the backyard." Although the two remarks denote the same event, they obviously do not "say" the same thing.

Words differ in amount of connotation. Some—like *boy, dog, food, small*—have almost none out of a given context; others—like *atom, rose,* and *heart*—have absorbed so much color from the backgrounds in which they have occurred that by themselves they are rich in connotation. Poets use both kinds. They may choose one word for its precise denotation, another for its complex associations.

EXERCISE 3

The following words are richly connotative for most readers. Briefly explain their denotations, using a dictionary if necessary, and then describe their connotations.

swaddling clothes	swashbuckler
Hun	occidental
epistle	kremlin
Hiroshima	Freudian
French postcard	peacock

Understanding a poem sometimes depends more on a reader's grasping the connotations of its words than on his knowing their denotations. For example, in the following poem much of a husband's bitter feelings toward his wife is conveyed by the connotations of the words he uses:

Sonnet 29

Am I failing? For no longer can I cast
A glory round about this head of gold.
Glory she wears, but springing from the mould;
Not like the consecration of the Past!

Is my soul beggared? Something more than earth   5
I cry for still: I cannot be at peace
In having Love upon a mortal lease.
I cannot take the woman at her worth!
Where is the ancient wealth wherewith I clothed
Our human nakedness, and could endow   10
With spiritual splendour a white brow
That else had grinned at me the fact I loathed?
A kiss is but a kiss now! and no wave
Of a great flood that whirls me to the sea.
But, as you will! we'll sit contentedly,   15
And eat our pot of honey on the grave.

GEORGE MEREDITH
(from *Modern Love*)

The word *mould* (line 3) suggests that whatever glory the wife still
has for her husband is just the efflorescence of decay. In the past her
glory was a "consecration" (line 4)—something holy. Now his soul is
not merely poor in love for her, but it is "beggared" (line 5). That
word summons up a picture of tattered and mendicant poverty. She is
no more than so much clay to him, and he desolately cries out (he does
not grieve or weep) for something better (lines 5–6). He cannot rest
in a love that he possesses only on a "mortal lease" (lines 6–7); the
adjective *mortal* suggests not only a human lease, but also a finite and a
fatal lease. *Lease* itself connotes a merely legal arrangement. In line 8
the important word is the basic and physiological *woman*: substitute
synonyms like *the lady, my mistress, my wife,* and the sense of the line
changes completely. In line 10 *nakedness* implies, with its sensual over-
tones, the nuptial relationship.

The word *grinned* (line 12) suggests the grimace of a skull because
it appears in the same context with *mould, earth, mortal,* and the final
word, *grave.* The horror of the situation culminates in the two final
lines of the poem: "we'll sit contentedly"—although there has not been
a moment of contentment in the poem—and "eat our pot" (not dish or
jar or bowl) of honey on the grave. The poem ends with the earthiest
word for interment: not *tomb,* which is dignified and noble; not
sepulchre, which is ecclesiastical; not *vault* nor *mausoleum,* words that
suggest an attempt to preserve what has been lost; but *grave,* which
connotes mould, decay, and worms.

Time

Unfathomable Sea! whose waves are years,
  Ocean of Time, whose waters of deep woe
Are brackish with the salt of human tears!
  Thou shoreless flood, which in thy ebb and flow
Claspest the limits of mortality,   5
And sick of prey, yet howling on for more,
Vomitest thy wrecks on its inhospitable shore;
Treacherous in calm, and terrible in storm,
  Who shall put forth on thee,
    Unfathomable Sea?   10

PERCY BYSSHE SHELLEY

1. What synonyms can you give for the words *unfathomable, woe, brackish, mortality, sick, prey, howling, inhospitable, treacherous, terrible*?
2. Describe as nearly as possible the difference between the synonyms and the words that Shelley uses.

Richard Cory

Whenever Richard Cory went down town,
We people on the pavement looked at him:
He was a gentleman from sole to crown,
Clean favored, and imperially slim.

And he was always quietly arrayed,   5
And he was always human when he talked;
But still he fluttered pulses when he said,
"Good-morning," and he glittered when he walked.

And he was rich—yes, richer than a king—
And admirably schooled in every grace: 10
In fine, we thought that he was everything
To make us wish that we were in his place.

So on we worked, and waited for the light,
And went without the meat, and cursed the bread;
And Richard Cory, one calm summer night,   15
Went home and put a bullet through his head.

EDWIN ARLINGTON ROBINSON

1. What words in this poem are effective primarily because of their connotation?
2. Compare this poem with "Call It a Good Marriage." In which poem does the ending come as the greater surprise?

POETIC DICTION

The words that a poet or any other writer or speaker chooses to use are called his **diction**. Critics and poets have long been interested in the relationship between the diction of poetry and the diction of ordinary speech. In some ages they have held that the two dictions resemble each other closely; in others, they have held the opposite view. In the so-called Augustan Age of English poetry (about 1660–1790), for instance, the authors of serious poems avoided words that had acquired "low" or familiar associations from extensive use; in place of these they used fancier or more dignified expressions. Thus Smollett's "Ode to Leven-Water" (page 262) has *swain* for *shepherd, lave* for *wash,* and *scaly brood* for *school of fish.* Against such embellished diction some poets of the late eighteenth and early nineteenth centuries protested. In 1800 Wordsworth asserted that "there neither is, nor can be, any essential difference between the language of prose and metrical composition." He thought that a poem should not have a special kind of language, but that it should be written in "a selection of the language really spoken by men." Consequently when he wrote about a shepherd, he called him "a shepherd"; sheep he called "sheep." Expressions like "keeper of the fleecy people" he labeled as "poetic diction"—a term that always had a derogatory connotation to him.

But Wordsworth had his own notions of what poetic diction should be; his own diction is no less poetic merely because it differs from the diction of the poets that preceded him. The word *selection* in the passage just quoted ("a selection of the language really spoken by men") implies that Wordsworth did not consider the language of poetry identical with the spoken language. He knew that a good poet selects his words much more carefully than a casual talker ever does.

The term **poetic diction,** then, need not be a term of abuse; it may instead refer to the total differences between the language of poetry and the language of common speech at any given time. In our own day T. S. Eliot has said that every age has its own poetic diction.

DECORUM

The basis on which a poet selects his diction from the general supply of words is called **decorum.** E. E. Cummings follows a different decorum in each of the two following poems, with the result that the diction in one poem is very different from that in the other.

All in Green Went My Love Riding

All in green went my love riding

on a great horse of gold
into the silver dawn.

four lean hounds crouched low and smiling
the merry deer ran before.   5

Fleeter be they than dappled dreams
the swift sweet deer
the red rare deer.

Four red roebuck at a white water
the cruel bugle sang before.   10

Horn at hip went my love riding
riding the echo down
into the silver dawn.

four lean hounds crouched low and smiling
the level meadows ran before.   15

Softer be they than slippered sleep
the lean lithe deer
the fleet flown deer.

Four fleet does at a gold valley
the famished arrow sang before.   20

Bow at belt went my love riding
riding the mountain down
into the silver dawn.

four lean hounds crouched low and smiling
the sheer peaks ran before.   25

Paler be they than daunting death
the sleek slim deer
the tall tense deer.

Four tall stags at a green mountain
the lucky hunter sang before.   30

All in green went my love riding
on a great horse of gold
into the silver dawn.

four lean hounds crouched low and smiling
my heart fell dead before.   35

E. E. CUMMINGS

Nobody Loses All the Time

nobody loses all the time

i had an uncle named
Sol who was a born failure and
nearly everybody said he should have gone
into vaudeville perhaps because my Uncle Sol could   5
sing McCann He Was a Diver on Xmas Eve like Hell Itself which
may or may not account for the fact that my Uncle

Sol indulged in that possibly most inexcusable
of all to use a highfalootin phrase
luxuries that is or to   10
wit farming and be
it needlessly
added

my Uncle Sol's farm
failed because the chickens   15
ate the vegetables so
my Uncle Sol had a
chicken farm till the
skunks ate the chickens when

my Uncle Sol   20
had a skunk farm but
the skunks caught cold and
died and so
my Uncle Sol imitated the
skunks in a subtle manner   25

or by drowning himself in the watertank
but somebody who'd given my Uncle Sol a Victor
Victrola and records while he lived presented to
him upon the auspicious occasion of his decease a
scrumptious not to mention splendiferous funeral with   30
tall boys in black gloves and flowers and everything and

i remember we all cried like the Missouri
when my Uncle Sol's coffin lurched because
somebody pressed a button
(and down went   35
my Uncle
Sol

and started a worm farm)

E. E. CUMMINGS

   No one would ever make the mistake of thinking that a line or
phrase quoted from one of these poems was taken from the other. The
diction of the first poem is romantic and heraldic, as if it were a
medieval troubadour's song or a description of a medieval tapestry.
The diction of the second has the distinctive twang of American
speech. Cummings would have violated decorum—that is, he would
have had two conflicting bases for choosing his words in one poem—if
he had used such adjectives as *scrumptious* and *splendiferous* in "All in
Green." These words are facetious, and they are therefore appropriate
in "Nobody Loses," a facetious poem. Decorum demands appropriate
diction.

Decorum of language is a very useful concept to a poet, for if he did not have a decorum he could not violate it. Poets in every age, but especially in the seventeenth and twentieth centuries, have delighted in violating decorum. Donne, for instance, begins a love poem with language appropriate to back-fence argument: "For God's sake, hold your tongue!" This opening is much more unexpected than it would be if a decorum for love poems had not been established. The unexpected always depends for its existence on the expected.

To Any Member of My Generation

What was it you remember—the summer mornings
Down by the river at Richmond with a girl,
And as you kissed, clumsy in bathing costumes,
History guffawed in a rosebush. O what a warning—
If only we had known, if only we had known!　　　　　5
And when you looked in mirrors was this meaning
Plain as the pain in the centre of a pearl?
Horrible tomorrow in Teutonic postures
Making absurd the past we cannot disown?

Whenever we kissed we cocked the future's rifles　　　10
And from our wild-oat words, like dragon's teeth,
Death underfoot now arises; when we were gay
Dancing together in what we hoped was life,
Who was it in our arms but the whores of death
Whom we have found in our beds today, today?　　　15

GEORGE BARKER

Richmond (2): resort city up the Thames River a short distance from London.　dragon's teeth (11): In Greek mythology, when Cadmus slew a dragon and sowed its teeth on a plain, armed men sprang up from them.

This poem opens nostalgically with an invitation to recall pleasant summer scenes of love-making by a river. Suddenly, in line 4, History is discovered lurking in a rosebush and watching the lovers like a dirty-minded old man. The reader is surprised, for he does not expect *History* to be followed by *guffawed;* decorum seems to require something more dignified. Yet this unexpected juxtaposition is essential to what the poem is saying. History gave a ribald jeer at the innocent young

lovers, even as the coming of World War II mocked a whole generation. Barker is saying that his generation led their usual lives, ignorant
of the coming war and unaware that they were soon to be swallowed
up in it.

POETIC LICENSE

Poets are allowed—and take—much greater freedom with language
than other writers and speakers. **Poetic license,** the right of a poet to
deviate from standard practices in order to achieve a certain effect,
allows him to ignore rules that prose writers customarily follow. Poetic
license takes many forms. A poet may, for instance, invent new words
or jam together old ones; he may leave their referents implied rather
than stated. He may use a noun to do the work of an adjective or verb,
an adjective to do the work of a noun. When Shakespeare's Cleopatra
says of Caesar,

> He words me, girls, he words me, that I should not
> Be noble to myself

she is turning the noun *word* into a verb. Among modern poets E. E.
Cummings especially uses this device:

What If a Much of a Which of a Wind

> what if a much of a which of a wind
> gives the truth to summer's lie;
> bloodies with dizzying leaves the sun
> and yanks immortal stars awry?
> Blow king to beggar and queen to seem   5
> (blow friend to fiend: blow space to time)
> —when skies are hanged and oceans drowned,
> the single secret will still be man
>
> what if a keen of a lean wind flays
> screaming hills with sleet and snow: 10
> strangles valleys by ropes of thing
> and stifles forests in white ago?

Blow hope to terror; blow seeing to blind
(blow pity to envy and soul to mind)
—whose hearts are mountains, roots are trees,   15
it's they shall cry hello to the spring

what if a dawn of a doom of a dream
bites this universe in two,
peels forever out of his grave
and sprinkles nowhere with me and you?   20
Blow soon to never and never to twice
(blow life to isn't: blow death to was)
—all nothing's only our hugest home;
the most who die, the more we live

E. E. CUMMINGS

Poets also take liberties with syntax, the order of words in a sentence. There are even a few poems consisting entirely of words and phrases rather than of complete sentences. But the most common syntactical liberties are various kinds of inversions of prose order. "All in green went my love riding," writes Cummings, rather than "My love went riding all in green." Requirements of rhyme and rhythm often make it necessary to change the normal order of words, though excessive use of this license, as in the metrical paraphrase of Psalm 23 (see page 175), is a defect in a poem. A poet is supposed to be able to control the form of his poem; it should not control him.

EXERCISE 5

What kinds of poetic license are found in these poems?

To-day and Thee

The appointed winners in a long-stretch'd game;
The course of Time and nations—Egypt, India, Greece and Rome;
The past entire, with all its heroes, histories, arts, experiments,
Its store of songs, inventions, voyages, teachers, books,
Garner'd for now and thee—To think of it!   5
The heirdom all converged in thee!

WALT WHITMAN

Spring and Fall: To a Young Child

Margaret, are you grieving
Over Goldengrove unleaving?
Leaves, like the things of man, you
With your fresh thoughts care for, can you?
Ah! as the heart grows older   5
It will come to such sights colder
By and by, nor spare a sigh
Though worlds of wanwood leafmeal lie;
And yet you will weep and know why.
Now no matter, child, the name: 10
Sorrow's springs are the same.
Nor mouth had, no nor mind, expressed
What heart heard of, ghost guessed:
It is the blight man was born for,
It is Margaret you mourn for.   15

GERARD MANLEY HOPKINS

PARAPHRASE

A bold use of poetic license, coupled with unfamiliar words, may
make it difficult for a reader to grasp the sense of a poem. One useful
way to help overcome the difficulty is to write a paraphrase. A **paraphrase** is a word-for-word rendering of a poem, or part of a poem, into
clear prose. Although it is seldom necessary to paraphrase a whole
poem, here, for purposes of demonstration, is a poem followed by a
complete paraphrase.

On My First Daughter

Here lies to each her parent's ruth,
Mary, the daughter of their youth;
Yet all heaven's gifts, being heaven's due,
It makes the father less to rue.
At six months' end she parted hence   5
With safety of her innocence;

Whose soul heaven's Queen (whose name she bears),
In comfort of her mother's tears,
Hath placed amongst her virgin-train;
Where, while that severed doth remain,   10
This grave partakes the fleshly birth,
Which cover lightly, gentle earth.

BEN JONSON

It is a cause of regret to both her parents that Mary, born to them when they were young, lies dead and buried here. But since her father understands that all of heaven's gifts ultimately belong to heaven, his sadness is lessened. After six months of life she left this world, secure in her sinlessness; the Queen of Heaven, for whom she was named, has placed her soul among the ranks of her attendant virgins in order to comfort the human mother's sorrow. So long as the child's soul remains in heaven separated from her flesh, this grave will hold her body. May the kind earth cover it lightly.

The paraphrase maintains, as far as possible, the person, tense, voice, and mood of the poem. It clarifies elliptical expressions by writing out the idea in full. It disentangles unusual syntax. It provides synonyms for unfamiliar words.

The advantages of such an exercise are almost self-evident. The need to make a paraphrase slows a reader down; it forces him to examine each word, to understand what it means, and then to find a close equivalent. Paraphrasing enforces on an inexperienced reader the kind of close attention that keeps him from racing through a poem at the rapid pace with which he reads most ordinary prose.

But it is imperative to remember that paraphrasing poems is merely an exercise, a device for training a reader to observe care and accuracy. No paraphrase, however exact it may be, is a substitute for, or an equivalent of, the poem itself. A paraphrase is never the poem "in other words." It cannot capture the total meaning or the whole experience of a poem (see Chapter 10). The sense of the words is only one small part of a poem's meaning; other parts are conveyed by sound, rhythm, phrasing, and the very uniqueness of each word used in the poem. These are matters that cannot be paraphrased.

EXERCISE 6

Write a paraphrase of one or more of the following poems. Point out the principal differences between your paraphrases and the poems.

To Blossoms

Fair pledges of a fruitful tree,
    Why do ye fall so fast?
    Your date is not so past,
But you may stay yet here awhile,
    To blush and gently smile,   5
    And go at last.

What, were ye born to be
    An hour or half's delight,
    And so to bid good night?
'Twas pity Nature brought ye forth   10
    Merely to show your worth,
    And lose you quite.

But you are lovely leaves, where we
    May read how soon things have
    Their end, though ne'er so brave: 15
And after they have shown their pride
    Like you a while, they glide
    Into the grave.

ROBERT HERRICK

My Heart Leaps Up

My heart leaps up when I behold
    A rainbow in the sky:
So was it when my life began;
So is it now I am a man;
So be it when I shall grow old,   5
    Or let me die!
The Child is father of the Man;
And I could wish my days to be
Bound each to each by natural piety.

WILLIAM WORDSWORTH

The Trojan Horse

A horse I am, whom bit,
Rein, rod, nor spur, not fear;
When I my riders bear,
Within my womb, not on my back, they sit.
No streams I drink, nor care for grass nor corn;   5
Art me a monster wrought,
All nature's works to scorn.
A mother, I was without mother born;
In end all armed my father I forth brought;
What thousand ships, and champions of renown   10
Could not do free, I captive razed a town.

WILLIAM DRUMMOND

Before Disaster

Evening traffic homeward burns,
Swift and even on the turns,
Drifting weight in triple rows,
Fixed relation and repose.
This one edges out and by,   5
Inch by inch with steady eye.
But should error be increased,
Mass and moment are released;
Matter loosens, flooding blind,
Levels drivers to its kind.   10
Ranks of nations thus descend,
Watchful to a stormy end.
By a moment's calm beguiled,
I have got a wife and child.
Fool and scoundrel guide the State.   15
Peace is whore to Greed and Hate.
Nowhere may I turn to flee:
Action is security.
Treading change with savage heel,
We must live or die by steel.   20

YVOR WINTERS

On Seeing a Hair of Lucretia Borgia

Borgia, thou once wert almost too august,
And high for adoration;—now thou'rt dust!
All that remains of thee these plaits infold,
Calm hair, meand'ring with pellucid gold!

WALTER SAVAGE LANDOR

Lucretia Borgia (Title): (1480–1519); daughter of Pope Alexander VI and wife of the Duke of Ferrara; patron of the arts and one of the most beautiful women of the Italian Renaissance.

2

THE READER
AND THE POEM

Some inexperienced readers have misconceptions about what—if anything—a poem is supposed to be or do. The first part of this chapter treats certain preconceived notions about poems that hamper understanding; then the chapter goes on to suggest some attitudes and habits of thinking that assist understanding.

"POETIC" SUBJECTS

Perhaps the most widespread misconception about poems is the belief that they must be written about "poetic" subjects. According to this view poetic subjects must be pleasant—love, nature, beauty; unpleasant subjects are unpoetic and are therefore unsuited to poems. To trace this circular absurdity to its origin would be neither a profitable nor an easy task. It seems to be related somehow to the stereotyped view of the poet as a pale esthete, so preoccupied with moonlight and rainbows that he never condescends to look at real life. Actually there are no limitations

27

on the suitability of subjects for poems, for there are good poems on almost every conceivable subject. A poet is as free to write about a rusty automobile radiator as about a sunset.

The Fly

O hideous little bat, the size of snot,
With polyhedral eye and shabby clothes,
To populate the stinking cat you walk
The promontory of the dead man's nose,
Climb with the fine leg of a Duncan Phyfe   5
   The smoking mountains of my food
      And in a comic mood
   In mid-air take to bed a wife.

Riding and riding with your filth of hair
On gluey foot or wing, forever coy,   10
Hot from the compost and green sweet decay,
Sounding your buzzer like an urchin toy—
You dot all whiteness with diminutive stool,
   In the tight belly of the dead
      Burrow with hungry head   15
   And inlay maggots like a jewel.

At your approach the great horse stomps and paws
Bringing the hurricane of his heavy tail;
Shod in disease you dare to kiss my hand
Which sweeps against you like an angry flail;   20
Still you return, return, trusting your wing
   To draw you from the hunter's reach
      That learns to kill to teach
   Disorder to the tinier thing.

My peace is your disaster. For your death   25
Children like spiders cup their pretty hands
And wives resort to chemistry of war.
In fens of sticky paper and quicksands
You glue yourself to death. Where you are stuck
   You struggle hideously and beg   30
      You amputate your leg
   Imbedded in the amber muck.

But I, a man, must swat you with my hate,
Slap you across the air and crush your flight,
Must mangle with my shoe and smear your blood,   35
Expose your little guts pasty and white,
Knock your head sidewise like a drunkard's hat,
   Pin your wings under like a crow's,
      Tear off your flimsy clothes
And beat you as one beats a rat.   40

Then like Gargantua I stride among
The corpses strewn like raisins in the dust,
The broken bodies of the narrow dead
That catch the throat with fingers of disgust.
I sweep. One gyrates like a top and falls   45
   And stunned, stone blind, and deaf
      Buzzes its frightful F
And dies between three cannibals.

KARL SHAPIRO

This poem presents some mildly nasty experiences in frank language. It will perhaps never be chanted at a ladies' club luncheon, but it has achieved another kind of success because its observations are comically accurate and because the poet has developed the subject with much imagination, ingenuity, and gusto.

EXERCISE 7

Study the language in these poems; then explain why certain words must necessarily be gross and harsh if the poet is to express his subject honestly.

Ask Not to Know This Man

Ask not to know this man. If fame should speak
   His name in any metal, it would break.
Two letters were enough the plague to tear
   Out of his grave, and poison every ear.
A parcel of court dirt, a heap and mass   5
   Of all vice hurled together, there he was:

Proud, false, and treacherous, vindictive, all
That thought can add, unthankful, the laystall
Of putrid flesh alive! Of blood, the sink!
And so I leave to stir him, lest he stink.   10

BEN JONSON

name . . . metal (2): that is, inscribed on a metal plate on his
tomb. court dirt (5): refuse of the court. laystall (8): dung
heap.

from *Hugh Selwyn Mauberley*

IV

These fought in any case,
and some believing,
            pro domo, in any case . . .

Some quick to arm,
some for adventure,   5
some from fear of weakness,
some from fear of censure,
some for love of slaughter, in imagination,
learning later . . .
some in fear, learning love of slaughter;   10

Died some, pro patria,
            non "dulce" non "et decor" . . .
walked eye-deep in hell
believing in old men's lies, then unbelieving
came home, home to a lie,   15
home to many deceits,
home to old lies and new infamy;
usury age-old and age-thick
and liars in public places.

Daring as never before, wastage as never before.   20
Young blood and high blood,
fair cheeks, and fine bodies;

fortitude as never before
frankness as never before,
disillusions as never told in the old days,   25
hysterias, trench confessions,
laughter out of dead bellies.

V

There died a myriad,
And of the best, among them,
For an old bitch gone in the teeth,   30
For a botched civilization,

Charm, smiling at the good mouth,
Quick eyes gone under earth's lid,

For two gross of broken statues,
For a few thousand battered books.   35

EZRA POUND

fought (1): in World War I. **pro domo** (3): for the home.
pro patria, non "dulce" non "et decor" (11–12): "for the
fatherland, not 'sweetly' and not 'fittingly' "; parody of the
famous line of Horace (65–8 B.C.): *Dulce et decorum est pro
patria mori* ("It is sweet and fitting to die for the fatherland").

STOCK RESPONSE AND IRRELEVANT ASSOCIATION

Stock response is a reader's automatic, unthinking reaction to certain
words or subjects because of the associations that they have with his
natural, conventional feelings. All human beings have certain reservoirs
of deep feeling that can be tapped by the appropriate verbal stimula-
tion. It is these feelings that a demagogue seeks to stir with his insincere references to "Old Glory" and "the land of the free, the home of
the brave." The "patriotic" orator in Cummings' poem (page 219) is
such a demagogue. It is these reservoirs of natural feelings that a
sentimentalist depends on when he refers to "happy hours of carefree
childhood," or "little toddlers lisping prayers at father's knee." In the
same way, an unskillful poet, unable to prompt fresh or genuine feel-

ings with his verses, may attempt to exploit the natural, ready-made emotions that lie just below the surface of most human beings.

Paradise

"What is it like, in Paradise?"
The look of love in your mother's eyes.

"What do they do there all day long?"
The little children go singing a song.

"If I were there would I sing too?"   5
Ay, shout and sing the whole day through.

"But I'd have no toys there at all!"
St. Peter would whittle you out a ball.

"If there were trees could I have the fruit?"
Apples and pears and plums to boot.   10

"But I'd want you when the dusk grew deep!"
Nay, Mary would rock my child to sleep.

"But surely, mother, I'd want you yet!"
My darling, no! For you would forget.

"Forget? Is that so good a thing?"   15
Better than flowers in the spring.

"But if I saw you over the wall?"
You would not cry for me at all.

"In Paradise should I never cry?"
They only laugh—those folk that die.   20

"Then let me go to that dear place!"
Nay—I'll keep you yet by God's good grace.

"Apples and pears I'd have, you say!"
Bitter my bread, yet shall you stay.

"But I cried to-day for a spoiled game!"   25
I'd have you cry and live the same.

"But they laugh and run beneath the tree!"
Your heart shall break—yet stay with me!

"Mother, O mother, let me go!"
Nay now, my child, for I love you so.   30

ANNA HEMPSTEAD BRANCH

Surely no comment on the foregoing lines is needed.

Closely related to stock response is **irrelevant association,** a reader's reaction to certain words or subjects because of their connections with his personal experiences or prejudices. One reader—to take a simple example—will respond to the word *lobster* by feeling nauseated; another, by feeling hungry. Thus an irrelevant association may dispose a reader either favorably or unfavorably toward whatever stimulates it.

Both stock responses and irrelevant associations are inevitable. No one could entirely rid himself of them, nor would he want to. But every reader should be aware of the existence of stock responses and of his own liability to irrelevant association. These reactions are insidious because they require no conscious thought. Because they occur automatically, they can prevent a reader from enjoying a poem that he might otherwise enjoy, or encourage a reader to admire a poem that is not worthy of admiration, or even cause a reader to assume that he understands a poem when actually he misunderstands it.

The last mentioned error is the worst. Suppose, for instance, that a reader of the following poem were the sort of person who automatically feels sympathy for any suffering animal.

The Slaughter-House

Under the big 500-watted lamps, in the huge sawdusted
    government inspected slaughter-house,
head down from hooks and clamps, run on trolleys over
    troughs,
the animals die.   5
Whatever terror their dull intelligences feel
    or what agony distorts their most protruding eyes
the incommunicable narrow skulls conceal.

Across the sawdusted floor,
ignorant as children, they see the butcher's slow   10
    methodical approach
in the bloodied apron, leather cap above, thick square
    shoes below,
struggling to comprehend this unique vision upside
    down,   15
and then approximate a human scream
    as from the throat slit like a letter
the blood empties, and the windpipe, like a blown valve,
    spurts steam.

But I, sickened equally with the ox and lamb,   20
    misread my fate,
mistake the butcher's love
    who kills me for the meat I am
to feed a hungry multitude beyond the sliding doors.
    I, too, misjudge the real   25
purpose of this huge shed I'm herded in: not for my love
    or lovely wool am I here,
but to make some world a meal.
    See, how on the unsubstantial air
I kick, bleating my private woe,   30
    as upside down my rolling sight
somersaults, and frantically I try to set my world upright;
    too late learning why I'm hung here,
whose nostrils bleed, whose life runs out from eye and
    ear.   35

ALFRED HAYES

The details in lines 1–9 could easily evoke a reaction of pity and indignation in any tender-hearted reader, who might sincerely but mistakenly assume that the poem is a protest against the wholesale killing of animals. After all, in the unlikely event that such a reader were himself to write a poem about a slaughterhouse, he would loudly denounce its practices, and so he assumes that Alfred Hayes has done the same. The reader might, on the other hand, assume that Hayes is rejoicing in the spectacle that he describes; he would then be so repelled by the poem that he would hardly be able to read it, let alone understand it. In both instances his automatic, unthinking reactions have kept him from seeing what is actually in the poem.

An unbiased reading shows that "The Slaughter-House" is much more concerned with pity for suffering mankind than with pity for animals. The "I" in the poem (line 20) regards himself as a sheep (the very name connotes dumb innocence) hanging upside down in an immense shed, waiting to have his throat slit. Just why he imagines himself in this dreadful predicament is not made explicit. Perhaps his "private woe" (line 30) is a private soldier's woe; perhaps he is about to be slaughtered in a great war, a war that has already turned his life upside down and made a shambles of it. Perhaps he is not actually going to be butchered, but only feels as though he were. At any rate, the poem seeks to evoke pity for a human animal in a world that seems to him like a slaughterhouse, rather than pity for the livestock in a real slaughterhouse.

The details in the poem are of a sort that automatically repels squeamish readers, automatically attracts readers who consider themselves hard-boiled and their view of the world "realistic." The hard-boiled reader tends to have favorable reactions to such words as *intestines, gore, stainless steel, claw, rape, dung, deceit, torture,* or *debauchery* in a poem; the tender-hearted reader reacts favorably when he encounters *mother-love, bluebird, rose, twilight, loyal, beautiful, love, patriotism, our Heavenly Father,* and so on. Both kinds of readers have ready-made emotional reactions that may easily prevent them from seeing a poem as it actually is.

EXERCISE 8

Carefully read and compare the two following poems.

My Mother's Hands

Such beautiful, beautiful hands!
  They're neither white nor small;
And you, I know, would scarcely think
  That they were fair at all.
I've looked on hands whose form and hue   5
  A sculptor's dream might be;
Yet are those wrinkled, aged hands
  Most beautiful to me.

Such beautiful, beautiful hands!
    Though heart were weary and sad,   10
These patient hands kept toiling on,
    That the children might be glad;
I always weep, as looking back
    To childhood's distant day,
I think how those hands rested not,   15
    When mine were at their play.

Such beautiful, beautiful hands!
    They're growing feeble now,
For time and pain have left their mark
    On hands, and heart, and brow.   20
Alas! alas! the nearing time,
    And the sad, sad day to me,
When 'neath the daisies, out of sight,
    These hands will folded be.

But oh, beyond this shadow land,   25
    Where all is bright and fair,
I know full well these dear old hands
    Will palms of victory bear;
Where crystal streams through endless years
    Flow over golden sands,   30
And where the old grow young again,
    I'll clasp my mother's hands.

                        ANONYMOUS
                    (*Nineteenth Century*)

To My Mother

Most near, most dear, most loved and most far,
Under the window where I often found her
Sitting as huge as Asia, seismic with laughter,
Gin and chicken helpless in her Irish hand,
Irresistible as Rabelais, but most tender for   5
The lame dogs and hurt birds that surround her,—
She is a procession no one can follow after
But be like a little dog following a brass band.

She will not glance up at the bomber, or condescend
To drop her gin and scuttle to a cellar,   10
But lean on the mahogany table like a mountain
Whom only faith can move, and so I send
O all my faith, and all my love to tell her
That she will move from mourning into morning.

GEORGE BARKER

1. What sort of reader might have an automatically favorable response to "My Mother's Hands"? What sort an unfavorable? Apply the same questions to "To My Mother."

2. In the latter poem comment on the connotations of *gin* (lines 4, 10), *Rabelais* (line 5), *mountain* (line 11), *morning* (line 14). What does the poet mean by *mourning* (line 14)?

3. Which of the poems resembles the sort of verse one finds inside a Mother's Day card?

4. Which of the two mothers is more particularly described and characterized? What traits of this mother are emphasized?

5. Which poem seems to portray almost any mother who has grown old? Can it be said, therefore, that this poem portrays nobody's mother?

6. Are the poems flattering or unflattering to the mothers they describe?

7. Which poem do you prefer? Why?

MESSAGES AND MORALS

The mistaken notion that the main purpose of a poem is to provide an inspirational message or to teach a moral can be held responsible for many a misreading. The notion stems, perhaps, from the fact that many poems, like many paintings, are on religious or moral subjects. A poem may incidentally edify or teach, but if it does nothing more, it will be a bad poem. The question of what a poem accomplishes in addition to these incidentals is a large one: it is, in fact, a chief concern of this whole book. The question of what makes one poem good and another bad is also large, but this question must be postponed until later (Chapter 11). It is enough to say here that poems with a message or a moral (**didactic** poems) are not necessarily better or worse than poems without, that some poems have no message and no moral, and that the attempt to read a moral or a message into a poem of the latter kind can be disastrous.

Suppose that a hardened message-hunter were to confront this song from *Love's Labor's Lost*.

Winter

When icicles hang by the wall,
   And Dick the shepherd blows his nail,
And Tom bears logs into the hall,
   And milk comes frozen home in pail,
When blood is nipped and ways be foul,   5
   Then nightly sings the staring owl:
      "Tu-whit, tu-who!"
      A merry note,
While greasy Joan doth keel the pot.

When all aloud the wind both blow,   10
   And coughing drowns the parson's saw,
And birds sit brooding in the snow,
   And Marian's nose looks red and raw,
When roasted crabs hiss in the bowl,
   Then nightly sings the staring owl: 15
      "Tu-whit, tu-who!"
      A merry note,
While greasy Joan doth keel the pot.

WILLIAM SHAKESPEARE

keel (9): cool; skim. **saw** (11) trite moral saying. **crabs** (14): crab apples.

Here the hunter will search in vain for Shakespeare's message. If he insists on messages, he will have to read them into the song: "Lay in a good supply of fuel"; "Feed the birds in winter"; "Cooks, you should not be greasy." Shakespeare, and his intelligent readers, feel no need for these saws. The poet is content with communicating a few wintry experiences, some of them familiar, and others, like the "merry note" of the proverbially mournful owl, strange. The reader should be content to enjoy the poem, and not look for advice on how to conduct his life.

EXERCISE 9

Read and compare these poems.

Up-Hill

Does the road wind up-hill all the way?
   Yes, to the very end.
Will the day's journey take the whole long day?
   From morn to night, my friend.

But is there for the night a resting-place?   5
   A roof for when the slow, dark hours begin.
May not the darkness hide it from my face?
   You cannot miss that inn.

Shall I meet other wayfarers at night?
   Those who have gone before.   10
Then must I knock, or call when just in sight?
   They will not keep you standing at that door.

Shall I find comfort, travel-sore and weak?
   Of labour you shall find the sum.
Will there be beds for me and all who seek?   15
   Yea, beds for all who come.

                     CHRISTINA G. ROSSETTI

The Road Not Taken

Two roads diverged in a yellow wood,
And sorry I could not travel both
And be one traveler, long I stood
And looked down one as far as I could
To where it bent in the undergrowth;   5

Then took the other, as just as fair,
And having perhaps the better claim,
Because it was grassy and wanted wear;
Though as for that the passing there
Had worn them really about the same,   10

And both that morning equally lay
In leaves no step had trodden black.
Oh, I kept the first for another day!
Yet knowing how way leads on to way,
I doubted if I should ever come back.   15

I shall be telling this with a sigh
Somewhere ages and ages hence:
Two roads diverged in a wood, and I—
I took the one less traveled by,
And that has made all the difference.   20

ROBERT FROST

1. In "Up-Hill" what are the connotations of *morn* (line 4), *night* (line 4), *roof* (line 6), *darkness* (line 7), and *inn* (line 8)? In answering the question, consider the context in which the words occur.
2. Does "Up-Hill" concern an actual trip? What words suggest something more than a mere trip? What do they suggest?
3. Could Frost's poem concern an actual walk through the woods? Where is something more than a walk suggested? What is suggested?
4. Which of the two poems implies a message that the reader might find edifying and helpful in his own personal life?
5. What unjustifiable messages might be read into the poem by Frost?

THE READER'S KNOWLEDGE

All writers count on their readers simply to know certain things. Poets especially have to make this assumption because communicating mere information is not their aim. In every age they have taken for granted the existence of a reading public well enough informed to understand them. In the seventeenth century, William Drummond did not think it necessary to tell the whole story of the Trojan War when he wrote his riddling poem (page 25); nor, in the twentieth, did George Barker take up valuable space in his two poems (pages 19 and 36) to say that World War II was then going on. Yet a reader who knows nothing about these two wars cannot make much sense of either Barker's or Drummond's poems. Even the simplest poem assumes some knowledge. To understand the following poem, for instance, a reader must know that all well-behaved swans are supposed to sing, for the first and last time, just before they die.

On a Volunteer Singer

Swans sing before they die—'twere no bad thing
Should certain persons die before they sing.

SAMUEL TAYLOR COLERIDGE

ALLUSION

A writer makes an allusion when he brings literary or historical material into his work from somewhere outside the work. When Barker mentions the bomber that does not frighten his mother, he is not alluding to the war; the war is going on concurrently with the other events of the poem. But he does make an allusion when he writes that his mother is "like a mountain/Whom only faith can move" because here he paraphrases St. Paul's words, "...though I have all faith, so that I could remove mountains." Barker brings these words into the poem from the Bible, where they have a very different context. An **allusion,** then, is an indirect reference, by means of mention or quotation, to something real or fictitious outside the work.

A good poet does not sprinkle his poems with allusions merely to display his vast learning or to make his works seem impressive and confusing to the average reader. He uses allusions because they enable him to say much in a small space. An allusion is functional rather than decorative, but it will not function unless it is recognized. When Frost gave the title "Out, Out" to his poem (page 6), he expected his readers to recall Macbeth's cry of despair.

> Tomorrow, and tomorrow, and tomorrow
> Creeps in this petty pace from day to day
> To the last syllable of recorded time;
> And all our yesterdays have lighted fools
> The way to dusty death. Out, out, brief candle!   5
> Life's but a walking shadow, a poor player
> That struts and frets his hour upon the stage
> And then is heard no more. It is a tale
> Told by an idiot, full of sound and fury,
> Signifying nothing.   10

WILLIAM SHAKESPEARE

The title of Frost's poem summons up this familiar passage. The reader who recognizes the allusion perceives that the life of the boy in the poem is an even briefer candle than Macbeth's, that his death is an even more meaningless performance than the poor player's.

EXERCISE 10

Using reference works in your library and your own literary and historical knowledge, provide whatever information is necessary for understanding these poems.

The Donkey

When fishes flew and forests walked
    And figs grew upon thorn,
Some moment when the moon was blood
    Then surely I was born;

With monstrous head and sickening cry   5
    And ears like errant wings,
The devil's walking parody
    On all four-footed things.

The tattered outlaw of the earth,
    Of ancient crooked will;   10
Starve, scourge, deride me: I am dumb,
    I keep my secret still.

Fools! For I also had my hour;
    One far fierce hour and sweet:
There was a shout about my ears,   15
    And palms before my feet.

GILBERT KEITH CHESTERTON

Mock on, Mock on Voltaire, Rousseau

Mock on, Mock on Voltaire, Rousseau:
Mock on, Mock on; 'tis all in vain!
You throw the sand against the wind,
And the wind blows it back again.

And every sand becomes a Gem   5
Reflected in the beams divine;
Blown back they blind the mocking eye,
But still in Israel's paths they shine.

The Atoms of Democritus
And Newton's Particles of light   10
Are sands upon the Red sea shore,
Where Israel's tents do shine so bright.

WILLIAM BLAKE

In a Prominent Bar in Secaucus One Day

To the tune of "The Old Orange Flute"
or the tune of "Sweet Betsy from Pike"

In a prominent bar in Secaucus one day
Rose a lady in skunk with a topheavy sway,
Raised a knobby red finger—all turned from their beer—
While with eyes bright as snowcrust she sang high and clear:

"Now who of you'd think from an eyeload of me   5
That I once was a lady as proud as could be?
Oh I'd never sit down by a tumbledown drunk
If it wasn't, my dears, for the high cost of junk.

"All the gents used to swear that the white of my calf
Beat the down of the swan by a length and a half.   10
In the kerchief of linen I caught to my nose
Ah, there never fell snot, but a little gold rose.

"I had seven gold teeth and a toothpick of gold,
My Virginia cheroot was a leaf of it rolled
And I'd light it each time with a thousand in cash—   15
Why the bums used to fight if I flicked them an ash.

"Once the toast of the Biltmore, the belle of the Taft,
I would drink bottle beer at the Drake, never draft,
And dine at the Astor on Salisbury steak
With a clean tablecloth for each bite I did take.   20

"In a car like the Roxy I'd roll to the track,
A steel-guitar trio, a bar in the back,
And the wheels made no noise, they turned over so fast,
Still it took you ten minutes to see me go past.

"When the horses bowed down to me that I might choose,   25
I bet on them all, for I hated to lose.
Now I'm saddled each night for my butter and eggs
And the broken threads race down the backs of my legs.

"Let you hold in mind, girls, that your beauty must pass
Like a lovely white clover that rusts with its grass.   30
Keep your bottoms off barstools and marry you young
Or be left—an old barrel with many a bung.

"For when time takes you out for a spin in his car
You'll be hard-pressed to stop him from going too far
And be left by the roadside, for all your good deeds,   35
Two toadstools for tits and a face full of weeds."

All the house raised a cheer, but the man at the bar
Made a phonecall and up pulled a red patrol car
And she blew us a kiss as they copped her away
From that prominent bar in Secaucus, N.J.   40

                    X. J. KENNEDY

POEMS AS AUTOBIOGRAPHIES

The relation of an artist to his work is such a complex matter that it cannot be given anything like a full treatment here. Most investigators of the problem believe that individual poets differ greatly in the degree to which they express their own personalities in their first-person poems. Few poets, however, express *merely* themselves; even the most subjective poets commonly create an *alter ego,* a second self, to speak for them. Critics, therefore, have adopted the useful term **persona** to refer to the voice, other than the poet's, that is heard in a poem. Some poets have a great variety of personae or masks through which they speak. Cummings's two poems (pages 16 and 17), for instance, are spoken by very different personae.

For these reasons a reader must beware of regarding every poem as pure autobiography or self-expression. Unlike a poet's birth certificate or his marriage license, his poems are not simply documents; in his poems a poet is not under oath to tell the literal truth about himself. The danger of regarding poems as mere biographical documents is this: the reader is likely to substitute interest in the poet's biography for interest in his poems. Then the poems evaporate amidst speculation about the fascinating details of the poet's life. Yet there is also a danger at the opposite extreme: the assumption that biographical data are irrelevant to every poem. There are many poems in which the persona resembles the poet very closely, and there are a few in which the two are virtually indistinguishable. For a full understanding of such poems, a reader needs some knowledge of the author. Blake's "Mock on, Mock on" (page 42) is much more meaningful to a reader who knows something about the events of Blake's life and the ideas he expresses in his other works than it is to a reader ignorant of this information. Even here, however, the reader must look on the poem as a poem, not as merely another piece of information about Blake.

POEMS AS DRAMAS

A reader can profitably regard this poem, or any other in which one person directly addresses someone else, as a small-scale drama.

Secrecy Protested

Fear not, dear love, that I'll reveal
Those hours of pleasure we two steal.
No eye shall see, nor yet the sun
Descry what thou and I have done;
No ear shall hear our love, but we   5
Silent as the night will be.
The god of love himself, whose dart
Did first wound mine and then thy heart,
Shall never know that we can tell
What sweets in stolen embraces dwell.   10
This only means may find it out:

If, when I die, physicians doubt
What caused my death, and, there to view
Of all their judgments which was true,
Rip up my heart—Oh then, I fear,   15
The world will see thy picture there.

THOMAS CAREW

There are two actors in this playlet. The one who refers to himself as "I"—in a discussion of the poem he would be called the "speaker"—is a man; he speaks to the woman whom he loves. Here, as in any other drama, there has been some antecedent action: the "hours of pleasure" (line 2) that the lovers have stolen. The scene of the drama is the place where they customarily meet in secret; the time is night. Just before the curtain goes up for line 1 of the poem, the woman has said, in a worried tone, something like this: "I am afraid that people are going to find out about us." This remark, which creates the conflict that a drama always needs, is one that the man cannot let pass without comment, because he wants her to feel confident that he will never betray her as long as he lives. His protestations make up the entire performance; the curtain comes down before the woman replies. The reader never knows whether she continues to be worried or why the lovers must meet secretly.

Notice that this discussion has not mentioned the author of the poem, but has assumed that Carew is writing dramatically rather than autobiographically, that he is not the man speaking in his poem. Since very little is known about Carew's personal life, an autobiographical element in the poem can neither be proved nor disproved. But two things seem certain. First, it would be an error to decide that Carew must have had a secret love affair (probably with a married woman?) just because he wrote a poem about two secret lovers. This view would deny that he had any imagination or ability to invent situations; it would imply that a poet is restricted to writing solely about the events of his own life. Second, even though Carew may have had such a love affair, the reader's knowledge of it would not necessarily increase his understanding and appreciation of the poem. And it might be a positive nuisance if a reader were to regard it as a substitute for directly experiencing the poem.

Carew's poem is an early and rather simple example of a **dramatic monologue:** a poem in which a fictitious or historical character, caught at an important moment in his life, speaks to one or more characters who remain silent. In Carew's monologue the main interest is the situation; in nineteenth- and twentieth-century monologues the main interest is the speaker's character.

EXERCISE 11

Look up the facts of Browning's life and decide whether any of them are useful in understanding these poems. If you decide that the poems are primarily dramatic, study them by answering these questions:

1. Who is the speaker? To whom does he speak?
2. What is the scene? The time?
3. What has happened immediately before the poem begins?
4. What are the speaker's traits?
5. How is the speaker in the first poem like the one in the second? How do the two speakers differ?

My Last Duchess

FERRARA

That's my last Duchess painted on the wall,
Looking as if she were alive. I call
That piece a wonder, now: Frà Pandolf's hands
Worked busily a day, and there she stands.
Will't please you sit and look at her? I said   5
"Frà Pandolf" by design, for never read
Strangers like you that pictured countenance,
The depth and passion of its earnest glance,
But to myself they turned (since none puts by
The curtain I have drawn for you, but I)   10
And seemed as they would ask me, if they durst,
How such a glance came there; so, not the first
Are you to turn and ask thus. Sir, 'twas not
Her husband's presence only, called that spot
Of joy into the Duchess' cheek: perhaps   15
Frà Pandolf chanced to say, "Her mantle laps
Over my lady's wrist too much," or "Paint
Must never hope to reproduce the faint
Half-flush that dies along her throat": such stuff

Was courtesy, she thought, and cause enough
For calling up that spot of joy. She had
A heart—how shall I say?—too soon made glad,
Too easily impressed: she liked whate'er
She looked on, and her looks went everywhere.
Sir, 'twas all one! My favour at her breast,   25
The dropping of the daylight in the West,
The bough of cherries some officious fool
Broke in the orchard for her, the white mule
She rode with round the terrace—all and each
Would draw from her alike the approving speech,   30
Or blush, at least. She thanked men,—good! but thanked
Somehow—I know not how—as if she ranked
My gift of a nine-hundred-years-old name
With anybody's gift. Who'd stoop to blame
This sort of trifling? Even had you skill   35
In speech—(which I have not)—to make your will
Quite clear to such an one, and say, "Just this
Or that in you disgusts me; here you miss,
Or there exceed the mark"—and if she let
Herself be lessoned so, nor plainly set   40
Her wits to yours, forsooth, and made excuse,
—E'en then would be some stooping, and I choose
Never to stoop. Oh Sir, she smiled, no doubt,
Whene'er I passed her; but who passed without
Much the same smile? This grew; I gave commands;   45
Then all smiles stopped together. There she stands
As if alive. Will't please you rise? We'll meet
The company below, then. I repeat,
The Count your master's known munificence
Is ample warrant that no just pretence   50
Of mine for dowry will be disallowed;
Though his fair daughter's self, as I avowed
At starting, is my object. Nay, we'll go
Together down, sir! Notice Neptune, though,
Taming a sea-horse, thought a rarity,   55
Which Claus of Innsbruck cast in bronze for me!

ROBERT BROWNING

Frá Pandolf (3): fictitious monk-artist. **Claus of Innsbruck**
(56): fictitious German metal-founder.

Confessions

What is he buzzing in my ears?
   "Now that I am come to die,
Do I view the world as a vale of tears?"
   Ah, reverend sir, not I!

What I viewed there once, what I view again   5
   Where the physic bottles stand
On the table's edge,—is a suburb lane,
   With a wall to my bedside hand.

That lane sloped, much as the bottles do,
   From a house you could descry   10
O'er the garden-wall; is the curtain blue
   Or green to a healthy eye?

To mine, it serves for the old June weather
   Blue above land and wall;
And that farthest bottle labelled "Ether"   15
   Is the house o'ertopping all.

At a terrace, somewhere near the stopper,
   There watched for me, one June,
A girl: I know, sir, it's improper,
   My poor mind's out of tune.   20

Only, there was a way . . . you crept
   Close by the side, to dodge
Eyes in the house, two eyes except:
   They styled their house "The Lodge."

What right had a lounger up their lane?   25
   But, by creeping very close,
With the good wall's help,—their eyes might strain
   And stretch themselves to Oes,

Yet never catch her and me together,
   As she left the attic, there,   30
By the rim of the bottle labelled "Ether,"
   And stole from stair to stair,

And stood by the rose-wreathed gate. Alas,
    We loved, sir—used to meet:
How sad and bad and mad it was—   35
    But then, how it was sweet!

ROBERT BROWNING

SUGGESTIONS TO READERS OF POEMS

1. Read all poems more than once and most poems many times. Use your dictionary, but think about connotations as well as denotations. Reading poems is a sport that demands active participators, not passive spectators.

2. Read every poem aloud (see page 205).

3. Pay attention to punctuation. The end of a line is almost never the end of a sentence.

4. Paraphrase (page 22) those passages in which the thoughts are difficult to grasp.

5. Read the poem that the poet wrote, not the one that you yourself would write on the same subject.

6. Beware of making assumptions about the poem that the entire text does not support.

7. Do not fear that close study will spoil the poem for you. Any poem worth reading at all is worth reading closely. A poem cannot be destroyed by analysis because it is not a living organism that dies when it is dissected. However much it is probed and picked apart, a poem still remains intact on the page, ready to be enjoyed after it has been understood.

EXERCISE 12

With the help of the questions read the following poems as carefully as you can.

Spring

When daisies pied and violets blue,
    And lady-smocks all silver white,
And cuckoo-buds of yellow hue
    Do paint the meadows with delight,
The cuckoo then, on every tree,   5
Mocks married men; for thus sings he:
        "Cuckoo,
Cuckoo, cuckoo!" O word of fear,
Unpleasing to a married ear!

When shepherds pipe on oaten straws,   10
   And merry larks are ploughmen's clocks,
When turtles tread, and rooks, and daws,
   And maidens bleach their summer smocks,
The cuckoo then, on every tree,
Mocks married men; for thus sings he: 15
     "Cuckoo,
Cuckoo, cuckoo!" O word of fear,
Unpleasing to a married ear!

WILLIAM SHAKESPEARE
(from *Love's Labor's Lost*)

cuckoo-buds (3): buttercups. **Unpleasing** (9): because *cuckoo*
sounds like *cuckold*. **turtles** (12): turtledoves.

1. How do you know that *smocks* in line 2 does not mean the same as *smocks* in line 13?
2. Why are the girls bleaching their smocks? How is this detail related to other details in the song?
3. Contrast the mood of this poem with that of "Winter" (page 38). Is one poem sad and the other merry?

The Line of an American Poet

That American Poet's future
Is bright because he began
With the know-how of Ford and Chrysler
And the faith of American Can.

He fathomed success's secret   5
And stuck to his P's and Q's
And urged himself, over and over,
To produce and produce and produce.

His very first verses were cleverly
Built; and the market boomed.   10
Some of the world's most critical
Consumers looked, and consumed.

Lines off his line became smoother
And smoother as more and more
Know-how came in the window   15
And verses rolled out the door.

Now everyone in the market
Knows his new works are sure
To be just as the country wants them:
Uniform, safe and pure.   20

REED WHITTEMORE

1. Explain *know-how* (line 3), *P's and Q's* (line 6), and *line* (line 13).
2. Does the speaker admire the poet whom he describes? How do you know?
3. What is the speaker's opinion of the people who like the poet's writings? How can you tell?

Leave Me, O Love

Leave me, O love which reachest but to dust,
And thou, my mind, aspire to higher things;
Grow rich in that which never taketh rust.
Whatever fades, but fading pleasure brings.

Draw in thy beams, and humble all thy might   5
To that sweet yoke where lasting freedoms be,
Which breaks the clouds and opens forth the light
That doth both shine and give us sight to see.

O take fast hold, let that light be thy guide
In this small course which birth draws out to death;   10
And think how evil becometh him to slide,
Who seeketh heaven and comes of heavenly breath.
   Then farewell, world, thy uttermost I see;
   Eternal love, maintain thy life in me.

SIR PHILIP SIDNEY

dust (1): **see** Genesis ii:7. **rust** (3): see Matthew vi:19, 20.
yoke (6): **see** Matthew xi:29, 30. **becometh** (11): it becomes.
slide (11): do wrong. **breath** (12): see Genesis ii:7.

1. What proof does the poet offer that one kind of love is "higher" than another?
2. To which of the two loves do the "beams" mentioned in line 5 belong? To which does the "yoke" (line 6) belong?
3. Why is the "course" (line 10) described as "small"?

3

IMAGES AND
THEMES IN POEMS

A good poet labors harder than any other kind of writer to say exactly what he means, because he wishes to expose his thoughts rather than to hide them. His passion for exactness is like the mathematician's. But unlike the mathematician, who thinks in abstractions, the poet not only thinks concretely but presents his thoughts concretely.

CONCRETENESS

Alexander Pope was thinking and writing concretely when he penned these lines in *Windsor Forest*.

> See! from the brake the whirring pheasant springs,
> And mounts exulting on triumphant wings:
> Short is his joy; he feels the fiery wound,
> Flutters in blood, and panting beats the ground.
> Ah! what avail his glossy, varying dyes,
> His purple crest, and scarlet-circled eyes,
> The vivid green his shining plumes unfold,
> His painted wings, and breast that flames with gold?

Pope makes the reader see and hear the pheasant—and even share something of its joy and pain. There is a world of difference between his description and the abstract statement "A beautiful bird, starting to fly, was killed." To a poet such an abstract statement is useless. Since it communicates nothing in particular and everything in general, it is a broad invitation for every reader to imagine whatever kind of bird-murder he pleases, from Australians boomeranging ostriches to eagles seizing parakeets. By avoiding abstractions, Pope has controlled the reader's response.

Pope is exact, but not as an ornithologist is exact; his pheasant is not a textbook pheasant, complete with data on size, shape, color, and mating habits. Pope could not include such information, however concrete, without introducing irrelevancies into his poem. On the other hand, the scientist could not say that the bird "mounts exulting on triumphant wings" because he is confined primarily to facts and verifiable hypotheses. The scientist communicates information; the poet, experience. Both rely on concrete details.

The poet who strays very far from the concrete is likely to get into trouble because poems made up entirely of abstractions are very difficult to understand.

Only a Thought

'Twas only a passing thought, my love,
   Only a passing thought,
That came o'er my mind like a ray o' the sun
   In the dimples of waters caught;
And it seemed to me, and I say to thee,   5
   That sorrow and shame and sin
Might disappear from our happy sphere,
   If we knew but to begin;
If we but knew how to profit
   By wisdom dearly bought: 10
It was only a passing thought, my love,
   Only a passing thought.

CHARLES MACKAY

Except for the comparison in lines 3 and 4 this poem contains nothing concrete—that is, nothing which the reader can touch, taste, hear, smell, or see. Words like *sorrow, shame, sin, happy sphere, profit, wisdom,* and *thought* are abstract; they stand for emotions, conditions, and states of mind that do of course exist, but that exist in a different way for each reader. Hence an individual reader can never be sure that his meaning of the terms is the same as Mackay's. In the poem a man seems to be telling a woman that "sorrow and shame and sin" would disappear from "our happy sphere" if we could learn how to make them disappear. But how can he be saying anything so obvious as that? Moreover, doesn't he contradict himself when he calls the world a "happy sphere," for how can it be happy if it has all that sorrow? This poem fails not because it is obvious but because it is excessively abstract. Unless there is something very definite and concrete in the poet's mind, there will be little or nothing in the reader's.

A good poet who uses an abstraction limits its meaning so that the reader will have the exact experience that the poet intends him to have. When Pope, for instance, mentions the joy (line 3) of the pheasant, he amplifies the abstraction by giving details of the speed and beauty that cause the bird's joy. He does not need to use the words *speed* and *beauty;* these "thoughts" are conveyed concretely.

EXERCISE 13

Adam's Dream

The sycamores and sidewalks of
His neighborhood were private park
And dark retreat, where he could walk
In congress sweet

With his kind neighbors, sleep and love,   5
And where their gossip, or nice talk,
Discriminated beast from bird
By proper word:

      Adam yawned, and there were cats;
      Blinked, and there were antelopes;   10
      Stretched, and everywhere he reached
      A mile of meadow bloomed.

He cocked his eye, and fishes leaped
In every brook to praise him;
He rose to walk, and rabbits ran   15
As couriers to every green
Community to tell of him.

He only glanced at any tree,
Its birds at once began to sing;
He nodded, and the region budded;   20
He put the bloom on everything.

He was the lord of all the park,
And he was lonely in the dark,
Till Eve came smiling out of his side
To be his bride.   25

"Sweet rib," he said, astonished at her,
"This is *my* green environ!"
Eve answered no word, but for reply
The wilderness was in her eye.

Adam awoke, the snow had come,   30
And drifts of daylight covered the park;
And his sweet friends, and their sweet talk,
Were dumb.

DAVID FERRY

1. List all the nouns in the poem that refer to animals or to places, and then arrange the words in each list beginning with the most abstract and ending with the most concrete.

2. Do the adjectives *private, dark, nice,* and *green* (lines 2, 3, 6, 16, and 27) make the nouns they modify more or less abstract? Why?

3. What is the difference between Adam's *green environ* (line 27) and Eve's *wilderness* (line 29)?

IMAGES

A concrete detail that appeals to any of the reader's senses is called an **image.** Although most of the image-making words in any language appeal to sight (and are therefore called visual images), there are also images of touch (tactile), sound (auditory), taste (gustatory), and smell (olfactory). The last two terms in parentheses, by the way, are mainly used by lovers of jargon. An image may also appeal to the reader's sense of motion: a verb like Pope's *springs* does so. An image is often a single word, like *birches;* or it may be a complete sentence, like Shakespeare's "Through the sharp hawthorn blows the cold wind" —a line that appeals simultaneously to the reader's senses of sight, sound, and touch.

These two stanzas from Keats's "The Eve of St. Agnes" are frequently used to illustrate all the kinds of images. In them a man is preparing an exotic midnight snack for a sleeping lady.

> Then by the bed-side, where the faded moon
> Made a dim, silver twilight, soft he set
> A table, and, half-anguish'd, threw thereon
> A cloth of woven crimson, gold, and jet:—
> O for some drowsy Morphean amulet!   5
> The boisterous, midnight, festive clarion,
> The kettle-drum, and far-heard clarionet,
> Affray his ears, though but in dying tone:—
> The hall door shuts again, and all the noise is gone.

> And still she slept an azure-lidded sleep,   10
> In blanched linen, smooth and lavender'd,
> While he from forth the closet brought a heap
> Of candied apple, quince, and plum, and gourd
> With jellies soother than the creamy curd,
> And lucent syrops, tinct with cinnamon;   15
> Manna and dates, in argosy transferr'd
> From Fez; and spiced dainties, every one,
> From silken Samarcand to cedar'd Lebanon.

In stanza 1 images of sight and sound predominate. The noise of a celebration going on downstairs (lines 6–9) penetrates the silence of the bedroom, where the man's every motion is soft (line 2) so that he will not awaken the lady. In stanza 2 sight and taste predominate, although *smooth* (line 11) is an image of touch and *spiced* (line 17) one of smell. Few poems have such a rich profusion of images as this excerpt has.

THE FUNCTIONS OF IMAGERY

A good poet does not use imagery—that is, images in general— merely to decorate his poems. He does not ask himself, "How can I dress up my subject so that it will seem fancier than it is?" Rather, he asks himself, "How can I make my subject appear to the reader exactly as it appears to me?" Imagery helps him solve his problem, for it enables him to present his subject as it is: as it looks, smells, tastes, feels, and sounds. To the reader imagery is equally important: it provides his imagination with something palpable to seize upon.

The Rhodora:
On Being Asked, Whence Is the Flower?

In May, when sea-winds pierced our solitudes,
I found the fresh Rhodora in the woods,
Spreading its leafless blooms in a damp nook,
To please the desert and the sluggish brook.
The purple petals, fallen in the pool,   5
Made the black water with their beauty gay;
Here might the red-bird come his plumes to cool,
And court the flower that cheapens his array.
Rhodora! if the sages ask thee why
This charm is wasted on the earth and sky,   10
Tell them, dear, that if eyes were made for seeing,
Then Beauty is its own excuse for being:
Why thou wert there, O rival of the rose!
I never thought to ask, I never knew:
But, in my simple ignorance, suppose   15
The self-same Power that brought me there brought you.

RALPH WALDO EMERSON

This poem divides into two distinct parts: lines 1–8, which contain many images, and lines 9–16, which have few. The first part is a kind of demonstration; instead of just saying that the rhodora is beautiful, Emerson exhibits its beauty. In this way he prepares the reader for the second part, which is a statement about beauty in general. The concrete first part presents the subject and supports the abstract conclusion.

EXERCISE 14

Study the imagery in the following poems and explain how it helps the poet present his subject.

Problem in History

At morning light the ark lay grounded fast
On top of Ararat; and Noah sent out
The raven flapping on jet-fingered wings
Unreturning; and thrice to look about
Sent the timid dove, that returned at last 5
Fluttering an olive bough. The robin sings

On the spattered rail and the sun shines
On the steaming earth, that like a bog stank
Greening at the clear blue sky. Asses bray
From the hold, the animals come down the plank 10
By twos and twos, in awkward-footed lines
Sniffing, while hawks and songbirds spray

Into the new air. Forgetful of the flood,
In a busy hour all are debarked and gone
Down from Ararat. By sunfall the voices 15
Of their going have vanished. The ark alone
Centers their outward footprints in the mud,
Settles through the night with creaking noises

Wearied with its long journey. In that repose
New suns will wreathe it with green-ivy vines, 20
Shade it with growing oaks and bushes round
There on the world's top, till it rots with rains
And snows and suns of time. And no one knows
What green the unreturning raven found.

ROBERT WALLACE

A White Rose

The red rose whispers of passion,
    And the white rose breathes of love;
O, the red rose is a falcon,
    And the white rose is a dove.

But I send you a cream-white rosebud   5
   With a flush on its petal tips;
For the love that is purest and sweetest
   Has a kiss of desire on the lips.

JOHN BOYLE O'REILLY

The Eagle

FRAGMENT

He clasps the crag with crooked hands;
Close to the sun in lonely lands,
Ring'd with the azure world, he stands.

The wrinkled sea beneath him crawls;
He watches from his mountain walls,   5
And like a thunderbolt he falls.

ALFRED, LORD TENNYSON

Hark, Hark, the Lark

Hark, hark! the lark at heaven's gate sings,
   And Phoebus 'gins arise,
His steeds to water at those springs
   On chalic'd flowers that lies;
And winking Mary-buds begin   5
   To ope their golden eyes.
With every thing that pretty is,
   My lady sweet, arise:
      Arise, arise!

WILLIAM SHAKESPEARE
(from Cymbeline)

'gins (2): begins. lies (4): lie. Mary-buds (5): marigolds.

It is a common practice for a poet to express his thoughts and feelings through his imagery.

Western Wind

Western wind, when will thou blow,
The small rain down can rain?
Christ, if my love were in my arms
And I in my bed again!

ANONYMOUS
(*Sixteenth Century*)

The speaker here is a lonely man who longs for two things: the western wind, which will bring a change in the weather, and a reunion with the woman whom he loves. In its context the visual-auditory-tactile image *small rain* (line 2) communicates the idea of relief from a dry spell. The speaker wants a mild spring shower, not a violent storm; he also wants love to renew his life, just as the rain renews nature in the spring. His desire for the lady is expressed in the imagery of lines 3-4. This anonymous poet has used images that convey many ideas— among them loneliness, nature, life, renewal, return, sex, and love. In its imagery "Western Wind" suggests more thoughts and emotions than the following poem, which is made up primarily of abstractions rather than images.

O That 'Twere Possible

O that 'twere possible
After long grief and pain
To find the arms of my true love
Round me once again!

.   .   .   .

A shadow flits before me,   5
Not thou, but like to thee:
Ah Christ, that it were possible
For one short hour to see
The souls we loved, that they might tell us,
What and where they be.   10

ALFRED, LORD TENNYSON
(from *Maud*)

EXERCISE 15

Study in the following poems the use of imagery to communicate thoughts.

All the World's a Stage

All the world's a stage,
And all the men and women merely players.
They have their exits and their entrances,
And one man in his time plays many parts,
His acts being seven ages. At first, the infant,   5
Mewling and puking in the nurse's arms.
Then the whining schoolboy, with his satchel
And shining morning face, creeping like snail
Unwillingly to school. And then the lover,
Sighing like furnace, with a woeful ballad   10
Made to his mistress' eyebrow. Then a soldier,
Full of strange oaths and bearded like the pard,
Jealous in honor, sudden and quick in quarrel,
Seeking the bubble reputation
Even in the cannon's mouth. And then the justice,   15
In fair round belly with good capon lined,
With eyes severe and beard of formal cut,
Full of wise saws and modern instances;
And so he plays his part. The sixth age shifts
Into the lean and slippered pantaloon,   20
With spectacles on nose and pouch on side;
His youthful hose, well saved, a world too wide
For his shrunk shank, and his big manly voice,
Turning again toward childish trebel, pipes
And whistles in his sound. Last scene of all,   25
That ends this strange eventful history,
Is second childishness and mere oblivion,
Sans teeth, sans eyes, sans taste, sans everything.

WILLIAM SHAKESPEARE
(from *As You Like It*)

1. Find all the auditory imagery and explain whether it is pleasant or unpleasant.
2. Is *justice* (line 15) abstract? Which of the seven descriptions contain no abstract terms? Which have many? Why are abstractions appropriate in some descriptions but not in others?

3. In the play Jaques speaks these famous lines. Is he so unobservant as to think that *every* man is successively a poet, a soldier, and a justice? What is his opinion of reputation (line 14)? How do you know?

4. Whether you have read the play or not, you can infer Jaques' character from these lines. Does he approve of anything that men do? Summarize his attitude toward each age and then toward life in general.

Cock at Sea

The wooden cage was wedged on the ship's prow
Between sails, vomit, chains that groaned all night.
The grey dawn broke, I heard the sick bird crow
Across the bitter water to the light.

The farm was dancing through that jagged cry—   5
Tall hay-stack, seed-rich field, barn, hedge and tree,
Cocks that could proudly strut, birds that could fly—
And he a captive of the grinding sea.

No answer from that farm, endless the blue,
Endless the waves, the slaps of salty breath.   10
He crowed again, the day was rising new
To feed the nightmare in the sleep of death.

C. A. TRYPANIS

A Noiseless Patient Spider

A noiseless patient spider,
I mark'd where on a little promontory it stood isolated,
Mark'd how to explore the vacant vast surrounding,
It launch'd forth filament, filament, filament, out of itself,
Ever unreeling them, ever tirelessly speeding them.   5

And you O my soul where you stand,
Surrounded, detached, in measureless oceans of space,
Ceaselessly musing, venturing, throwing, seeking the spheres to connect them,
Till the bridge you will need be form'd, till the ductile anchor hold,
Till the gossamer thread you fling catch somewhere, O my   10
soul.

WALT WHITMAN

1. Explain the relationship between lines 1–5 and 6–10.
2. What thoughts are suggested by *bridge, ductile anchor* (line 9), and *gossamer thread* (line 10)?
3. Does the speaker know where his thread will reach?

His Desire

Give me a man that is not dull,
When all the world with rifts is full;
But unamazed dares clearly sing,
Whenas the roof's a-tottering;
And, though it falls, continues still   5
Tickling the citterne with his quill.

ROBERT HERRICK

Whenas (4): when.   **citterne** (6): a musical instrument, like a guitar.

THEME AND SUBJECT

The **subject** of a poem is the topic that the poet has chosen to write about; it can be almost anything: a person, scene, emotion, event. Pope's subject is a pheasant; Emerson's, a rhodora; Shakespeare's, the ages of man. Goldsmith's, in this poem, is women betrayed by men.

Song

When lovely woman stoops to folly,
    And finds too late that men betray,
What charm can soothe her melancholy,
    What art can wash her guilt away?

The only art her guilt to cover,   5
    To hide her shame from every eye,
To give repentance to her lover,
    And wring his bosom—is to die.

OLIVER GOLDSMITH
(from *The Vicar of Wakefield*)

Goldsmith's theme is what he has to say about "fallen" women: they must die. The **theme** of a poem, then, is the main thought that it expresses about the subject. A theme may be explicit, as in Goldsmith's poem, or it may be implied.

Composed upon Westminster Bridge

Earth has not anything to show more fair:
Dull would he be of soul who could pass by
A sight so touching in its majesty:
This City now doth, like a garment, wear
The beauty of the morning; silent, bare,   5
Ships, towers, domes, theatres, and temples lie
Open unto the fields, and to the sky;
All bright and glittering in the smokeless air.
Never did sun more beautifully steep
In his first splendour, valley, rock, or hill;   10
Ne'er saw I, never felt, a calm so deep!
The river glideth at his own sweet will:
Dear God! the very houses seem asleep;
And all that mighty heart is lying still!

WILLIAM WORDSWORTH

The theme of this poem is implicit rather than explicit, although the opening sentence may seem to state a thought explicitly and even bluntly. But the first line is not Wordsworth's theme; it states, rather, his subject—the beauty of the city. Wordsworth wishes to say something more precise about the city's beauty than the abstract opening statement; he wishes to show that the city, as much as the country, is a part of nature and that early in the morning the city shares in the natural majesty and peace of all created things. These thoughts are communicated by images: the buildings of the city, like "valley, rock, or hill" (line 10), lie "Open unto the fields, and to the sky" (line 7). The poet is not comparing the city with the country to the disadvantage of either; instead, he is saying that they are the same. He attributes human qualities to the works of both God and man: the city wears its beauty "like a garment" (line 4); the houses "seem asleep" (line 13); the river has a "will" (line 12). To summarize: Wordsworth announces his subject—the beauty of the city—in line 1. The rest of the poem implies the theme: the *natural* beauty of the city.

EXERCISE 16

Study each of these poems to determine whether its theme is implicit or explicit.

A Description of the Morning

Now hardly here and there an Hackney-Coach
Appearing, show'd the Ruddy Morns Approach.
Now Betty from her Masters Bed had flown,
And softly stole to discompose her own.
The Slipshod Prentice from his Masters Door,   5
Had par'd the Dirt, and Sprinkled round the Floor.
Now Moll had whirl'd her Mop with dex'trous Airs,
Prepar'd to Scrub the Entry and the Stairs.
The Youth with Broomy Stumps began to trace
The Kennel-Edge, where Wheels had worn the Place.   10
The Smallcoal-Man was heard with Cadence deep,
'Till drown'd in Shriller Notes of Chimney-Sweep,
Duns at his Lordships Gate began to meet,
And Brickdust Moll had Scream'd through half the Street.
The Turnkey now his Flock returning sees,   15
Duly let out a Nights to Steal for Fees.
The watchful Bailiffs take their silent Stands,
And School-Boys lag with Satchels in their Hands.

JONATHAN SWIFT

1. How does the speaker know that morning has arrived?
2. Why does Betty (a standard nickname for a housemaid) "discompose" (line 4) her bed?
3. What are "Broomy Stumps" (line 9) and "Duns" (line 13)? What is the connotation of *Flock* (line 15)?
4. What are the bailiffs watching for (line 17)? What do you imagine causes Brickdust Moll to scream? Why can you assume that she screams every morning?
5. Make some general comments on the characters depicted in the poem.
6. Compare Swift's subject and theme with Wordsworth's.

Preludes

I

The winter evening settles down
With smell of steaks in passageways
Six o'clock.
The burnt-out ends of smoky days.
And now a gusty shower wraps   5
The grimy scraps
Of withered leaves about your feet
And newspapers from vacant lots;
The showers beat
On broken blinds and chimney-pots,   10
And at the corner of the street
A lonely cab-horse steams and stamps.
And then the lighting of the lamps.

T. S. ELIOT

1. Should line 3 be read aloud in a solemn or in a matter-of-fact tone?
2. Explain the image in line 4. Does *ends* imply a particular kind of end?
3. Commentators on this poem say that when it was written *steaks* (line 2) connoted a typical working-class meal. Does this information help a reader understand the poem?
4. What thoughts have guided the speaker in his choice of images?
5. Summarize the speaker's attitude toward the scene.

Song

Still to be neat, still to be drest,
As you were going to a feast;
Still to be powdered, still perfumed:
Lady, it is to be presumed,
Though art's hid causes are not found,   5
All is not sweet, all is not sound.

Give me a look, give me a face
That makes simplicity a grace;
Robes loosely flowing, hair as free:

Such sweet neglect more taketh me,   10
Than all the adulteries of art.
They strike mine eyes, but not my heart.

BEN JONSON
(from *Epicoene*)

Still (1, 3): always. **As** (2): as if.

1. What does *adulteries* (line 11) mean?
2. Explain the antithesis in the last line.
3. Compare the poem with the following, on the subject of women's dress. Are the themes identical?

Delight in Disorder

A sweet disorder in the dress
Kindles in clothes a wantonness:
A lawn about the shoulders thrown
Into a fine distraction,
An erring lace, which here and there   5
Enthralls the crimson stomacher,
A cuff neglectful, and thereby
Ribands to flow confusedly,
A winning wave (deserving note)
In the tempestuous petticoat,   10
A careless shoe-string, in whose tie
I see a wild civility,
Do more bewitch me than when art
Is too precise in every part.

ROBERT HERRICK

After Death Nothing Is

After death nothing is, and nothing death:
The utmost limits of a gasp of breath.
Let the ambitious zealot lay aside
His hopes of heaven, where faith is but his pride;

Let slavish souls lay by their fear,   5
Nor be concerned which way or where
After this life they shall be hurled.
Dead, we become the lumber of the world;
And to that mass of matter shall be swept,
Where things destroyed with things unborn are kept.   10
Devouring time swallows us whole;
Impartial death confounds body and soul.
For hell and the foul fiend that rules
God's everlasting fiery jails,
Devised by rogues, dreaded by fools   15
(With his grim, grisly dog that keeps the door),
Are senseless stories, idle tales,
Dreams, whimseys, and no more.

SENECA
(translated by John Wilmot,
Earl of Rochester)

dog (16): Cerberus.

THEME VERSUS "HIDDEN MESSAGE"

The notion that poems must convey messages (see page 37) is likely to creep unnoticed into discussions of theme, especially when a reader states the theme of a particular poem in a complete sentence. There is a temptation, for instance, to say that the theme of Wordsworth's poem about London is this: "The city is as beautiful a place to live in as the country." A sentence of this sort comes perilously close to giving advice; it is almost like the recommendation "People ought to live in the city"—or something of that kind. The danger of regarding theme as message or moral decreases when a noun with appropriate modifiers replaces the complete sentence. The theme of "Composed upon Westminster Bridge" is then said to be *the natural beauty of the city;* the theme of "Western Wind," *a man's yearning for refreshment in his life;* the theme of "A Noiseless Patient Spider," *the soul's efforts to make contact with something outside itself.* The nouns *beauty, yearning,* and *efforts* are not, of course, the only nouns that could be used to express the themes of these poems, since all readers cannot be expected to think in identical words. Regardless of the inevitable differences in readers, every reader must make certain that the nouns and modifiers he uses to express the theme reflect the poem and not merely his private response to the poem. The images of the poem rather than the reader's internal impulses must be allowed to control the response.

A theme, then, is not a message; nor is it something hidden in the poem. The reader's ability to express a theme does not depend on his powers as a detective, but on his capacity for making valid generalizations. A theme generalizes what is specific in the poem; it renders concrete details into abstract thoughts. It has something of the same relationship to the poem as the formula *NaCl* has to the product on the dining table. The formula is useful to those who want to understand common salt, but it is in no way a salt substitute. One cannot put the formula on roast beef. Similarly, formulating a theme is an exercise that helps a reader understand what the poem says about its subject. It thus helps the reader experience the poem, but it is neither a substitute for the poem itself nor the total meaning of the poem (see Chapter 10).

EXERCISE 17

Study each of these poems and state its theme as a noun with modifiers.

A Birthday

My heart is like a singing bird
    Whose nest is in a watered shoot;
My heart is like an apple-tree
    Whose boughs are bent with thickset fruit;
My heart is like a rainbow shell   5
    That paddles in a halcyon sea;
My heart is gladder than all these
    Because my love is come to me.

Raise me a dais of silk and down;
    Hang it with vair and purple dyes;   10
Carve it in doves and pomegranates,
    And peacocks with a hundred eyes;
Work it in gold and silver grapes,
    In leaves and silver fleurs-de-lys;

Because the birthday of my life   15
   Is come, my love is come to me.

CHRISTINA G. ROSSETTI

Get Up and Bar the Door

It fell about the Martinmas time,
   And a gay time it was then,
When our goodwife got puddings to make,
   And she's boiled them in the pan.

The wind sae cauld blew south and north,   5
   And blew into the floor;
Quoth our goodman to our goodwife,
   "Gae out and bar the door."

"My hand is in my hussyfskap,
   Goodman, as ye may see;   10
An it shoud nae be barred this hundred year,
   It's no be barred for me."

They made a paction 'tween them twa,
   They made it firm and sure,
That the first word whaeer shoud speak,   15
   Shoud rise and bar the door.

Then by there came two gentlemen,
   At twelve o'clock at night,
And they could neither see house nor hall,
   Nor coal nor candle-light.   20

"Now whether is this a rich man's house,
   Or whether is it a poor?"
But neer a word wad ane o' them speak,
   For barring of the door.

And first they ate the white puddings,   25
   And then they ate the black;
Tho' muckle thought the goodwife to hersel,
   Yet neer a word she spake.

Then said the one unto the other,
  "Here, man, tak ye my knife;   30
Do ye tak aff the auld man's beard,
  And I'll kiss the goodwife."

"But there's nae water in the house,
  And what shall we do than?"
"What ails ye at the pudding-broo,   35
  That boils into the pan?"

O up then started our goodman,
  An angry man was he:
"Will ye kiss my wife before my een,
  And scad me wi' pudding-bree?"   40

Then up and started our goodwife,
  Gied three skips on the floor:
"Goodman, you've spoken the foremost word,
  Get up and bar the door."

ANONYMOUS
(Eighteenth Century)

sae cauld (5): spelling of *so cold* that reflects Scottish pronunciation of the vowels; found throughout the poem. **hussyfskap**
(9): housework. **muckle** (27): much. **een** (39): eyes. **scad**
(40): scald.

A Poison Tree

I was angry with my friend:
I told my wrath, my wrath did end.
I was angry with my foe:
I told it not, my wrath did grow.

And I water'd it in fears,   5
Night and morning with my tears;
And I sunned it with smiles,
And with soft deceitful wiles.

And it grew both day and night,
Till it bore an apple bright;   10
And my foe beheld it shine,
And he knew that it was mine,

And into my garden stole
When the night had veil'd the pole:
In the morning glad I see   15
My foe outstretch'd beneath the tree.

WILLIAM BLAKE

I Taste a Liquor Never Brewed

I taste a liquor never brewed—
From Tankards scooped in Pearl—
Not all the Frankfort Berries
Yield such an Alcohol!

Inebriate of Air—am I—   5
And Debauchee of Dew—
Reeling—thro endless summer days—
From inns of Molten Blue—

When "Landlords" turn the drunken Bee
Out of the Foxglove's door—   10
When Butterflies—renounce their "drams"—
I shall but drink the more!

Till Seraphs swing their snowy Hats—
And Saints—to windows run—
To see the little Tippler   15
From Manzanilla come!

EMILY DICKINSON

Frankfort Berries (3): An earlier version read "Vats upon the
Rhine." Manzanilla (16): in Cuba; associated with rum.
There are two other versions of line 16: "Leaning against the
—Sun—" and "Come staggering toward the sun."

I May, I Might, I Must

If you will tell me why the fen
appears impassable, I then
will tell you why I think that I
can get across it if I try.

MARIANNE MOORE

Out of the Night That Covers Me

Out of the night that covers me,
  Black as the Pit from pole to pole,
I thank whatever gods may be
  For my unconquerable soul.

In the fell clutch of circumstance   5
  I have not winced nor cried aloud.
Under the bludgeonings of chance
  My head is bloody, but unbowed.

Beyond this place of wrath and tears
  Looms but the Horror of the shade,   10
And yet the menace of the years
  Finds, and shall find, me unafraid.

It matters not how strait the gate,
  How charged with punishments the scroll,
I am the master of my fate: 15
  I am the captain of my soul.

WILLIAM ERNEST HENLEY

Pit (2): Hell.

4

THE POET'S USE
OF SIMILE
AND METAPHOR

A poet or any other writer or speaker makes two kinds of statements: literal and figurative. "I am sick"; "Yonder is a mountain"; "The sky is cloudy"—these are literal statements, and they mean exactly what they say. Figurative statements, in contrast, always have another meaning than the literal one. Like lies, they depart from literal truth, though not with the intention of deceiving. Thus a man may say, "I am heartsick," and not be advertising a cardiac condition; "I have mountains of work," and not be preparing to ascend the Alps. He may ask, as King Claudius asks of Hamlet, "How is it that the clouds still hang on you?" without being taken for a weather observer.

FIGURATIVE STATEMENTS

Figurative statements are by no means the exclusive property of poets; they also abound in common talk and writing. Use has even made some of them lose their figurative quality. Thus shoes have tongues, combs have teeth, needles have eyes—as though these objects were living creatures. Use has made other figurative statements trite ("He is old as the hills"; "She has a baby face'; "He is foxy"). When a student says that his parents "rolled out the red carpet" for him when he arrived home for Christmas vacation, he certainly does not mean that his father and mother painfully laid a long rug down the front walk. A sociologist who writes about the "role" of clergymen in community affairs is not consciously thinking of the theater. Unlike these speakers and writers, the good poet invents new figurative statements. Poets, therefore, are necessary to the welfare of a language because they keep it from becoming stale and exhausted.

SIMILE AND METAPHOR

A statement becomes figurative when it contains one of the **figures of language,** or **tropes.** The most common of these are simile and metaphor. A **simile** uses *like, as,* or *than* to express a resemblance between two essentially unlike entities: "Her hair drooped down her pallid cheeks like seaweed on a clam." Though literally untrue, this comparison creates the desired image of something lank, dank, and dull-colored. It should be observed that not every comparison is figurative: "Her wig, like Jane's, is red" is a literal statement because it compares two entities of the same kind, two wigs. "John knows Greek better than Jim" is literal; "John can speak Greek as naturally as a pig can squeak" is figurative.

A **metaphor** is a figure of language which omits the comparative term (*like, as, than*) and says or implies that one thing is another that it cannot literally be: "All the world's a stage." A simile says that *x* is like *y;* a metaphor, in its explicit form, says that *x* is *y.* This anonymous sixteenth-century song consists of four explicit metaphors.

> April is in my mistress' face,
> And July in her eyes hath place;
> Within her bosom is September,
> But in her heart a cold December.

Here, as in a simile, both terms of the comparisons are explicitly stated: *April–face, July–eyes,* etc.

IMPLICIT METAPHORS

In another anonymous song the metaphors are implicit rather than explicit.

> Injurious hours, whilst any joy doth bless me,
> With speedy wings you fly, and so release me.
> But if some sorrow do oppress my heart,
> You creep as if you never meant to part.

When the poet says that the hours have wings (line 2), he is obviously comparing them to a fast-flying bird. This metaphor is an implicit metaphor because one of the comparative terms—*bird*—is implied rather than stated. Similarly, in line 4, the hours are said to creep; here the omitted term is *slow-moving creature*. A metaphor, then, will not necessarily be in the form *x* is *y;* more commonly, the metaphor assumes that *x* is *y* and then goes on to say something about *x* as though it were *y*. These figurative statements contain implicit metaphors: "I will drink life to the lees" (understood explicit metaphor: life is a glass of wine); "She whispered into her husband's long, furry ear" (he is a jackass); "He glittered when he walked" (he was a shiny jewel). In the last example the whole metaphor has been concentrated into the single word *glittered*.

EXERCISE 18

In the following poems distinguish literal from figurative statements, and identify the similes and metaphors. Classify the metaphors as implicit or explicit.

Sic Vita

> Like to the falling of a star,
> Or as the flights of eagles are,
> Or like the fresh spring's gaudy hue,
> Or silver drops of morning dew,
> Or like a wind that chafes the flood,   5
> Or bubbles which on water stood—

Even such is man, whose borrowed light
Is straight called in, and paid to night.
The wind blows out, the bubble dies;
The spring entombed in autumn lies;   10
The dew dries up, the star is shot;
The flight is past, and man forgot.

HENRY KING

Title: "Thus Is Life."

I Wandered Lonely as a Cloud

I wandered lonely as a cloud
That floats on high o'er vales and hills,
When all at once I saw a crowd,
A host, of golden daffodils;
Beside the lake, beneath the trees,   5
Fluttering and dancing in the breeze.

Continuous as the stars that shine
And twinkle on the milky way,
They stretched in never-ending line
Along the margin of a bay: 10
Ten thousand saw I at a glance,
Tossing their heads in sprightly dance.

The waves beside them danced; but they
Out-did the sparkling waves in glee:
A poet could not but be gay,   15
In such a jocund company:
I gazed—and gazed—but little thought
What wealth the show to me had brought:

For oft, when on my couch I lie
In vacant or in pensive mood,   20
They flash upon that inward eye
Which is the bliss of solitude;
And then my heart with pleasure fills,
And dances with the daffodils.

WILLIAM WORDSWORTH

On the Head of a Stag

So we some antique hero's strength
Learn by his lance's weight and length;
As these vast beams express the beast,
Whose shady brows alive they dressed.
Such game, while yet the world was new,   5
The mighty Nimrod did pursue.
What huntsman of our feeble race,
Or dogs, dare such a monster chase,
Resembling, with each blow he strikes,
The charge of a whole troop of pikes?   10
O fertile head! which every year
Could such a crop of wonder bear!
The teeming earth did never bring
So soon, so hard, so huge a thing;
Which, might it never have been cast   15
(Each year's growth added to the last)
These lofty branches had supplied
The earth's bold sons' prodigious pride;
Heaven with these engines had been scaled,
When mountains heaped on mountains failed.   20

EDMUND WALLER

Nimrod (6): See Genesis x:8–9. sons (18): in Greek mythology the Titans, who waged unsuccessful war on heaven.

The Moon

And, like a dying lady lean and pale,
Who totters forth, wrapp'd in a gauzy veil,
Out of her chamber, led by the insane
And feeble wanderings of her fading brain,
The moon arose up in the murky east   5
A white and shapeless mass.

Art thou pale for weariness
Of climbing heaven and gazing on the earth,

Wandering companionless
Among the stars that have a different birth,   10
And ever changing, like a joyless eye
That finds no object worth its constancy?

                                    PERCY BYSSHE SHELLEY

Piazza di Spagna, Early Morning

I can't forget
How she stood at the top of that long marble stair
Amazed, and then with a sleepy pirouette
Went dancing slowly down to the fountain-quieted square;

Nothing upon her face   5
But some impersonal loneliness,--not then a girl
But as it were a reverie of the place,
A called-for falling glide and whirl;

As when a leaf, petal, or thin chip
Is drawn to the falls of a pool and, circling a moment above it, 10
Rides on over the lip—
Perfectly beautiful, perfectly ignorant of it.

                                    RICHARD WILBUR

Title: The Spanish Square in Rome. A vast, baroque stairway
descends from the church of Santa Trinita del Monte on a hill
overlooking the piazza to the square below.

LITERALISM

Literalism—mistaking figurative for literal statements—is a bad and
frequently a comic blunder.

On a Horse Who Bit a Clergyman

The steed bit his master;
How came this to pass?
He heard the good pastor
Say, "All flesh is grass."

                                    ANONYMOUS
                                    (Eighteenth Century)

In a horse literalism is probably excusable; in a reader of poems it is certainly not. A reader with an excessively literal mind will find nothing but nonsensical rubbish in poems. Of course such a reader has been using similes and metaphors all his life, but he has never stopped to think analytically about them. Learning to analyze figures is the best remedy for literalism.

ANALYZING A FIGURE OF COMPARISON

Every simile and every metaphor consists of two parts: an x, or a main entity, and a y, or a secondary entity to which the main entity is compared. Simile and explicit metaphor keep the two parts separate; implicit metaphor fuses the two, sometimes into a single word. Analysis of the figure consists first of identifying the two parts and then of explaining the basis on which the comparison is made—that is, the grounds of similarity between the two parts. Sometimes the grounds are stated:

> As flies to wanton boys are we to the gods:
> They kill us for their sport.

The two figures (gods are like boys; men are like flies) are followed by a statement of the grounds for the comparison: the gods kill men as heartlessly as reckless boys kill flies.

When the grounds of the comparison are not stated, analysis of the figure must concentrate on the connotations of the second part.

A Red, Red Rose

> O, my luve is like a red, red rose,
>   That's newly sprung in June.
> O, my luve is like the melodie,
>   That's sweetly play'd in tune.
>
> As fair art thou, by bonie lass,
>   So deep in luve am I,
> And I will luve thee still, my dear,
>   Till a' the seas gang dry.

5

Till a' the seas gang dry, my dear,
And the rocks melt wi' the sun!   10
And I will luve thee still, my dear,
While the sands o' life shall run.

And fare thee weel, my only luve,
And fare thee weel a while!
And I will come again, my luve,   15
Tho' it were ten thousand mile!

ROBERT BURNS

luve (1): beloved. **bonie:** (5) beautiful. **a'** (8): all. **gang**
(8): go. **weel** (13): well.

An analysis of the two similes in stanza 1 supplies all the relevant
connotations of *rose* and *melody:*

The girl is like a rose because she is beautiful in the way a rose is—not
just any rose, but a red, red rose. This image suggests something vibrant
and startling about her beauty. (A pale pink rose would suggest a fragile
beauty and a shy, withdrawn personality.) Since this girl is like a rose
that's newly sprung in June, she is the first, not the last rose of summer.
She is fresh and young. According to the second simile in the stanza she
is like a melody; she lifts up the lover's heart and pleases him in the same
way music does—not just any tune whistled in the street, but a melody
that has a kind of simple and artfully artless perfection.

Rather than rambling on in prose about the lady, Burns uses two
similes to express, more sharply and precisely than any prosaic inven-
tory could express, both the qualities of the girl and the man's feelings
for her. The figures help to communicate the experience because they
appeal to the reader's own experience. It is as if the speaker of the
poem were saying, "I know this girl and how I feel about her, but you
don't. But you *do* know what roses and lovely tunes are like. Well,
that's what *she* is like."

In addition to the figures of overstatement (see page 106) in stanzas
2, 3, and 4 of Burns's poem, there is an implicit metaphor in line 12:
"sands o' life." Here life is compared to an hourglass in which running
sand indicates the passing of time. An analysis of this metaphor, then,
would first identify the submerged term, *hourglass,* and then point out
that it connotes the passing of time. Burns wants the reader to think of

a very long period of time; it would take a long time for the sand to run out in a "lifetime glass," if there were such a thing.

EXERCISE 19

Analyze the metaphors and similes in these poems.

With Rue My Heart Is Laden

With rue my heart is laden
    For golden friends I had,
For many a rose-lipt maiden
    And many a lightfoot lad.

By brooks too broad for leaping   5
    The lightfoot boys are laid;
The rose-lipt girls are sleeping
    In fields where roses fade.

A. E. HOUSMAN

1. What are the possible meanings of *rue* (line 1)?
2. What are the various metaphors implied by *golden* (line 2)?

Fear No More the Heat o' the Sun

Fear no more the heat o' the sun,
    Nor the furious winter's rages;
Thou thy worldly task hast done,
    Home art gone, and ta'en thy wages;
Golden lads and girls all must,   5
As chimney-sweepers, come to dust.

Fear no more the frown o' the great,
    Thou art past the tyrant's stroke;
Care no more to clothe and eat,
    To thee the reed is as the oak.   10
The scepter, learning, physic, must
All follow this and come to dust.

Fear no more the lightning flash,
Nor the all-dreaded thunder-stone;
Fear not slander, censure rash;   15
Thou hast finished joy and moan.
All lovers young, all lovers must
Consign to thee and come to dust.

WILLIAM SHAKESPEARE
(from *Cymbeline*)

stone (14): bolt. **consign to** (18): consent to follow your example.

1. In the play two young men address this song to a dead girl. Contrast the attitude toward death here with the attitude in Housman's poem.
2. What are the connotations of *reed* and *oak* (line 10)?

She Walks in Beauty

She walks in Beauty, like the night
Of cloudless climes and starry skies;
And all that's best of dark and bright
Meet in her aspect and her eyes:
Thus mellowed to that tender light   5
Which Heaven to gaudy day denies.

One shade the more, one ray the less,
Had half impaired the nameless grace
Which waves in every raven tress,
Or softly lightens o'er her face;   10
Where thoughts serenely sweet express,
How pure, how dear their dwelling-place.

And on that cheek, and o'er that brow,
So soft, so calm, yet eloquent,
The smiles that win, the tints that glow,   15
But tell of days in goodness spent,
A mind at peace with all below,
A heart whose love is innocent!

GEORGE GORDON, LORD BYRON

1. The description of this lady is based on a contrast. What is the contrast?
2. What irrelevant connotations of *raven* (line 9) must the reader banish from his mind?

THE SOURCES OF FIGURATIVE LANGUAGE

Poets derive the secondary terms of their figures of comparison from every area of human experience. In the figurative statement "Silence, like a poultice, heals the wounds of sound," the secondary terms come from medicine; in

> To sleep I give my powers away;
> My will is bondsman to the dark . . .

the secondary terms come from legal practice. The metaphors in the following poem are drawn from government, architecture, clothing, and warfare:

Complaint of a Lover Rebuked

> Love that liveth and reigneth in my thought,
> That built his seat within my captive breast,
> Clad in the arms wherein with me he fought,
> Oft in my face he doth his banner rest.
> She that me taught to love and suffer pain,   5
> My doubtful hope and eke my hot desire
> With shamefast cloak to shadow and refrain,
> Her smiling grace converteth straight to ire;
> And coward love then to the heart apace
> Taketh his flight, whereas he lurks and plains   10
> His purpose lost, and dare not show his face.
> For my lord's guilt thus faultless bide I pains;
> Yet from my lord shall not my foot remove:
> Sweet is his death that takes his end by love.

> HENRY HOWARD, EARL OF SURREY

Campion's song beginning

> There is a garden in her face
> Where roses and white lilies blow . . .

draws on horticulture for its metaphorical images. Nature, religion, business, eating, drinking, objects of every kind, animals, games, studies—all these and many more provide poets with their figures.

EXERCISE 20

Sonnet 73

That time of year thou mayest in me behold
When yellow leaves, or none, or few, do hang
Upon those boughs which shake against the cold,
Bare ruined choirs, where late the sweet birds sang.
In me thou seest the twilight of such day   5
As after sunset fadeth in the west,
Which by and by black night doth take away,
Death's second self, that seals up all in rest.
In me thou seest the glowing of such fire
That on the ashes of his youth doth lie,   10
As the death-bed whereon it must expire,
Consumed with that which it was nourished by.
   This thou perceiv'st, which makes thy love more strong,
   To love that well which thou must leave ere long.

WILLIAM SHAKESPEARE

1. What is the source of the implicit metaphors that run through lines 1–4? Through lines 5–8? Through lines 9–12?
2. What do these metaphors have in common?
3. Do lines 13–14 make a literal or a figurative statement? What is the relationship between these lines and the rest of the poem?

EXTENDED FIGURES

A single metaphor or simile that runs through several lines, as in Shakespeare's "That time of year," is called an **extended figure;** a figure may even be extended throughout an entire poem. Such a poem is embedded in the dialogue of *Romeo and Juliet,* in the scene where Romeo, having come uninvited to a masked ball given by the enemies of his family, suddenly sees their daughter and, unaware of who she is, falls in love with her. In disguise he approaches her:

Romeo. If I profane with my unworthiest hand
This holy shrine, the gentle fine is this:
My lips, two blushing pilgrims, ready stand
To smooth that rough touch with a tender kiss.

Juliet. Good pilgrim, you do wrong your hand too much,   5
Which mannerly devotion shows in this;
For saints have hands that pilgrims' hands do touch,
And palm to palm is holy palmers' kiss.

Romeo. Have not saints lips, and holy palmers too?

Juliet. Ay, pilgrim, lips that they must use in prayer.   10

Romeo. O, then, dear saint, let lips do what hands do:
They pray; grant thou, lest faith turn to despair.

Juliet. Saints do not move, though grant for prayers' sake.

Romeo. Then move not, while my prayers' effect I take.

The implicit metaphor in these lines likens the meeting of Romeo and Juliet to a pilgrim's approaching the shrine of a saint. All the imagery of the poem, and all its subsidiary metaphors, derive directly from this central comparison. That human love should be spoken of as religious devotion may seem strange, but such language is valid in this poem. The young lovers feel a kind of awe in the presence of each other that is not unlike the devout person's feeling of unworthiness in a holy place.

EXERCISE 21

Sonnet 34

Like as a ship, that through the ocean wide
By conduct of some star, doth make her way,
When as a storm hath dimmed her trusty guide,
Out of her course doth wander far astray;
So I, whose star, that wont with her bright ray   5
Me to direct, with clouds is overcast,
Do wander now in darkness and dismay,
Through hidden perils round about me placed.
Yet hope I well that, when this storm is passed,
My Helice, the lodestar of my life,   10

Will shine again and look on me at last
With lovely light to clear my cloudy grief.
Till then I wander carefull, comfortless,
In secret sorrow, and sad pensiveness.

EDMUND SPENSER
(from *Amoretti*)

Helice (10): Ursa Major.

1. Who is being compared with the ship? Who with the star?
2. How far in the poem does the comparison extend?
3. For what is *storm* (line 9) a metaphor?

On First Looking into Chapman's Homer

Much have I travell'd in the realms of gold,
  And many goodly states and kingdoms seen;
  Round many western islands have I been
Which bards in fealty to Apollo hold.
Oft of one wide expanse had I been told   5
  That deep-brow'd Homer ruled as his demesne;
  Yet did I never breathe its pure serene
Till I heard Chapman speak out loud and bold:
Then felt I like some watcher of the skies
  When a new planet swims into his ken;   10
Or like stout Cortez when with eagle eyes
  He star'd at the Pacific—and all his men
Look'd at each other with a wild surmise—
  Silent, upon a peak in Darien.

JOHN KEATS

Chapman's Homer (Title): the translation of the *Iliad* and the
Odyssey by George Chapman (1559–1634).

1. What is being compared with traveling in line 1?
2. What, literally, are the "western islands" (line 3)?
3. How does line 4 help the reader supply the omitted part of the metaphor in lines 1–4?
4. What metaphor extends throughout the poem?

5. What is the connection between the metaphor in lines 9–10 and the extended metaphor?
6. Keats forgot that Balboa (not Cortez) discovered the Pacific. Does this error injure the poem in any way? Why or why not?
7. Why is the "surmise" (line 13) said to be "wild"?
8. What is the theme of the poem?

THE USES OF FIGURATIVE LANGUAGE

First, what does figurative language *not* do? It emphatically does not merely embellish or decorate a thought. A figurative statement is not a more effective or more vivid way of saying something that could be just as well said literally. Compare, for instance, "Shut up!" (an implicit metaphor that likens a human being to a box and thus takes from him all his humanity) and "Stop speaking!" These two commands do not say the same thing; they are not interchangeable. Similarly, the command "Don't butt in!" compares a human being with a goat and is thus not the equivalent of "Don't interfere in my affairs," which makes no comparison at all. What has been said about these colloquial figures applies equally to figures in poems. If figures were merely fancier ways of making literal statements, good poets would have no use for them because a good poet says what he means and nothing else. Figures help him accomplish this purpose.

Suppose that a poet wished to express the feeling of disillusionment. If he were a bad poet, he might scribble some literal doggerel like this:

> A thought that once was dear to me
> (How sad is what I say!)
> Is not what it appeared to be,
> As I found out today.

—Very disappointing lines, because they communicate no experience, evoke no images, and actually say very little.

A good poet, in contrast, will find a metaphor to help him say what he has to say.

It Dropped So Low in My Regard

It dropped so low—in my Regard—
I heard it hit the Ground—
And go to pieces on the Stones
At bottom of my Mind—

Yet blamed the Fate that fractured—*less*   5
Than I reviled Myself,
For entertaining Plated Wares
Upon my Silver Shelf—

EMILY DICKINSON

This poem is about something more than an accident in a china closet or the mistaking of silver-plate for sterling. The accident in stanza one is obviously the second term of an extended metaphor implied by the words *low, Regard* (line 1), and *Mind* (line 4). These words suggest that whatever has fallen has been more than a dish, because dishes do not break on the floor of the mind. The mind contains ideas, not dishes. An idea that is "high" in the mind is an ideal. In the first stanza, then, an ideal is being compared with a dish; disillusionment is being compared with the fall of the dish to a stone floor, where it breaks.

In the second stanza the poet shifts her metaphor slightly in order to say something about her mistaken evaluation of her ideal. What was highly valued as true sterling turns out to be nothing more than cheap silver-plate, the sort of ware that should never have been kept from the very beginning on a high shelf with the valuable sterling pieces. The shift in the metaphor is probably a flaw in the poem. Though both figures in the poem are drawn from closely related areas of housekeeping, they tend to cancel each other out logically. Plated ware may dent, but it does not shatter on a stone floor; moreover, since sterling is softer, it is apt to be even more damaged in a fall than silver-plate. Someone might argue that what the poet had in mind was a china or glass vessel overlaid with silver; many people are familiar with such lusterware, but no one would mistake it for true silver and, in any event, it was never called *plated ware*. There is nothing inherently wrong with shifted or mixed metaphors as long as they work harmoniously together and do not cancel each other out or seem absurd (as in "Aubade," page 10). In fact many poets deliberately use them to organize or develop their poems, or to achieve special effects. In Emily Dickinson's poem, however, the shift appears to be a flaw.

In spite of this weakness, the poem usefully illustrates a number of the functions that metaphor can perform. First, it makes the abstract appear to be concrete. Nobody has ever seen or heard an ideal go to pieces in a mind, yet everybody has had accidents with dishes. Thus the metaphor appeals to the reader's experience and imagination because it creates images, images lacking in the literal statement "I overvalued something, and now I am disillusioned." Second, a metaphor, if it is successfully developed, can give a poem its structure. It provides the poet with a concise narrative. Third, the metaphor enables the poet to express a judgment without wasting space on such bald exclamations as "How false was my ideal!" The judgment is implicit in the metaphors *go to pieces* (line 3) and *Plated* (line 7). Fourth, the metaphor enables the reader to recreate the speaker's feeling so that he can feel something like it himself. The important word *entertaining* (line 7) tells the reader how the speaker felt before she discovered that her ideal was spurious. Once she entertained (that is, cherished as well as maintained and kept up) the false ideal; now that it has been exposed as worthless, she blames herself. Fate may have brought about the exposure, but only she put the dish (the ideal) high in her cupboard (her mind).

Thus a metaphor enables a poet to say precisely what he means because (1) it creates images that make abstract statements appear concrete, (2) it gives shape and structure to statements, (3) it conveys judgments, and (4) it communicates feelings.

EXERCISE 22

Determine the functions of the figurative statements in these poems.

The Last Word

Creep into thy narrow bed,
Creep, and let no more be said!
Vain thy onset! all stands fast;
Thou thyself must break at last.

Let the long contention cease!   5
Geese are swans, and swans are geese.
Let them have it how they will!
Thou art tired; best be still!

They out-talk'd thee, hiss'd thee, tore thee.
Better men fared thus before thee;   10
Fired their ringing shot and pass'd,
Hotly charged—and broke at last.

Charge once more, then, and be dumb!
Let the victors, when they come,
When the forts of folly fall,   15
Find thy body by the wall!

MATTHEW ARNOLD

The Silver Swan

The silver swan, who living had no note,
When death approached, unlocked her silent throat;
Leaning her breast against the reedy shore,
Thus sung her first and last, and sung no more:
"Farewell, all joys! O death, come close mine eyes;   5
More geese than swans now live, more fools than wise."

ANONYMOUS
(*Seventeenth Century*)

By the Road to the Air-Base

The calloused grass lies hard
Against the cracking plain:
Life is a grayish stain;
The salt-marsh hems my yard.

Dry dikes rise hill on hill: 5
In sloughs of tidal slime
Shell-fish deposit lime,
Wild sea-fowl creep at will.

The highway, like a beach,
Turns whiter, shadowy, dry: 10
Loud, pale against the sky,
The bombing planes hold speech.

Yet fruit grows on the trees;
Here scholars pause to speak;
Through gardens bare and Greek,   15
I hear my neighbor's bees.

                    YVOR WINTERS

Driving Home

Nothing. Not even you, Dave, speak
at this speed. We have flattened out
a little toward that radiant
silhouette science talks about:—
mass moving at the speed of light.   5
Dusk wounds our windshield;
townships divide; the winding creek
unwinds; forest and field
flicker and slant. We have lost weight.
What syllable's not too ponderous   10
for us—two headlights twinkling
across country—small double star
in its untranquil firmament
of route and suburb. Inkling
of the Immaterial—we mount,   15
accelerate without effort, pass
through throngs unnoticed . . . . All the same,
we saw a girl step from a car—
calves chiaroscuro; through blurred wood
watched a rotund old gelding plod   20
his moving pasture . . . . These reclaim
our lost gravity: "Let me out!"
eh, Dave? Observance of the mass
for us. Let angels levitate.

                    PETER KANE DUFAULT

Easter Wings

Lord, who createdst man in wealth and store,
  Though foolishly he lost the same,
    Decaying more and more
      Till he became
        Most poor: 5
        With thee
      O let me rise,
    As larks, harmoniously,
  And sing this day thy victories;
Then shall the fall further the flight in me.   10

My tender age in sorrow did begin;
  And still with sicknesses and shame
    Thou didst so punish sin,
      That I became
        Most thin.   15
        With thee
      Let me combine
    And feel this day thy victory;
  For, if I imp my wing on thine,
Affliction shall advance the flight in me.   20

GEORGE HERBERT

To the Senses

When conquering love did first my heart assail,
Unto mine aid I summoned every sense,
Doubting, if that proud tyrant should prevail,
My heart should suffer for mine eyes' offence;
But he with beauty first corrupted sight,   5
My hearing bribed with her tongue's harmony,
My taste, by her sweet lips drawn with delight,
My smelling won with her breath's spicery;
But when my touching came to play his part
(The king of senses, greater than the rest),   10

He yields love up the keys unto my heart,
And tells the other how they should be blest;
  And thus by those of whom I hoped for aid,
  To cruel love my soul was first betrayed.

MICHAEL DRAYTON

1. Analyze the extended metaphor.
2. How are the five senses corrupted by the heart's assailant?
3. Why is touch called the king of senses (line 10)?
4. In what way is love cruel (line 14)? Why does the lover think of himself as having been betrayed?

CONCEITS

A figurative comparison of two strikingly dissimilar entities is called a **conceit**.

> Nature's confectioner, the bee
> (Whose suckets are moist alchemy,
> The still of his refining mold
> Minting the garden into gold),
> Having rifled all the fields   5
> Of what dainties Flora yields,
> Ambitious now to take excise
> Of a more fragrant paradise,
> At my Fuscara's sleeve arrived
> Where all delicious sweets are hived.   10

In these lines from John Cleveland's "Fuscara" a honeybee is compared to a manufacturer of suckets, or candies (line 1), to an alchemist (line 2), to a coiner of money (lines 3–4), to a thief (line 5), and to a tax-collector (line 7). Except for the first and perhaps the second comparison, all these comparisons are conceits. The distance between a bee and a tax-collector is so great that the comparison may be considered far-fetched. Comparing a girl's sleeve to a beehive (line 10) is also far-fetched. Surely the poet wants the reader to admire his cleverness rather than to form an image of this particular dress. Cleveland's lines are cited here because they provide such unmistakable examples of conceits, not because they contain especially effective conceits.

PETRARCHAN CONCEITS

Several writers of love poems in sixteenth-century England used stock comparisons that literary historians call **Petrarchan conceits,** after Francesco Petrarch (1304–1374), the Italian poet whom the English poets imitated. In a Petrarchan poem the lover, who is usually the speaker, describes himself as a worshiper of his lady's beauty and virtue. Regardless of what the lady does, the lover suffers. When she is aloof and haughty, he freezes; if she so much as smiles at him, he burns and fries. Sometimes her eyes shoot arrows at him and wound him; then his weeping becomes a shower of rain, and his sighs turn into a windstorm. Petrarchan ladies usually have hair of gold, complexions of lilies and roses, teeth of pearls, necks and breasts of milky whiteness. Their virtue is an impregnable fortress.

These conceits provided a would-be poet with a ready-made set of metaphors that he could string together without thinking about the experience of love or the beauty of a particular lady. Yet it would be an error to condemn all Petrarchan conceits merely because some bad poets abused them. The Petrarchan poets who avoided excessively farfetched and hackneyed conceits wrote some fine poems idealizing love and womanhood. (See the poems by Shakespeare, Surrey, Spenser, and Drayton in this chapter.)

EXERCISE 23

Identify among the following a poem that uses the Petrarchan conceits successfully, a poem that does not use them successfully, and a poem that ridicules them. Defend your choices.

Burn On, Sweet Fire

Burn on, sweet fire, for I live by that fuel
  Whose smoke is as an incense to my soul.
Each sigh prolongs my smart. Be fierce and cruel,
  My fair Parthenophe. Frown and control,
Vex, torture, scald, disgrace me. Do thy will!   5
  Stop up thine ears; with flint immure thine heart,
And kill me with thy looks, if they would kill.

Thine eyes, those crystal phials which impart
The perfect balm to my dead-wounded breast;
   Thine eyes, the quivers whence those darts were drawn   10
Which me to thy love's bondage have addressed;
   Thy smile and frown, night-star and daylight's dawn,
Burn on, frown on, vex, stop thine ears, torment me!
   More, for thy beauty borne, would not repent me.

BARNABY BARNES

Parthenophe (4): the girl's name.

Sonnet 130

My mistress' eyes are nothing like the sun;
Coral is far more red than her lips' red;
If snow be white, why then her breasts are dun;
If hairs be wires, black wires grow on her head.
I have seen roses damasked, red and white,   5
But no such roses see I in her cheeks;
And in some perfumes is there more delight
Than in the breath that from my mistress reeks.
I love to hear her speak, yet well I know
That music hath a far more pleasing sound;   10
I grant I never saw a goddess go;
My mistress, when she walks, treads on the ground.
   And yet, by heaven, I think my love as rare
   As any she belied with false compare.

WILLIAM SHAKESPEARE

go (11): walk.

To Delia

Fair is my love, and cruel as she's fair:
   Her brow shades frowns, although her eyes are sunny;
   Her smiles are lightning, though her pride despair;
   And her disdains are gall, her favors honey.
A modest maid, decked with a blush of honor,   5
   Whose feet do tread green paths of youth and love;

> The wonder of all eyes that look upon her,
> Sacred on earth, designed a saint above.
> Chastity and beauty, which were deadly foes,
> Live reconcilèd friends within her brow;   10
> And had she pity to conjoin with those,
> Then who had heard the plaints I utter now?
> For had she not been fair and thus unkind,
> My muse had slept, and none had known my mind.

SAMUEL DANIEL

METAPHYSICAL CONCEITS

The figurative comparisons found in the poems of John Donne (1572–1631) and his imitators are called **metaphysical conceits.** Samuel Johnson described this kind of conceit as "a combination of dissimilar images, or discovery of occult resemblances." A metaphysical conceit is likely to be more unexpected and more original than a Petrarchan. A marriage bed may be compared to a grave, the union of two lovers to an alchemist's mixture, the parting of friends to an eclipse of the sun. "The most heterogeneous ideas are yoked by violence together," said Dr. Johnson, who did not admire these conceits; "nature and art are ransacked for illustrations, comparisons, and allusions." The metaphors of a single poem may be drawn from such difficult studies as theology and astronomy, and from such ordinary activities as commerce and housekeeping. In general the metaphysical poets display more learning in their poems than do the Petrarchans.

Another difference between the metaphysicals and the Petrarchans is that the former do not ordinarily idealize womanhood and love. Instead, they attempt to define attitudes toward particular women—and their attitudes are not always respectful. Sometimes the speaker of a metaphysical poem argues ingeniously in defense of an outrageous proposition.

The Flea

Mark but this flea, and mark in this
How little that which thou deniest me is;
It sucked me first, and now sucks thee,
And in this flea our two bloods mingled be.
Thou knowest that this cannot be said   5
A sin, nor shame, nor loss of maidenhead;
   Yet this enjoys before it woo,
   And pampered swells with one blood made of two,
   And this, alas, is more than we would do.

O stay! Three lives in one flea spare,   10
Where we almost, yea, more than married are;
This flea is you and I, and this
Our marriage bed and marriage temple is.
Though parents grudge, and you, we're met
And cloistered in these living walls of jet.   15
   Though use make you apt to kill me,
   Let not to that, self-murder added be,
   And sacrilege, three sins in killing three.

Cruel and sudden! Hast thou since
Purpled thy nail in blood of innocence?   20
Wherein could this flea guilty be,
Except in that drop which it sucked from thee?
Yet thou triumph'st and saist that thou
Find'st not thyself, nor me, the weaker now.
   'Tis true. Then learn how false, fears be;   25
   Just so much honor, when thou yield'st to me,
   Will waste, as this flea's death took life from thee.

JOHN DONNE

    This lover's way of persuading his lady to yield to him is certainly unusual; the last thing in the world a "romantic" lover would do would be to compare love-making to flea-bites. In using this metaphor, the speaker shows that he is cynical about romance and artificial etiquette. He is seeking his own gratification, and he will use any means to achieve his ends. His metaphor minimizes the importance of what he seeks. In effect what he keeps saying through the metaphor is "What I want of you is just as unimportant as a flea-bite."

Donne's "Flea" represents one extreme in metaphysical poetry; his divine poems represent another. Unlike the Petrarchans, Donne and his followers also wrote passionately ingenious poems on religious subjects.

The Windows

Lord, how can man preach thy eternal word?
 He is a brittle, crazy glass;
Yet in thy temple thou dost him afford
 This glorious and transcendent place,
 To be a window through thy grace.   5

But when thou dost anneal in glass thy story,
 Making thy life to shine within
The holy preacher's, then the light and glory
 More reverend grows, and more doth win,
 Which else shows waterish, bleak, and thin. 10

Doctrine and life, colors and light in one,
 When they combine and mingle, bring
A strong regard and awe; but speech alone
 Doth vanish like a flaring thing,
 And in the ear, not conscience, ring.   15

GEORGE HERBERT

Stanza 1 compares a clergyman to a plain glass window. As a mere man, he is all too imperfect for the holy task assigned to him. He is "brittle" (that is, unstable and insecure) and "crazed" (full of fine cracks and imperfections). He can transmit light (the word of God) only glaringly and imperfectly to his congregation—and only with the help of God's grace. Stanza 2 continues the metaphor by comparing the holy minister—the man who has shaped his life according to God's teachings—to a stained-glass window. His life is a colorfully pictured example of God's doctrine (line 11) because he practices what he preaches. The words of a clergyman in whom God has annealed his

101

story ring (line 15) in the consciences, not the ears, of his congregation. Herbert makes the unlikely and artificial comparison of a man to a window seem inevitable and right. The best metaphysical conceits appeal simultaneously to a reader's mental and emotional apparatus—to his mind and heart.

EXERCISE 24

A Valediction Forbidding Mourning

As virtuous men pass mildly away,
    And whisper to their souls to go,
Whilst some of their sad friends do say,
    The breath goes now, and some say, no:

So let us melt, and make no noise,   5
    No tear-floods, nor sigh-tempests move;
'Twere profanation of our joys
    To tell the laity our love.

Moving of the earth brings harms and fears;
    Men reckon what it did and meant;   10
But trepidation of the spheres,
    Though greater far, is innocent.

Dull sublunary lovers' love
    (Whose soul is sense) cannot admit
Absence, because it doth remove   15
    Those things which elemented it.

But we, by a love so much refined
    That ourselves know not what it is,
Inter-assurèd of the mind,
    Care less, eyes, lips, and hands to miss. 20

Our two souls, therefore, which are one,
    Though I must go, endure not yet
A breach, but an expansion,
    Like gold to airy thinness beat.

If they be two, they are two so   25
  As stiff twin compasses are two:
Thy soul, the fixed foot, makes no show
  To move, but doth, if the other do.

And though it in the center sit,
  Yet when the other far doth roam,   30
It leans and harkens after it,
  And grows erect as that comes home.

Such wilt thou be to me, who must,
  Like the other foot, obliquely run;
Thy firmness makes my circle just,   35
  And makes me end where I begun.

JOHN DONNE

trepidation of the spheres (11): precession of the equinoxes.
innocent (12): harmless. **elemented** (16): constituted.

1. To what does the speaker compare the dying of men described in stanza 1? What is the basis of this comparison?
2. Analyze the metaphor implied by *melt* (line 5) and *laity* (line 8).
3. From what studies are the metaphors in stanza 3 drawn?
4. Should *sublunary* (line 13) be understood figuratively or literally?
5. From what activity is the simile in line 24 drawn?
6. What is the speaker's attitude toward Petrarchan conceits?
7. What kind of compass is referred to in line 26?
8. Compare the extended simile in lines 25–36 with the following poem:

The Man and Wife That Kind and Loving Are

The man and wife that kind and loving are,
I fitly may to compasses compare;
The compasses are two, conjoined at the head,
So man and wife in Christ are couplèd.
One part steps forth and doth the circle trace,   5
The other firmly keeps the center's place.
So while the man doth travel for his gain,
The wife at home doth what is got maintain.

They being in part disjoined by circles wide,
Do yet in part united still abide;   10
And when the circle's drawn, and figure done,
They are conjoined again as 'twere in one.
So though far business the man and wife do part,
They are together still in love and heart;
And when the man returneth to his place,   15
They both as one do lovingly embrace.
Nothing but force can separate those twain;
These never part till one by death is slain.
One part being broken, then out of use the other lies;
Without joy the one lives when the other dies.   20
If art conjoin a new part to the old,
Yet will not they due correspondence hold;
If man and wife procure a second mate,
They seldom pass their time without some bate.
Thus loving couples, as we plainly see,   25
Like compasses in everything agree;
Thus do they join, thus live, thus love, thus die;
Thus they join, live, love, and die, most happily.

ANONYMOUS
(*Seventeenth Century*)

1. Does the metaphor in the anonymous poem receive any additional development after line 5?
2. What bases of comparison does the unknown poet use that Donne does not?
3. Agree or disagree with this statement: "In Donne's poem the metaphor is subordinated to the total idea of the poem: the metaphor is used for the sake of the poem. The other poem seems to exist solely for the sake of the metaphor."
4. What other important differences are there between these poems?

Holy Sonnet 13

What if this present were the world's last night?
Mark in my heart, O soul, where thou dost dwell,
The picture of Christ crucified, and tell
Whether that countenance can thee affright:
Tears in his eyes quench the amazing light;   5
Blood fills his frowns, which from his pierced head fell.

And can that tongue adjudge thee unto hell,
Which prayed forgiveness for his foes' fierce spite?
No, no; but, as in my idolatry
I said to all my profane mistresses,   10
Beauty, of pity; foulness only is
A sign of rigor, so I say to thee,
To wicked spirits are horrid shapes assigned;
This beauteous form assures a piteous mind.

JOHN DONNE

1. To what event does line 1 refer?
2. Why does the prospect of that event trouble the speaker?
3. The phrase *in my idolatry* (line 9) apparently refers to the time when **Donne** wrote poems like "The Flea." What he said to the ladies in this period of his life is expressed elliptically in lines 11–12: "Beauty is a sign of pity; foulness (i.e., ugliness) is a sign of rigor." Show the relevance of this argument (the simile running from *as* in line 9 to *so* in line 12) to his present spiritual plight.
4. Explain whether or not the prospect envisioned in line 1 still troubles the speaker in line 14.

On Donne's Poetry

With Donne, whose muse on dromedary trots,
Wreathe iron pokers into true-love knots;
Rhyme's sturdy cripple, fancy's maze and clue,
Wit's forge and fire-blast, meaning's press and screw.

SAMUEL TAYLOR COLERIDGE

1. Analyze Coleridge's metaphors. What attitudes toward Donne do they imply?
2. Cite examples from Donne's poems that illustrate Coleridge's remarks.

5

THE POET'S USE
OF OTHER FIGURES

Poets have available for their use many different figures of language—over two hundred, in fact, according to the traditional rhetoricians who identified the various kinds and gave them such formidable labels as *litotes, asyndeton,* and *hendiadys.* Of all these possible figures, the beginning reader of poems needs to know, in addition to simile and metaphor, only six: overstatement, understatement, metonymy, apostrophe, personification, and paradox. Labeling and classifying the various figures is less important, however, than understanding why and how poets use them. The study of figures is not an end in itself, but a means for better understanding poems.

OVERSTATEMENT AND UNDERSTATEMENT

She Dwelt among the Untrodden Ways

She dwelt among the untrodden ways
  Beside the springs of Dove,
A Maid whom there were none to praise
And very few to love:

A violet by a mossy stone   5
  Half hidden from the eye!
—Fair as a star, when only one
  Is shining in the sky.

She lived unknown, and few could know
  When Lucy ceased to be;   10
But she is in her grave, and, oh,
  The difference to me!

WILLIAM WORDSWORTH

Dove (2): a stream in the Midlands of England.

Had Wordsworth been writing directly and literally, he might have begun his account of Lucy by saying, "She lived in a very remote place"; but this statement is inexact compared with the first line of the poem. Lucy dwelt in a place so remote that *nobody* walked on the roads: the "ways" were "untrodden." Here, clearly, Wordsworth is exaggerating. A poet makes an **overstatement** (sometimes called **hyperbole**) when he exaggerates, not to deceive the reader but to create a special effect (see stanzas 2, 3, and 4 of Burns's poem, page 81). Wordsworth may have wanted to emphasize, in a single word, how remote and lonely Lucy's dwelling-place was. The last line of the poem, in contrast, is an **understatement,** because it not only says much less than it could have said, but less than the occasion warrants. Understatement is effective because of what it leaves unsaid. The effect would have been much less poignant had Wordsworth written "The misery to me!"

EXERCISE 25

Find examples of overstatement and understatement in these poems.

Dread

Beside a chapel I'd a room looked down,
Where all the women from the farms and town,
On Holy-days and Sundays used to pass
To marriages, and christenings, and to Mass.

Then I sat lonely watching score and score,   5
Till I turned jealous of the Lord next door. . . .
Now by this window, where there's none can see,
The Lord God's jealous of yourself and me.

JOHN MILLINGTON SYNGE

1. What is happening by the window (line 7)?
2. Why does Synge use overstatement?
3. If you think that the title is inappropriate, suggest a better one.

How Annandale Went Out

"They called it Annandale—and I was there
To flourish, to find words, and to attend:
Liar, physician, hypocrite, and friend,
I watched him; and the sight was not so fair
As one or two that I have seen elsewhere: 5
An apparatus not for me to mend—
A wreck, with hell between him and the end,
Remained of Annandale; and I was there.

"I knew the ruin as I knew the man;
So put the two together, if you can,   10
Remembering the worst you know of me.
Now view yourself as I was, on the spot—
With a slight kind of engine. Do you see?
Like this . . . You wouldn't hang me? I thought not."

EDWIN ARLINGTON ROBINSON

1. The key to this poem is the proper identification of *slight kind of engine* (line 13). For what word or words is this expression a metaphor?
2. What does *it* (line 1) refer to? Why is *it* used?
3. Why does the speaker repeatedly emphasize that he was there? What does the phrase *on the spot* (line 12) suggest?
4. Characterize the speaker. What is his opinion of himself?

Upon Julia's Voice

So smooth, so sweet, so silv'ry is thy voice,
As, could they hear, the damned would make no noise,
But listen to thee, walking in thy chamber,
Melting melodious words to lutes of amber.

ROBERT HERRICK

Eight O'Clock

He stood, and heard the steeple
  Sprinkle the quarters on the morning town.
One, two, three, four, to market-place and people
  It tossed them down.

Strapped, noosed, nighing his hour,   5
  He stood and counted them and cursed his luck;
And then the clock collected in the tower
  Its strength, and struck.

A. E. HOUSMAN

METONYMY

Metonymy is a figure of language in which a thing is not designated by its own name, but by the name of a thing resembling it or closely related to it. Metonymies are very common in everyday speech. "Give me a light," a man says, when he literally means that he wants some fire. "He is addicted to the bottle" is another way of saying that he drinks too much liquor. "I am studying Shakespeare" means that I am studying Shakespeare's plays, not the man himself. In each of these remarks a closely related object is substituted for the object itself.

Poets use metonymy to emphasize a significant detail and thereby to suggest something that the literal word does not suggest. Thus when Shakespeare, for example, says (page 38) that "Dick the shepherd blows his *nail*," he draws particular attention to one part of the hand, and we are reminded of how hard and blue-looking a very cold hand is, as though it were not flesh and blood, but all fingernail. This particular effect would be missing if Shakespeare had used the literal word *hand* instead of the metonymy *nail*.

EXERCISE 26

Identify the metonymies and discuss their use in these poems.

The Glories of Our Blood and State

The glories of our blood and state
   Are shadows, not substantial things;
There is no armor against fate;
   Death lays his icy hand on kings:
      Scepter and crown   5
      Must tumble down,
And in the dust be equal made,
With the poor crooked scythe and spade.

Some men with swords may reap the field,
   And plant fresh laurels where they kill;   10
But their strong nerves at last must yield;
   They tame but one another still:
      Early or late
      They stoop to fate,
And must give up their murmuring breath,   15
When they, pale captives, creep to death.

The garlands wither on your brow;
   Then boast no more your mighty deeds;
Upon death's purple altar now,
   See where the victor-victim bleeds: 20
      Your heads must come
      To the cold tomb.
Only the actions of the just
Smell sweet and blossom in their dust.

JAMES SHIRLEY
(from The Contention of Ajax and Ulysses)

With You a Part of Me Hath Passed Away

With you a part of me hath passed away;
For in the peopled forest of my mind
A tree made leafless by this wintry wind
Shall never don again its green array.
Chapel and fireside, country road and bay,   5
Have something of their friendliness resigned;
Another, if I would, I could not find,
And I am grown much older in a day.
But yet I treasure in my memory
Your gift of charity, your mellow ease,   10
And the dear honour of your amity;
For these once mine, my life is rich with these.
And I scarce know which part may greater be,—
What I keep of you, or you rob from me.

GEORGE SANTAYANA

Disdain Returned

He that loves a rosy cheek,
    Or a coral lip admires,
Or from star-like eyes doth seek
    Fuel to maintain his fires;
As old Time makes these decay,   5
So his flames must waste away.

But a smooth and steadfast mind,
    Gentle thoughts and calm desires,
Hearts with equal love combined,
    Kindle never-dying fires.   10
Where these are not, I despise
Lovely cheeks, or lips, or eyes.

No tears, Celia, now shall win
    My resolved heart to return;
I have searched thy soul within,   15
    And find nought but pride and scorn;

I have learned thy arts, and now
    Can disdain as much as thou.
Some power, in my revenge, convey
    That love to her I cast away.   20

THOMAS CAREW

1. How and why does the poet avoid using the word *girl* or one of its synonyms in the first two stanzas?
2. For what experience is *fires* (lines 4, 10) a metonymy? Why has the poet not mentioned the experience directly?
3. Would the poem be improved by lopping off stanza 3? Justify your answer.

Epitaph on Himself

Good friend, for Jesus' sake forbear
To dig the dust enclosed here;
Blest be the man that spares these stones,
And curst be he that moves my bones.

WILLIAM SHAKESPEARE

A great many metonymies—the *fires* of "Disdain Returned," for example—can also be regarded as metaphors. The label is of no importance, because the various figures of language cannot be separated into exclusive categories. Whether one calls *fires* a metonymy or a metaphor depends on how one looks at the figure. Understanding the functions of figures is more important than giving them tags. Many of the best figures, moreover, escape notice that they *are* figures until they have been carefully examined. And frequently the best figures invite examination from more than one angle.

PERSONIFICATION

Personification is a figure that bestows human traits on anything nonhuman. It compares the nonhuman with the human and is thus a kind of metaphor in which one member is always a human being. Animals, objects, natural phenomena, and ideas may be personified. Like metonymy, personification occurs frequently in common speech.

"She won't run," a driver says of a stalled car. "Money talks." "Let's get out of this raging storm." In personifying car, money, and storm nobody visualizes them as people. Similarly, poets do not always expect their readers to visualize their personifications, but they sometimes do.

EXERCISE 27

Study the personifications in these poems.

Drinking

The thirsty earth soaks up the rain,
And drinks and gapes for drink again;
The plants suck in the earth, and are
With constant drinking fresh and fair;
The sea itself, which one would think   5
Should have but little need of drink,
Drinks ten thousand rivers up,
So filled that they o'erflow the cup.
The busy sun—and one would guess
By's drunken fiery face no less—   10
Drinks up the sea, and when he's done,
The moon and stars drink up the sun:
They drink and dance by their own light
They drink and revel all the night.
Nothing in nature's sober found,   15
But an eternal health goes round.
Fill up the bowl, then, fill it high!
Fill all the glasses there: for why
Should every creature drink but I?
Why, man of morals, tell me why?   20

ABRAHAM COWLEY

1. Which of these personifications are also visual images? Which are not?
2. In what order are the drinkers presented? Can the order be changed without damaging the poem?
3. Why are there so many overstatements in the poem?
4. What is the main flaw in the argument? Does the flaw increase the reader's enjoyment of the poem?

On the Death of Dr. Robert Levet

Condemn'd to hope's delusive mine,
   As on we toil from day to day,
By sudden blasts, or slow decline,
   Our social comforts drop away.

Well tried through many a varying year,   5
   See Levet to the grave descend;
Officious, innocent, sincere,
   Of ev'ry friendless name the friend.

Yet still he fills affection's eye,
   Obscurely wise, and coarsely kind;   10
Nor, letter'd arrogance, deny
   Thy praise to merit unrefin'd.

When fainting nature call'd for aid,
   And hov'ring death prepar'd the blow,
His vig'rous remedy display'd   15
   The power of art without the show.

In misery's darkest caverns known,
   His useful care was ever nigh,
Where hopeless anguish pour'd his groan,
   And lonely want retir'd to die.   20

No summons mock'd by chill delay,
   No petty gain disdain'd by pride,
The modest wants of ev'ry day
   The toil of ev'ry day supplied.

His virtues walk'd their narrow round,   25
   Nor made a pause, nor left a void;
And sure th' Eternal Master found
   The single talent well employ'd.

SAMUEL JOHNSON

Levet (Title): a physician who practiced among the poor of London, lived more or less at Johnson's expense, and died in Johnson's house in 1782. **officious** (7): helpful. **talent** (28): see page 249.

1. Who is "condemned" (line 1)? Who is "tried" (line 5)?
2. Why is hope's mine called "delusive" (line 1)?
3. Why are the words *letter'd arrogance* (line 11) set off by commas?
4. What opinion does the poet seem to have of most physicians other than Levet?
5. Show how the figure of personification enables the poet to say much in a small space.

To Autumn

Season of mists and mellow fruitfulness,
    Close bosom-friend of the maturing sun;
Conspiring with him how to load and bless
    With fruit the vines that round the thatch-eves run;
To bend with apples the moss'd cottage-trees,   5
    And fill all fruit with ripeness to the core;
        To swell the gourd, and plump the hazel shells
With a sweet kernel; to set budding more,
    And still more, later flowers for the bees,
    Until they think warm days will never cease,   10
        For Summer has o'er-brimm'd their clammy cells.

Who hath not seen thee oft amid thy store?
    Sometimes whoever seeks abroad may find
Thee sitting careless on a granary floor,
    Thy hair soft-lifted by the winnowing wind;   15
Or on a half-reap'd furrow sound asleep,
    Drows'd with the fume of poppies, while thy hook
        Spares the next swath and all its twined flowers:
And sometimes like a gleaner thou dost keep
    Steady thy laden head across a brook;   20
    Or by a cyder-press, with patient look,
        Thou watchest the last oozings hours by hours.

Where are the songs of Spring? Ay, where are they?
    Think not of them, thou hast thy music too,—
While barred clouds bloom the soft-dying day,   25
    And touch the stubble-plains with rosy hue;
Then in a wailful choir the small gnats mourn
    Among the river sallows, borne aloft
        Or sinking as the light wind lives or dies;

And full-grown lambs loud bleat from hilly bourn;   30
    Hedge-crickets sing; and now with treble soft
The red-breast whistles from a garden-croft;
    And gathering swallows twitter in the skies.

JOHN KEATS

1. Where is the first suggestion of personification? As what is Autumn personified? Is the personification effective and appropriate? Does it continue to the end of the poem?

2. Explain these metonymies: *hook* (line 17); *treble* (line 31); *red-breast* (line 32).

3. Does the same kind of imagery predominate in each stanza?

4. Locate every word that relates to time. Then discuss the truth or falsity of these statements: the poem covers the period of a year; the poem covers a period of about three months; the poem covers the period of a day.

5. What words have unpleasant connotations? Why are they in the poem?

6. Where are there suggestions of melancholy? What causes this melancholy?

The Chestnut Casts His Flambeaux

The chestnut casts his flambeaux, and the flowers
    Stream from the hawthorn on the wind away,
The doors clap to, the pane is blind with showers.
    Pass me the can, lad; there's an end of May.

There's one spoilt spring to scant our mortal lot,   5
    One season ruined of our little store.
May will be fine next year as like as not:
    Oh, ay, but then we shall be twenty-four.

We for a certainty are not the first
    Have sat in taverns while the tempest hurled   10
Their hopeful plans to emptiness, and cursed
    Whatever brute and blackguard made the world.

It is in truth iniquity on high
    To cheat our sentenced souls of aught they crave,
And mar the merriment as you and I   15
    Fare on our long fool's-errand to the grave.

Iniquity it is; but pass the can.
My lad, no pair of kings our mothers bore;
Our only portion is the estate of man:
We want the moon, but we shall get no more.　　　　20

If here to-day the cloud of thunder lours
　To-morrow it will hie on far behests;
The flesh will grieve on other bones than ours
Soon, and the soul will mourn in other breasts.

The troubles of our proud and angry dust　　　　25
Are from eternity, and shall not fail.
Bear them we can, and if we can we must.
Shoulder the sky, my lad, and drink your ale.

A. E. HOUSMAN

1. Describe the setting in a single sentence.

2. Are the personifications in stanza 1 also visual images?

3. For what is *can* (line 4) a metonymy?

4. What annoys the speaker? Is it merely the weather?

5. Express the idea in line 5 in your own words.

6. Explain how the personification in stanza 3 reflects the speaker's annoyance.

7. At what point does the speaker's vexation diminish? What causes it to diminish?

8. What is meant by *estate of man* (line 19)? Where in the poem is that estate summarized?

9. Is the speaker optimistic or pessimistic?

A Description of the Spring

And now all nature seemed in love;
The lusty sap began to move;
New juice did stir the embracing vines,
And birds had drawn their valentines.
The jealous trout, that low did lie,　　　　5
Rose at a well-dissembled fly;
There stood my friend with patient skill,
Attending of his trembling quill.
Already were the eaves possessed
With the swift pilgrim's daubèd nest;　　　　10

The groves already did rejoice
In Philomel's triumphing voice.
The showers were short, the weather mild,
The morning fresh, the evening smiled.
Joan takes her neat-rubbed pail, and now   15
She trips to milk the sand-red cow;
Where, for some sturdy football swain,
Joan strokes a syllabub or twain.
The fields and gardens were beset
With tulip, crocus, violet;   20
And now, though late, the modest rose
Did more than half a blush disclose.
Thus all looked gay, all full of cheer,
To welcome the new liveried year.

SIR HENRY WOTTON

APOSTROPHE

Apostrophe is a figure in which the absent are addressed as though present, the dead as though living, the inanimate as though animate. In its last-mentioned use it is closely related to personification, for if a poet addresses inanimate things he necessarily personifies them. The root meaning of *apostrophe* is "a turning away." In the last line of "Drinking" the speaker turns away from his course of thought and directly addresses an imaginary man who, he pretends, has been listening to him all along. An apostrophe may come at the very beginning of a poem, as in Blake's "Tyger" (page 142) or any other poem written in the second person. Successful apostrophes add immediacy, excitement, and intensity to a poem. There is nothing, however, more frigid and absurd than an unsuccessful apostrophe. A disaster occurs when a feeble poet embellishes a confused thought with apostrophe and personification.

Stay with me, Poesy! playmate of childhood!
    Friend of my manhood! delight of my youth!
Roamer with me over valley and wildwood,
    Searcher for loveliness, groping for Truth.

CHARLES MACKAY
(from "An Invocation to Poesy")

For an effective apostrophe to contrast with this excerpt, see Wordsworth's sonnet addressed to Milton (page 225).

EXERCISE 28

Adieu, Farewell, Earth's Bliss

Adieu, farewell, earth's bliss!
This world uncertain is;
Fond are life's lustful joys,
Death proves them all but toys,
None from his darts can fly;   5
I am sick, I must die:
    Lord, have mercy on us!

Rich men, trust not in wealth,
Gold cannot buy you health;
Physic himself must fade;   10
All things to end are made.
The plague full swift goes by;
I am sick, I must die:
    Lord, have mercy on us!

Beauty is but a flower   15
Which wrinkles will devour;
Brightness falls from the air,
Queens have died young and fair,
Dust hath closed Helen's eye.
I am sick, I must die: 20
    Lord, have mercy on us!

Strength stoops unto the grave,
Worms feed on Hector brave,
Swords may not fight with fate;
Earth still holds ope her gate.   25
Come! come! the bells do cry.
I am sick, I must die:
    Lord, have mercy on us!

Wit with his wantonness
Tasteth death's bitterness;   30
Hell's executioner
Hath no ears for to hear
What vain art can reply.
I am sick, I must die:
    Lord, have mercy on us!   35

Haste, therefore, each degree,
To welcome destiny.
Heaven is our heritage,
Earth but a player's stage;
Mount we unto the sky.   40
I am sick, I must die:
    Lord, have mercy on us!

THOMAS NASHE
(from *Summer's Last Will and Testament*)

1. Is the last line of each stanza on apostrophe? If it is, how does it differ from the other apostrophes in the poem?
2. Why are the two characters from the Troy legend mentioned?
3. Give the literal equivalents of *gate* (line 25), *hell's executioner* (line 31), *vain art* (line 33), and *degree* (line 36).
4. Would line 17 be improved if it read, as some scholars have said it was meant to be read, "Brightness falls from the hair"? Why or why not?
5. Does the world seem attractive or unattractive to this dying man? Support your answer with details from the poem.

PARADOX

A **paradox** is a statement that seems at first glance self-contradictory or opposed to common sense; yet upon investigation or explanation it will be found to express a truth. "Make haste slowly" seems to be contradictory advice; a moment's thought about *haste,* however, will show that it is being used here in the sense of long-run progress. The paradox depends on the various possible meanings of *haste* in this context. We have resolved the paradox when we have reconciled the apparent contradiction and discovered the truth behind it.

A Lame Beggar

"I am unable," yonder beggar cries,
"To stand or move!" If he say true, he lies.

JOHN DONNE

The paradox of Donne's beggar who simultaneously lies and tells the truth is easily resolved. The word *lies* is a pun, or play on words. A **pun** is an intentional confusion of two words that sound similar but differ in meaning. Many oral riddles are paradoxical because they contain puns; "black and white and red (read) all over," for example, describes a newspaper. "Whether life is worth living or not depends on the liver" is another punning statement. All puns, by the way, are not necessarily contemptible.

EXERCISE 29

The Pulley

When God at first made man,
Having a glass of blessings standing by,
Let us, said he, pour on him all we can.
Let the world's riches, which dispersèd lie,
    Contract into a span.   5

So strength first made a way,
Then beauty flowed, then wisdom, honor, pleasure.
When almost all was out, God made a stay,
Perceiving that alone of all his treasure
    Rest in the bottom lay.   10

For if I should, said he,
Bestow this jewel also on my creature,
He would adore my gifts instead of me,
And rest in nature, not the God of nature:
    So both should losers be.   15

Yet let him keep the rest,
But keep them with repining restlessness.
Let him be rich and weary, that at least
If goodness lead him not, yet weariness
    May toss him to my breast.   20

GEORGE HERBERT

1. Describe the situation in the first stanza.
2. In the Greek myth Pandora let everything out of the chest except Hope. Here all good things except one are poured on man. What is left in the glass?
3. Give some synonyms for the first word of line 10.
4. Explain why this particular gift is kept back.
5. Resolve the punning paradox of lines 16–17.
6. What is the significance of the title?

Paradox can be much more than wordplay. When a serious poet suggests that black is white, or that love is hate, he is doing more than juggling language. He is using paradox to shock his readers into realizing the complexity and mystery of the universe. He is forcing his readers to plunge beneath the surface of things. He is disturbing their complacency by suggesting that contraries are not so contrary as they had always assumed. Some truths, especially the truths of religion, demand paradoxical statement: "Whosoever will save his life shall lose it: but whosoever will lose his life for my sake, the same shall save it."

EXERCISE 30

Examine the paradoxes in these poems and resolve them.

Holy Sonnet 14

Batter my heart, three-personed God, for you
As yet but knock, breathe, shine, and seek to mend;
That I may rise and stand, o'erthrow me, and bend
Your force to break, blow, burn, and make me new.

I, like an usurped town to another due,   5
Labor to admit you, but oh, to no end;
Reason, your viceroy in me, me should defend,
But is captived, and proves weak or untrue.
Yet dearly I love you, and would be lovèd fain
But am betrothed unto your enemy;   10
Divorce me, untie or break that knot again;
Take me to you, imprison me, for I,
Except you enthrall me, never shall be free,
Nor ever chaste, except you ravish me.

JOHN DONNE

1. What metaphor is extended through lines 1–4? Lines 5–8? Lines 9–14?

2. Is there an element of meaning common to all three of these extended metaphors?

3. Who is the enemy referred to in line 10? Has he been referred to previously
   in the poem?

4. What paradox underlies the poem?

5. Characterize the speaker.

To Lucasta. Going to the Wars

Tell me not, sweet, I am unkind,
    That from the nunnery
Of thy chaste breast and quiet mind,
    To war and arms I fly.

True, a new mistress now I chase: 5
    The first foe in the field;
And with a stronger faith embrace
    A sword, a horse, a shield.

Yet this inconstancy is such
    As you, too, shall adore;   10
I could not love thee, dear, so much,
    Loved I not honor more.

RICHARD LOVELACE

1. What is the relationship between the speaker and the listener? What is the occasion?
2. What has the speaker decided to do even before the poem begins?
3. Cite evidence that the listener wants him to do something else.
4. What means does the speaker use to convince the listener?
5. Discuss the language of the poem, using the terms *metaphor, paradox, pun,* and *personification*.

Of Treason

Treason doth never prosper. What's the reason?
For if it prosper, none dare call it treason.

SIR JOHN HARINGTON

Non Sum Qualis Eram Bonae sub Regno Cynarae

Last night, ah, yesternight, betwixt her lips and mine
There fell thy shadow, Cynara! thy breath was shed
Upon my soul between the kisses and the wine;
And I was desolate and sick of an old passion,
    Yea, I was desolate and bowed my head: 5
I have been faithful to thee, Cynara! in my fashion.

All night upon mine heart I felt her warm heart beat,
Night-long within mine arms in love and sleep she lay;
Surely the kisses of her bought red mouth were sweet;
But I was desolate and sick of an old passion,   10
    When I awoke and found the dawn was gray:
I have been faithful to thee, Cynara! in my fashion.

I have forgot much, Cynara! gone with the wind,
Flung roses, roses riotously with the throng,
Dancing, to put thy pale, lost lilies out of mind;   15
But I was desolate and sick of an old passion,
    Yea, all the time, because the dance was long:
I have been faithful to thee, Cynara! in my fashion.

I cried for madder music and for stronger wine,
But when the feast is finished and the lamps expire,   20
Then falls thy shadow, Cynara! the night is thine;
And I am desolate and sick of an old passion,
    Yea, hungry for the lips of my desire:
I have been faithful to thee, Cynara! in my fashion.

ERNEST DOWSON

Title: "I am not what I was under the rule of the good
Cynara."

Crazy Jane Talks with the Bishop

I met the Bishop on the road
And much said he and I.
"Those breasts are flat and fallen now,
Those veins must soon be dry;
Live in a heavenly mansion   5
Not in some foul sty."

"Fair and foul are near of kin,
And fair needs foul," I cried.
"My friends are gone, but that's a truth
Nor grave nor bed denied,   10
Learned in bodily lowliness
And in the heart's pride.

"A woman can be proud and stiff
When on love intent;
But Love has pitched his mansion in   15
The place of excrement;
For nothing can be sole or whole
That has not been rent."

WILLIAM BUTLER YEATS

AMBIGUITY IN POEMS

A poem communicates an experience that cannot be communicated
by ordinary literal language. It does so by means of figurative language,
which gives depth and richness to the experience. Some poems are so

rich that they convey two or even more experiences simultaneously. Since 1930, when William Empson published his *Seven Types of Ambiguity,* the term **ambiguity** has been given to the multiple meanings that a single poem may communicate. The term is perhaps not the best one that might be chosen to describe this phenomenon, because in nonpoetic discourse it denotes two or more incompatible meanings. For instance, the statement "My old uncle has a hearty appetite, and he is very fond of babies" contains the ambiguous word *fond*. In this context the word has two incompatible meanings: "feels affection for" and "likes to eat." The statement is a very inexact one because the old gentleman cannot be fond of babies in both these ways. Ambiguities in prose are either comic or puzzling or both: "This monument was erected to the memory of John Smith, who was shot, as a mark of affection by his brother." "Mr. Jones has just received a letter from Mr. Smith, saying that he will deliver the next annual address." "Lost: a cow belonging to Mrs. Brown, who has brass knobs on her horns." But as it has come to be applied to poems, the term *ambiguity* denotes multiple meanings that are compatible with each other.

They Flee from Me

> They flee from me that sometime did me seek,
>   With naked foot stalking in my chamber.
> I have seen them gentle, tame, and meek,
>   That now are wild, and do not remember
>   That sometime they put themself in danger   5
> To take bread at my hand; and now they range
> Busily seeking with a continual change.
>
> Thanked be fortune, it hath been otherwise
>   Twenty times better; but once, in special,
> In thin array, after a pleasant guise,   10
>   When her loose gown from her shoulders did fall,
>   And she me caught in her arms long and small,
> Therewith all sweetly did me kiss,
> And softly said, "Dear heart, how like you this?"
>
> It was no dream; I lay broad waking.   15
>   But all is turned thorough my gentleness,
> Into a strange fashion of forsaking;

And I have leave to go of her goodness,
And she also to use newfangleness.
But since that I so kindly am served,   20
I would fain know what she hath deserved.

SIR THOMAS WYATT

small (12): slender.   thorough (16): through.   use newfangleness (19): search for new experiences.

This famous poem has an air of mystery about it that no amount of analysis can dispel. The mystery is an integral part of the poem because the speaker himself does not know exactly what has happened to him, or why it has happened. He knows only that circumstances have changed and that he is unhappy. In any discussion of the poem, there-fore, it is frequently necessary to use the word *perhaps*.

Lines 1–7 contrast the past and the present. In the past visitors came to the speaker's room at night. The implicit metaphor extended through these lines compares the visitors to small, shy creatures, per-haps birds, who were not afraid of the speaker, but sought him out, took his favors, and gave him theirs. Now all that has changed; far from seeking him out, they flee from him and seek out others.

Lines 8–14 describe one particular visitor who made a special im-pression. *Pleasant guise* (line 10) suggests that this girl came to his room after a court party of some sort. Perhaps she invited him to compliment her, or even to fall in love with her, when she asked him the question (line 14). Perhaps he did fall in love.

Lines 15–21 have several ambiguities. *It was no dream* (line 15) has this possible implication: the girl who asked the question was real enough, but the others (lines 1–7) were only dreams. Or it may mean, "You think that everything I'm saying never happened. But it did." Or it may have both meanings. The reason for the change is also stated ambiguously. The speaker blames himself for the fact that she has forsaken him, but just how he is to blame is not clear to him, nor to the reader. Does *gentleness* (line 16) mean that he was gentle with her—that is, he did not press her to swear fidelity to him? Or does it mean that he generously permitted her to visit other men? Or does it have some other meaning? The ambiguity is right because the speaker does not know how the separation came about. *Strange* (line 17) seems to be an understatement; the speaker could have used a much stronger adjective. The word *newfangleness* (line 19), which has unfavorable connotations, shows that he disapproves of her present conduct. But he does not know whether to blame her or not. *Kindly* (line 20, probably pronounced *kindely*) is perhaps the most ambiguous word in the poem. In Wyatt's day it had its present meanings, and it also meant "naturally." She has served him kindly, he says with sarcasm—meaning that she has been unkind. Or perhaps he is saying that her conduct is only natural, because she made no commitment to him. At any rate, he does not know whether she deserves any blame (line 21).

The man has his freedom; the girl has hers. But why? And who is to blame? These questions are not answered because they have no answers—or, rather, they have many answers. Only an ambiguous poem could justly represent this complex experience. Multiple meanings are calamitous in utilitarian prose, but they make poems rich and interesting.

At this point two distinctions are necessary. First, the reader must distinguish between an ambiguity that enriches a poem and one that does not. A poem like Mackay's "Only a Thought" (page 54) is ambiguous in a bad sense; it does not communicate even a single definite experience, let alone two experiences. Second, the reader must distinguish between ambiguities that he finds in a poem because he does not thoroughly understand it and ambiguities that are actually in the poem. Making this distinction is not easy. It becomes easier as the reader learns to focus his attention on the poem itself rather than on his own reactions to it. Poems may be ambiguous, but there is no poem so ambiguous that it can mean anything that a particular reader would like it to mean.

EXERCISE 31

Discuss the contribution made by figurative language to the experiences in these poems. If any poem seems hard to understand, write out some questions about the figures of language, the answers to which would make the poem more comprehensible.

Each More Melodious Note

Each more melodious note I hear
Brings sad reproach to me,
That I alone afford the ear,
Who would the music be.

HENRY DAVID THOREAU

At Birth

Come from a distant country,
Bundle of flesh, of blood,
Demanding painful entry,
Expecting little good:
There is no going back   5
Among those thickets where
Both night and day are black
And blood's the same as air.

Strangely you come to meet us,
Stained, mottled, as if dead: 10
You bridge the dark hiatus
Through which your body slid
Across a span of muscle,
A breadth my hand can span.
The gorged and brimming vessel   15
Flows over, and is man.

Dear daughter, as I watched you
Come crumpled from the womb,
And sweating hands had fetched you
Into this world, the room   20
Opened before your coming
Like water struck from rocks
And echoed with your crying
Your living paradox.

ANTHONY THWAITE

To Althea. From Prison

When love with unconfinèd wings
    Hovers within my gates,
And my divine Althea brings
    To whisper at the grates;
When I lie tangled in her hair,   5
    And fettered to her eye,
The gods that wanton in the air
    Know no such liberty.

When flowing cups run swiftly round
   With no allaying Thames,   10
Our careless heads with roses bound,
   Our hearts with loyal flames;
When thirsty grief in wine we steep,
   When healths and draughts go free,
Fishes that tipple in the deep   15
   Know no such liberty.

When, like committed linnets, I
   With shriller throat shall sing
The sweetness, mercy, majesty,
   And glories of my King;   20
When I shall voice aloud how good
   He is, how great should be,
Enlargèd winds that curl the flood
   Know no such liberty.

Stone walls do not a prison make,   25
   Nor iron bars a cage;
Minds innocent and quiet take
   That for an hermitage;
If I have freedom in my love,
   And in my soul am free,   30
Angels alone that soar above
   Enjoy such liberty.

RICHARD LOVELACE

King (20): Charles I, in whose cause Lovelace was imprisoned in 1642, just before civil war broke out between the King and the Parliament.

Naming of Parts

To-day we have naming of parts. Yesterday,
We had daily cleaning. And to-morrow morning,
We shall have what to do after firing. But to-day,
To-day we have naming of parts. Japonica
Glistens like coral in all of the neighbouring gardens,   5
   And to-day we have naming of parts.

This is the lower sling swivel. And this
Is the upper sling swivel, whose use you will see,
When you are given your slings. And this is the piling swivel,
Which in your case you have not got. The branches   10
Hold in the gardens their silent, eloquent gestures,
    Which in our case we have not got.

This is the safety-catch, which is always released
With an easy flick of the thumb. And please do not let me
See anyone using his finger. You can do it quite easy   15
If you have any strength in your thumb. The blossoms
Are fragile and motionless, never letting anyone see
    Any of them using their finger.

And this you can see is the bolt. The purpose of this
Is to open the breech, as you see. We can slide it   20
Rapidly backwards and forwards: we call this
Easing the spring. And rapidly backwards and forwards
The early bees are assaulting and fumbling the flowers:
    They call it easing the Spring.

They call it easing the Spring: it is perfectly easy   25
If you have any strength in your thumb: like the bolt,
And the breech, and the cocking-piece, and the point of balance,
Which in our case we have not got; and the almond-blossom
Silent in all of the gardens and the bees going backwards
    and forwards,
    For to-day we have naming of parts.

                            HENRY REED
                    (from "Lessons of the War")

Still, Citizen Sparrow

Still, citizen sparrow, this vulture which you call
Unnatural, let him but lumber again to air
Over the rotten office, let him bear
The carrion ballast up, and at the tall

Tip of the sky lie cruising. Then you'll see   5
That no more beautiful bird is in heaven's height,
No wider more placid wings, no watchfuller flight;
He shoulders nature there, the frightfully free,

The naked-headed one. Pardon him, you
Who dart in the orchard aisles, for it is he   10
Devours death, mocks mutability,
Has heart to make an end, keeps nature new.

Thinking of Noah, childheart, try to forget
How for so many bedlam hours his saw
Soured the song of birds with its wheezy gnaw,   15
And the slam of his hammer all the day beset

The people's ears. Forget that he could bear
To see the towns like coral under the keel,
And the fields so dismal deep. Try rather to feel
How high and weary it was, on the waters where   20

He rocked his only world, and everyone's.
Forgive the hero, you who would have died
Gladly with all you knew; he rode that tide
To Ararat; all men are Noah's sons.

RICHARD WILBUR

The Waking

I wake to sleep, and take my waking slow.
I feel my fate in what I cannot fear.
I learn by going where I have to go.

We think by feeling. What is there to know?
I hear my being dance from ear to ear.   5
I wake to sleep, and take my waking slow.

Of those so close beside me, which are you?
God bless the Ground! I shall walk softly there,
And learn by going where I have to go.

Light takes the Trees; but who can tell us how?   10
The lowly worm climbs up a winding stair;
I wake to sleep, and take my waking slow.

Great Nature has another thing to do
To you and me; so take the lively air,
And, lovely, learn by going where to go.   15

This shaking keeps me steady. I should know.
What falls away is always. And is near.
I wake to sleep, and take my waking slow.
I learn by going where I have to go.

                              THEODORE ROETHKE

6

THE POET'S USE
OF SYMBOL
AND ALLEGORY

Defined broadly, a symbol is a sign that does not exist for its own sake, but instead points to a meaning beyond itself. In this sense all words and all signs of every kind are symbols. A spoken or a written word in its context stands for a certain meaning; a plus sign in arithmetic indicates a certain process; the notes and other marks on a staff of music signify certain sounds and their duration; a striped pole outside a shop announces that hair is cut inside the shop. As applied to literature, however, the term *symbol* necessarily has a somewhat narrower meaning. Poems are made of words, but not every word is a literary symbol, nor does every poem contain symbolism.

SYMBOLS IN LITERATURE

Literary symbols are best defined functionally—that is, according to how they work. A **literary symbol** is a thing (or an event, a person, a quality, or a relationship) that functions simultaneously in two ways:

as itself and as a sign of something outside itself. Hence a literary symbol differs greatly from such a symbol as the dollar sign. A dollar sign merely points to the fact that the number it precedes is to be understood as that much money; the sign is not part of the money itself, nor does it have anything more than an arbitrary connection with the money. A literary symbol, in contrast, seems to be part of what it stands for.

An examination of a particular symbol will make the definition clearer. The moon is a symbol in the following poem; in this text every reference to it has been italicized.

Strange Fits of Passion Have I Known

Strange fits of passion have I known:
And I will dare to tell,
But in the Lover's ear alone,
What once to me befell.

When she I loved looked every day   5
Fresh as a rose in June,
I to her cottage bent my way,
Beneath an *evening-moon.*

Upon the *moon* I fixed my eye,
All over the wide lea;   10
With quickening pace my horse drew nigh
Those paths so dear to me.

And now we reached the orchard-plot;
And, as we climbed the hill,
The *sinking moon* to Lucy's cot   15
Came near, and nearer still.

In one of those sweet dreams I slept,
Kind Nature's gentlest boon!
And all the while my eyes I kept
On the *descending moon.*   20

My horse moved on; hoof after hoof
He raised, and never stopped:
When down behind the cottage roof,
At once, the *bright moon dropped.*

What fond and wayward thoughts will slide   25
Into a Lover's head!
"O mercy!" to myself I cried,
"If Lucy should be dead!"

WILLIAM WORDSWORTH

Notice that the moon functions first as a moon and only gradually takes on symbolical significance. A bright object in the sky, it lights the lover on his way as he rides to visit his sweetheart. Along with the hill, the orchard-plot, and the cottage, it is part of the landscape described in the poem. But the moon is also an actor in the drama. At first only an "evening moon" (line 8), it becomes a "sinking moon" (line 15) and a "descending moon" (line 20); then suddenly (line 24) it vanishes. Lucy's cottage, of course, blocks the lover's view of it. But this common-sense explanation never occurs to the lover, who has been gazing at it and thinking of Lucy until she and the moon have merged in his waking dream. The sudden blotting out of the moon's brightness symbolizes to him the death of Lucy. She is the light of his life, and that light may go out as the moon has gone out. The moon, then, functions as a literary symbol: (1) it is literally a moon; (2) it also stands for a possible disaster—the death of Lucy; (3) by suddenly disappearing, it behaves in such a way that it seems to participate in the disaster—that is, it has been identified with Lucy in the lover's mind.

It is useful to make a distinction between two kinds of literary symbols: conventional and nonce.

CONVENTIONAL SYMBOLS

Conventional symbols are objects that, by customary association and general agreement, have a certain significance. They are common in both art and life. A Christian's cross, a country's flag, a married person's ring, a bereaved person's black band on his sleeve—these are all conventional symbols. Similarly, the statue of a blindfolded woman holding scales in one hand and a sword in the other is a symbol of Justice; a naked and blind boy carrying a bow and arrows symbolizes Love. In literature darkness conventionally symbolizes death; light, wisdom; roses, romantic love. A reader of Robert Frost's "The Road Not Taken" (page 39) inevitably associates the diverging paths in that poem with a decision. Christina Rossetti's "Up-Hill" (page 39) uses one of a large number of conventional symbols for life—a journey. Some of the other symbols for life are found in Bacon's "In Vitam Humanam" (page 187).

The Funeral Rites of the Rose

The Rose was sick and, smiling, died;
And, being to be sanctified,
About the bed there sighing stood
The sweet and flowery sisterhood:
Some hung the head, while some did bring,   5
To wash her, water from the spring;
Some laid her forth, while other wept,
But all a solemn fast there kept.
The holy sisters, some among,
The sacred dirge and trental sung.   10
But ah! what sweets smelt everywhere,
As Heaven had spent all perfumes there.
At last, when prayers for the dead
And rites were all accomplishèd,
They, weeping, spread a lawny loom,   15
And closed her up as in a tomb.

ROBERT HERRICK

trental (10): Originally a set of thirty requiem masses; but here used loosely to mean a dirge. **lawny loom** (15): a finely spun pall or shroud.

That this rose is more than a literal flower is clearly indicated by the anthropomorphic language—that is, the kind of language referring to human beings and human events; roses do not smile (line 1), nor are they sanctified (line 2). Although other flowers might be regarded as figuratively weeping (a metaphor for the dew on them) when a rose dies, they certainly do not, even figuratively, fast or sing trentals (lines 8, 10). And it is ludicrous to suppose that they would cover a dead rose with a shroud (line 15). Thus while the poem talks about flowers, it is signifying—or symbolizing—something more.

The further significance becomes clear when the reader reflects that the rose is a conventional symbol of love, of beauty, and of the beloved person. The poem can accommodate all three of these significations.

Herrick may be dramatizing his love for another person, a love that has died and has been buried "as in a tomb." He may be lamenting the death of a beautiful woman, whose passing is regretted by all the "sisterhood" of lovely women whose beauty is equally perishable. He may even be mourning his own sweetheart's untimely death. Literally he is talking about the death of a rose, but in so doing he is simultaneously talking about all these other things.

EXERCISE 32

Identify and discuss the conventional symbols in these poems.

Sixty-Eighth Birthday

As life runs on, the road grows strange
With faces new, and near the end
The milestones into headstones change,
'Neath every one a friend.

JAMES RUSSELL LOWELL

On a Squirrel Crossing the Road in Autumn, in New England

It is what he does not know,
Crossing the road under the elm trees,
About the mechanism of my car,
About the Commonwealth of Massachusetts,
About Mozart, India, Arcturus,   5

That wins my praise. I engage
At once in whirling squirrel-praise.

He obeys the orders of nature
Without knowing them.
It is what he does not know   10
That makes him beautiful.
Such a knot of little purposeful nature!

I who can see him as he cannot see himself
Repose in the ignorance that is his blessing.

It is what man does not know of God   15
Composes the visible poem of the world.

. . . Just missed him!

RICHARD EBERHART

Opportunity

This I beheld, or dreamed it in a dream:—
There spread a cloud of dust along a plain;
And underneath the cloud, or in it, raged
A furious battle, and men yelled, and swords
Shocked upon swords and shields. A prince's banner   5
Wavered, then staggered backward, hemmed by foes.
A craven hung along the battle's edge,
And thought, "Had I a sword of keener steel—
That blue blade that the king's son bears,—but this
Blunt thing—!" he snapt and flung it from his hand,   10
And lowering crept away and left the field.
Then came the king's son, wounded, sore bestead,
And weaponless, and saw the broken sword,
Hilt-buried in the dry and trodden sand,
And ran and snatched it, and with battle-shout   15
Lifted afresh he hewed his enemy down,
And saved a great cause that heroic day.

EDWARD   ROWLAND   SILL

Crossing the Bar

Sunset and evening star,
    And one clear call for me!
And may there be no moaning of the bar,
    When I put out to sea,

But such a tide as moving seems asleep,   5
   Too full for sound and foam,
When that which drew from out the boundless deep
   Turns again home.

Twilight and evening bell,
   And after that the dark!   10
And may there be no sadness of farewell,
   When I embark;

For tho' from out our bourne of Time and Place
   The flood may bear me far,
I hope to see my Pilot face to face   15
   When I have crost the bar.

ALFRED, LORD TENNYSON

NONCE SYMBOLS

A **nonce symbol** is a symbol that a writer himself invents "for the
nonce"—that is, for a particular purpose or occasion. Wordsworth's
moon is such a symbol because the moon does not conventionally
symbolize a girl's death. It does, however, have conventional associations with romantic love, as every popular song-writer knows. Wordsworth has expanded and developed the conventional symbol into something unique.

Wordsworth's moon, however, differs from most nonce symbols in
two respects: it has only one signification—Lucy's possible death—and
this signification is explicitly stated in the poem, in the last stanza. It is
more usual for a nonce symbol, like the conventional symbols in Herrick's "Funeral Rites of the Rose," to have several possible interpretations, all of which the poet implies rather than clearly explains.

Nonce symbols occur mainly in poems written during the last century and a half. Before that time poets and other writers drew their
symbolism from a large body of traditional symbolism, especially from
the symbolism of Christianity and the rituals of Christian churches.
With the decline of universally accepted religious beliefs and rituals,
poets, including Christian poets, began to invent private symbols. But
like the religious symbols of older poets, the private symbols of more
recent poets emphasize the correspondence between the visible world
and an unseen world.

The Sick Rose

O Rose, thou art sick!
The invisible worm
That flies in the night,
In the howling storm,

Has found out thy bed   5
Of crimson joy:
And his dark secret love
Does thy life destroy.

WILLIAM BLAKE

If the reader takes the rose in this poem to be a conventional symbol for love or for beauty or for both love and beauty, he still faces the problem of what the worm (line 2) symbolizes. Whatever it is, it is not good. By devoting as much of his poem to the worm as to the sick rose, Blake communicates images of nastiness that are quite different from the pretty images in Herrick's poem on the same subject. The adjective *invisible* (line 2) suggests that the worm comes from the unseen world of evil; real worms do not make "dark secret love" (line 7). The "howling storm" (line 4) suggests a catastrophe far greater than the destruction of a literal rose. Blake's worm seems (*seems* is a very useful word in any discussion of symbolism) to symbolize the unseen forces that destroy love and beauty: materialism, greed, hypocrisy, deceit, prudery, neurosis—the list is endless. The symbol cannot be paraphrased as one particular evil; Blake apparently used a symbol because it enabled him to suggest many kinds of evil.

IDENTIFYING AND INTERPRETING SYMBOLS

A symbol may be regarded as a figure that goes two steps beyond a simile and one step beyond a metaphor. "My love is like a star" is a simile; "My love is a star," a metaphor. "My star" could be, in the right context, a symbol for "my love." In a symbol there is no question of comparison; one part of the figure completely replaces the other. Blake would have expressed his thoughts metaphorically rather than symbolically had he said or implied, "Evil is a worm." Instead, he concentrated entirely on the worm. The method of symbolism is to dwell on the subject with such particularity and in such a way that it takes on more than a literal meaning.

The difference between symbols and figures of comparison can be illustrated by contrasting two poems of Rainer Maria Rilke. First, a poem that uses an explicit figure of comparison.

The Swan

This toiling to go through something yet
undone, heavily and as though in bonds,
is like the ungainly gait of the swan.

And dying, this no longer grasping
of that ground on which we daily stand,   5
like his anxious letting-himself-down—:

into the waters, which receive him smoothly
and which, as though happy and bygone,
draw back underneath him, flow on flow;
while he, infinitely still and sure,   10
ever more maturely and more royally
and more serenely deigns to draw along.

(translated by M. D. Herter Norton)

Here the actions of a swan laboriously waddling across land to the bank of a stream, letting himself down, and then smoothly sailing along are compared with the life of a man: first the struggle through a life to be lived; then the anxiety-ridden dying; then, finally, the masterful serenity of death. The poet has seen the actions of a swan as the metaphorical equivalent of man's life. A symbolical poem would not mention living and dying, but would concentrate on the swan's actions.

The Panther

His vision from the passing by of bars
Has grown so tired that it holds nothing more.
It seems to him there are a thousand bars,
And out beyond those thousand bars no world.

His supple lope and flexibly strong strides,   5
That always in the smallest circle turn,
Are like a dance of strength around a middle
In which, benumbed, a great will stands.

Just sometimes does the veil upon his eye
Silently rise; then goes an image in,   10
Goes through the nervous poise of his still limbs,
And ceases, in his heart, to be.

(translated by Peter J. Seng)

Here Rilke concentrates entirely on a restless, caged panther. But he intuits the psychology of the beast in such a way as to suggest that the panther is simultaneously a beast and something more. A caged panther may feel that many bars hold him in; the generalization in line 4, however, is far beyond the mental powers of any animal. Rilke invites the reader to regard the panther as any caged being, caught behind the bars of a limited world and yearning for a greater world beyond, but deadened to that greater world by the years of his captivity. One of the possible interpretations of the symbol might be as follows:

The panther represents man, who is a caged animal in the physical world: he longs for a world of changeless perfection, but is trapped in this world which is mutable and stained. His years of captivity to matter and flesh have dulled his vision so that only rarely is he aware of a world outside his cage; in the rare moments when he does have a vision of the changeless perfection of another world, that vision fades when it reaches his practical and human heart. But the numbed longing persists, and whatever he does in his cage-world is simply a dance around a will doomed to frustration.

EXERCISE 33

The Tyger

Tyger! Tyger! burning bright
In the forests of the night,
What immortal hand or eye
Could frame thy fearful symmetry?

In what distant deeps or skies   5
Burnt the fire of thine eyes?
On what wings dare he aspire?
What the hand dare seize the fire?

And what shoulder, and what art,
Could twist the sinews of thy heart?   10
And when thy heart began to beat,
What dread hand? and what dread feet?

What the hammer? what the chain?
In what furnace was thy brain?
What the anvil? what dread grasp   15
Dare its deadly terrors clasp?

When the stars threw down their spears,
And water'd heaven with their tears,
Did he smile his work to see?
Did he who made the Lamb make thee?   20

Tyger! Tyger! burning bright
In the forests of the night,
What immortal hand or eye,
Dare frame thy fearful symmetry?

WILLIAM BLAKE

1. Is the speaker's wonder caused solely by the tiger or by something else?
2. Could the tiger symbolize all the things in the world that are cunning, powerful, and rapacious? If so, what could the lamb (line 20) represent?
3. Could the tiger symbolize all the beauty in the world?
4. The Bible compares the devil to a "roaring lion, [that] walketh about, seeking whom he may devour." Is the tiger perhaps meant to be the devil?
5. What is the effect of so many unanswered questions?
6. Does the poem anywhere suggest that the tiger and the lamb are one and the same?
7. What event could be referred to in lines 17–18?
8. Agree or disagree with this statement: "The last stanza is unnecessary because it merely repeats the first."

Neither Out Far Nor In Deep

The people along the sand
All turn and look one way.
They turn their back on the land.
They look at the sea all day.

As long as it takes to pass   5
A ship keeps raising its hull;
The wetter ground like glass
Reflects a standing gull.

The land may vary more;
But wherever the truth may be—   10
The water comes ashore,
And the people look at the sea.

They cannot look out far.
They cannot look in deep.
But when was that ever a bar   15
To any watch they keep?

ROBERT FROST

1. What peculiarity of human behavior has Frost observed? Do your observations agree with his? What do you think causes this behavior?
2. If the poem ended at line 12, would it seem complete? Would it seem significant?
3. Does Frost make the behavior of the people in the poem seem symbolic? What does this behavior symbolize?

The Windhover: To Christ Our Lord

I caught this morning morning's minion, king-
    dom of daylight's dauphin, dapple-dawn-drawn Falcon, in his riding
    Of the rolling level underneath him steady air, and striding
High there, how he rung upon the rein of a wimpling wing
In his ecstasy! then off, off forth on swing,   5
    As a skate's heel sweeps smooth on a bow-bend: the hurl and gliding
    Rebuffed the big wind. My heart in hiding
Stirred for a bird,—the achieve of, the mastery of the thing!

Brute beauty and valour and act, oh, air, pride, plume, here
   Buckle! AND the fire that breaks from thee then, a billion   10
Times told lovelier, more dangerous, O my chevalier!

No wonder of it: sheer plod makes plough down sillion
Shine, and blue-bleak embers, ah my dear,
   Fall, gall themselves, and gash gold-vermilion.

                        GERARD MANLEY HOPKINS

> **rung upon the rein** (4): described a circle, as a horse walking about its trainer. **wimpling** (4): curving, plaited. **bow-bend** (6): a bow-shaped figure in skating. **Buckle** (10): clasp, crumple. **sillion** (12): furrow.

1. What liberties has the poet taken with syntax and parts of speech?
2. What is the subject of the poem? Study and explain the images in lines 1–7.
3. What indicates that the poem is not merely a description of a bird's flight?
4. Where is the first indication of a connection between the windhover and Christ? What is the connection?
5. Interpret the symbols of the field (lines 12–13) and the fire (lines 13–14).

Since symbolism is by no means a universal phenomenon in poems, the reader who has just learned to identify symbols must beware of assuming that *every* poem contains a symbol whose hidden meaning he must ferret out. Reading poems is not solving puzzles. Poets, moreover, do not hide their meaning behind symbols; instead they use symbols to present their meaning. The poem itself will indicate whether or not a given object or event is to be understood symbolically. If a poem contains symbolism, its language will ordinarily be more serious and intense than the language required in a literal treatment of the subject. And, since a reader can seldom be absolutely certain that a particular symbol has a particular significance, he should avoid dogmatism in all his discussions of symbolism.

EXERCISE 34

Do any of the following poems contain symbols?

The Woodspurge

The wind flapped loose, the wind was still,
Shaken out dead from tree and hill:
I had walked on at the wind's will,—
I sat now, for the wind was still.

Between my knees my forehead was,—   5
My lips, drawn in, said not Alas!
My hair was over in the grass,
My naked ears heard the day pass.

My eyes, wide open, had the run
Of some ten weeds to fix upon;   10
Among those few, out of the sun,
The woodspurge flowered, three cups in one.

From perfect grief there need not be
Wisdom or even memory:
One thing then learnt remains to me,—   15
The woodspurge has a cup of three.

DANTE GABRIEL ROSSETTI

Woodspurge (Title): plant with clusters of yellowish-green flowers.

There Was a Lady Loved a Swine

There was a lady loved a swine.
    "Honey," quoth she,
"Pig-hog, wilt thou be mine?"
    "Hoogh," quoth he.

"I'll build thee a silver sty,   5
    Honey," quoth she,
"And in it thou shalt lie."
    "Hoogh," quoth he.

"Pinned with a silver pin,
     "Honey," quoth she,   10
"That thou may go out and in."
     "Hoogh," quoth he.

"Wilt thou have me now,
     Honey?" quoth she.
"Speak, or my heart will break!"   15
     "Hoogh," quoth he.

ANONYMOUS
(Seventeenth Century)

The Boat

The boat that took my love away
He sent again to me
To tell me that he would not sleep
Alone beneath the sea.

The flower and fruit of love are mine   5
The ant, the fieldmouse and the mole,
But now a tiger prowls without
And claws upon my soul.

Love is not love that wounded bleeds
And bleeding sullies slow.   10
Come death within my hands and I
Unto my love will go.

STEVIE SMITH

ant (6): see page 233.   Love (9): see page 294.

Do Not Go Gentle into That Good Night

Do not go gentle into that good night,
Old age should burn and rave at close of day;
Rage, rage against the dying of the light.

Though wise men at their end know dark is right,
Because their words had forked no lightning they   5
Do not go gentle into that good night.

Good men, the last wave by, crying how bright
Their frail deeds might have danced in a green bay,
Rage, rage against the dying of the light.

Wild men who caught and sang the sun in flight,   10
And learn, too late, they grieved it on its way,
Do not go gentle into that good night.

Grave men, near death, who see with blinding sight
Blind eyes could blaze like meteors and be gay,
Rage, rage against the dying of the light.   15

And you, my father, there on the sad height,
Curse, bless, me now with your fierce tears, I pray.
Do not go gentle into that good night.
Rage, rage against the dying of the light.

                           DYLAN   THOMAS

Two Realities

A waggon passed with scarlet wheels
    And a yellow body, shining new.
"Splendid!" said I. "How fine it feels
To be alive, when beauty peels
    The grimy husk from life." And you   5

Said, "Splendid!" and I thought you'd seen
    That waggon blazing down the street;
But I looked and saw that your gaze had been
On a child that was kicking an obscene
    Brown ordure with his feet.   10

Our souls are elephants, thought I,
    Remote behind a prisoning grill,
With trunks thrust out to peer and pry
And pounce upon reality;
    And each at his own sweet will   15

Seizes the bun that he likes best
And passes over all the rest.

ALDOUS HUXLEY

ALLEGORY

Allegory is narration or description in which each of the main elements stands for something else—something else that is not mentioned by name. It is seldom used in short poems because it requires more space for development than a short poem affords. Two of the world's most famous poetic allegories—Dante's *Divine Comedy* and Spenser's *Faerie Queene*—are also famous for their length. An allegory usually tells a story that contains one or more other stories; it is like a telegraph wire that transmits several messages simultaneously.

A Rose

A rose, as fair as ever saw the North,
Grew in a little garden all alone;
A sweeter flower did Nature ne'er put forth,
Nor fairer garden yet was never known:
The maidens danced about it morn and noon,   5
And learnèd bards of it their ditties made;
The nimble fairies by the pale-faced moon
Watered the root and kissed her pretty shade.
But well-a-day!—the gard'ner careless grew;
The maids and fairies both were kept away,   10
And in a drought the caterpillars threw
Themselves upon the bud and every spray.
   God shield the stock! If heaven send no supplies,
   The fairest blossom of the garden dies.

WILLIAM BROWNE
(from "Visions")

Concealed beneath the surface of Browne's poem there runs another story, each element of which parallels an element in the surface story. A series of equations can be set up between the surface and the submerged narratives: perhaps the rose is a beautiful little girl, an only child on whom her parents and friends dote; the garden (line 2) is her home; the gardener (line 9) is her parents; the caterpillars (line 11) are a disease that strikes her. Certain elements (the other maidens, the fairies, the bards, and heaven) have similar functions in both narratives, and therefore they serve as a link between the two. The submerged narrative might be paraphrased as follows:

A beautiful child, the fairest ever seen in the north country, lived all alone with her parents. Her radiance was everywhere celebrated: maidens of the village praised it, and poets wrote of it; it seemed as though the fairies themselves visited her by night to cherish her beauty. But as she grew to womanhood, her beauty faded because her parents no longer protected her, and the attendant maids and fairies no longer visited her. In the absence of love she became a prey to disease. But if heaven is gracious, she will recover and will perhaps have a child of her own, who will perpetuate her beauty.

Other allegorical interpretations might be made. The caterpillars, for instance, might stand for evil men who take advantage of the girl after her friends and parents withdraw their protection. But whatever interpretation is made, it must establish a coherent pattern of equivalents between the surface and what lies under the surface.

ALLEGORY AND SYMBOLISM

The method of allegory resembles, but is essentially different from, the method of symbolism. First, allegory is more systematic than symbolism. In the surface narrative of George Orwell's *Animal Farm,* for instance, some domestic animals overthrow the farmer who owns them and set up a new government under the rule of pigs. Every event in this animal revolution systematically parallels an event in Russian history. In an allegory one pattern of characters and events runs alongside another in such a way that a series of equations can be set up between the two patterns. A work could not contain a single allegorical character or event—though it might contain a single symbol. Allegory implies a system of correspondences.

A second difference is that the surface story in an allegory may be read and enjoyed without any awareness of the submerged story. Generations of little children have enjoyed the first book of *Gulliver's Travels* without being aware of the political and moral allegory running beneath the surface. A symbolic work, in contrast, means little to a reader unaware of the symbols. Neither Rilke's poem on a panther nor Blake's on a tiger tells an interesting animal story.

Third, the symbolist writer selects objects and events of this world and presents them in such a way that they communicate insights into an unseen world; Blake's real rose and worm stand simultaneously for themselves and for the unseen forces of love and the unseen forces that destroy love. The allegorist, in contrast, invents an imaginary world that reflects the real world. In its crudest form an allegory might tell the story of a knight named Love who is devoured by a dragon named Hate. Unlike worms and roses, knights named Love and dragons named anything exist only in the writer's imagination; the writer invents them to dramatize the opposition between love and hate in the real world. Many allegories contain personified abstractions: Love, Hate, Courage, Rumor. Symbolism concentrates on the concrete, visible world; allegory is likely to be fantastic.

Finally, allegory can usually be mechanically interpreted, since it is systematic; symbolism cannot. Once the key to an allegory is known, each element in the submerged story comes to the surface and falls into place. The submerged story can then be paraphrased. A symbol is more elusive; its contents cannot be exhausted by paraphrase.

Yet, despite these differences, the reader should beware of considering allegory and symbolism as mutually exclusive categories. Literary works of any merit refuse to be pigeonholed. Probably no writer has ever started to work thinking, "I shall now produce an allegory, and I must carefully avoid all suggestions of symbolism." Writers are more sensible than to place such absurd restrictions upon themselves. Readers, therefore, should regard symbolism and allegory as tendencies that a work may have rather than as categories into which a work may be put. Both tendencies may exist in the same work. A work is allegorical insofar as its images fit together to form a coherent pattern of meaning in addition to the surface meaning. It is symbolical insofar as it contains any image that is simultaneously itself and something more significant than itself.

EXERCISE 35

Discuss the use of allegory and symbolism in these poems.

Excelsior

The shades of night were falling fast,
As through an Alpine village passed
A youth, who bore, 'mid snow and ice,
A banner with the strange device,
Excelsior!   5

His brow was sad; his eye beneath,
Flashed like a falchion from its sheath,
And like a silver clarion rung
The accents of that unknown tongue,
Excelsior!   10

In happy homes he saw the light
Of household fires gleam warm and bright;
Above, the spectral glaciers shone,
And from his lips escaped a groan,
Excelsior!   15

"Try not the Pass!" the old man said;
"Dark lowers the tempest overhead,
The roaring torrent is deep and wide!"
And loud that clarion voice replied,
Excelsior!   20

"O stay," the maiden said, "and rest
Thy weary head upon this breast!"
A tear stood in his bright blue eye,
But still he answered, with a sigh,
Excelsior!   25

"Beware the pine tree's withered branch!
Beware the awful avalanche!"
This was the peasant's last Good-night;
A voice replied, far up the height,
Excelsior!   30

At break of day, as heavenward
The pious monks of Saint Bernard
Uttered the oft-repeated prayer,
A voice cried through the startled air,
Excelsior!   35

A traveller, by the faithful hound,
Half-buried in the snow was found,
Still grasping in his hand of ice
That banner with the strange device,
　　Excelsior!   40

There in the twilight cold and gray,
Lifeless, but beautiful, he lay,
And from the sky, serene and far,
A voice fell, like a falling star,
　　Excelsior!   45

HENRY WADSWORTH LONGFELLOW

O Where Are You Going

"O where are you going?" said reader to rider,
"That valley is fatal when furnaces burn,
Yonder's the midden whose odours will madden,
That gap is the grave where the tall return."

"O do you imagine," said fearer to farer,   5
"That dusk will delay on your path to the pass,
Your diligent looking discover the lacking
Your footsteps feel from granite to grass?"

"O what was that bird," said horror to hearer,
"Did you see that shape in the twisted trees?   10
Behind you swiftly the figure comes softly,
The spot on your skin is a shocking disease?"

"Out of this house"—said rider to reader,
"Yours never will"—said farer to fearer,
"They're looking for you"—said hearer to horror,   15
As he left them there, as he left them there.

W. H. AUDEN

The Wayfarer

The wayfarer,
Perceiving the pathway to truth,
Was struck with astonishment.
It was thickly grown with weeds.
"Ha," he said,   5
"I see that none has passed here
In a long time."
Later he saw that each weed
Was a singular knife.
"Well," he mumbled at last,   10
"Doubtless there are other roads."

STEPHEN CRANE

When the Prophet, a Complacent Fat Man

When the prophet, a complacent fat man,
Arrived at the mountain-top,
He cried: "Woe to my knowledge!
I intended to see good white lands
And bad black lands,   5
But the scene is grey."

STEPHEN CRANE

The Heavy Bear Who Goes with Me

"the withness of the body"
—WHITEHEAD

The heavy bear who goes with me,
A manifold honey to smear his face,
Clumsy and lumbering here and there,
The central ton of every place,
The hungry beating brutish one   5
In love with candy, anger, and sleep,

Crazy factotum, dishevelling all,
Climbs the building, kicks the football,
Boxes his brother in the hate-ridden city.

Breathing at my side, that heavy animal,   10
That heavy bear who sleeps with me,
Howls in his sleep for a world of sugar,
A sweetness intimate as the water's clasp,
Howls in his sleep because the tight-rope
Trembles and shows the darkness beneath.   15
—The strutting show-off is terrified,
Dressed in his dress-suit, bulging his pants,
Trembles to think that his quivering meat
Must finally wince to nothing at all.

That inescapable animal walks with me,   20
Has followed me since the black womb held,
Moves where I move, distorting my gesture,
A caricature, a swollen shadow,
A stupid clown of the spirit's motive,
Perplexes and affronts with his own darkness,   25
The secret life of belly and bone,
Opaque, too near, my private, yet unknown,
Stretches to embrace the very dear
With whom I would walk without him near,
Touches her grossly, although a word   30
Would bare my heart and make me clear,
Stumbles, flounders, and strives to be fed,
Dragging me with him in his mouthing care,
Amid the hundred million of his kind,
The scrimmage of appetite everywhere.   35

DELMORE SCHWARTZ

Question

Body my house
my horse my hound
what will I do
when you are fallen

Where will I sleep   5
How will I ride
What will I hunt

Where can I go
without my mount
all eager and quick   10
How will I know
in thicket ahead
is danger or treasure
when Body my good
bright dog is dead   15

How will it be
to lie in the sky
without roof or door
and wind for an eye

With cloud for shift   20
how will I hide?

MAY SWENSON

The Horse Chestnut Tree

Boys in sporadic but tenacious droves
Come with sticks, as certainly as Autumn,
To assault the great horse chestnut tree.

There is a law governs their lawlessness.
Desire is in them for a shining amulet   5
And the best are those that are highest up.

They will not pick them easily from the ground.
With shrill arms they fling to the higher branches,
To hurry the work of nature for their pleasure.

I have seen them trooping down the street   10
Their pockets stuffed with chestnuts shucked, unshucked.
It is only evening keeps them from their wish.

Sometimes I run out in a kind of rage
To chase the boys away: I catch an arm,
Maybe, and laugh to think of being the lawgiver.   15

I was once such a young sprout myself
And fingered in my pocket the prize and trophy.
But still I moralize upon the day

And see that we, outlaws on God's property,
Fling out imagination beyond the skies,   20
Wishing a tangible good from the unknown.

And likewise death will drive us from the scene
With the great flowering world unbroken yet,
Which we held in idea, a little handful.

RICHARD EBERHART

7

THE RHYTHM
AND METER
OF A POEM

Poetry, according to Coleridge, is "the best words in their best order." Although this remark hardly satisfies the requirements of formal definition, it does assert an important fact: the order of the words in a poem is as material as the words themselves. Consider this stanza from Coleridge's "Rime of the Ancient Mariner."

> He prayeth best, who loveth best
> All things both great and small;
> For the dear God who loveth us,
> He made and loveth all.

To demonstrate the importance of word order, one has only to rearrange the first two lines:

> He who loves all things both great
> And small prayeth best.

158

Tampered with in this way, the words still make sense, but they neither please the ear nor slip easily off the tongue. They obviously lack something that the original had. That something is measurable rhythm.

RHYTHM AND METER

Rhythm implies alternation: something is here, then it is replaced by something else, then the first thing returns. People speak of the rhythm of the tides, of the seasons, of the heavenly bodies. All human utterances are rhythmical: the voice rises, falls, then rises again; stressed words precede and follow unstressed words; words said hastily alternate with words said slowly. The rewritten lines from the "Ancient Mariner" are rhythmical when read aloud, because all speech is rhythmical. But unlike the original lines they are not metrical. **Meter is rhythm that can be measured in poems.**

SCANSION

Since meter is to a poem approximately what beat is to music, any literate person who has ever tapped his foot in time with a march or a waltz can learn to scan a poem—that is, to mark it in such a way that its meter is made evident. **Scansion** is the act of marking a poem to show the metrical units of which it is composed.

The smallest of these metrical units is the syllable. English syllables are of two kinds: accented or stressed, and unaccented or unstressed. An **accented syllable** requires more wind and push behind it than an **unaccented;** it also may be pitched slightly higher or held for a slightly longer time. In the following words the two kinds of syllables have been marked according to a widely used system of scansion:

$$\acute{\text{lear}}\breve{\text{ned}} \qquad \breve{\text{un}}\acute{\text{til}} \qquad \acute{\text{flat}}\breve{\text{tery}} \qquad \acute{\text{for}}\breve{\text{ceps}} \qquad \acute{\text{al}}\breve{\text{a}}\acute{\text{bas}}\breve{\text{ter}}$$

Observe that the first word in the list could just as well have been

treated as a monosyllable and marked leárned. This word must be seen in a context before the number of syllables it contains can be determined. Notice also that the last word has two accented syllables. The fact that one of these is a secondary accent has been ignored; both have been marked as having equal stress. In actual speech there are many degrees of accent that any system of scansion must ignore if it is to remain manageable. The first step in learning to scan, then, is learning to recognize syllables and to determine whether they are accented or unaccented.

EXERCISE 36

Mark, according to the system used above, the syllables in these words. Which of the words can be marked in more than one way? Why?

tremble	proceeds	heroic	cities
anon	apostle	Corinthian	aged
hours	spotted	sunset	knitted
syllable	over	desperate	hire
through	office	abhorrence	conduct
record	offices	flourish	pierce

FEET

After the syllable, the next largest metrical unit is the **foot,** which is a group of two or more syllables. The six most common kinds of feet in English metrics have names derived from Greek:

1. The **iambic** foot, or **iamb,** consists of an unaccented syllable followed by an accented. It is marked like this: ⌣ /
2. The **trochaic** foot, or **trochee,** consists of an accented syllable followed by an unaccented. It is marked like this: / ⌣
3. The **dactylic** foot, or **dactyl,** consists of an accented syllable followed by two unaccented syllables. It is marked like this: / ⌣ ⌣
4. The **anapestic** foot, or **anapest,** consists of two unaccented syllables followed by an accented syllable. It is marked like this: ⌣ ⌣ /
5. The **spondaic** foot, or **spondee,** consists of two accented syllables. It is marked like this: / /
6. The **pyrrhic** foot, or **pyrrhic,** consists of two unaccented syllables. It is marked like this: ⌣ ⌣

LINES

The next largest metrical unit is the line. A **line** is a regular succession of feet, and, though it is not necessarily a sentence, it customarily begins with a capital letter. These lines from four different poems illustrate the four kinds of meter:

1. Iambic: With loads | of lear | ned lum | ber in | his head.

2. Trochaic: Pleasant | was the | landscape | round him.

3. Dactylic: One more un | fortunate.

4. Anapestic: With his nos | trils like pits | full of blood | to the brim.

Lines consisting entirely of spondaic feet are extremely rare, and, entirely of pyrrhic feet, nonexistent because of the accentual nature of our language. A line containing only one foot is called a **monometer** line; one with two feet, a **dimeter** line; and so on through **trimeter, tetrameter, pentameter, hexameter, heptameter,** and **octameter.** Since each of these eight lengths may be composed of any of the four kinds of feet, thirty-two different varieties of line are theoretically possible. In practice, however, lines containing more than six feet are rare because they are too long to strike the ear as a unit. When read aloud, the heptameter line

> O, rest ye, brother mariners, we will not wander more

sounds as though it were written

> O, rest ye, brother mariners,
> We will not wander more.

Similarly, iambic octameter usually splits into two iambic tetrameter lines. Dactylic lines, of whatever length, are the rarest of the four kinds in English, perhaps because their movement is not suitable to many subjects, as Coleridge observed:

This is a | galloping | measure, || a | hop and a | trot and a | gallop.

The bulk of traditional English poetry is in iambic pentameter or tetrameter. A line of iambic hexameter is called an **alexandrine.**

Ă nĕed | lĕss Ă | lĕxăn | drĭne ĕnds | thĕ sŏng,
Thăt lĭke | ă wŏun | dĕd snăke | drăgs ĭts | slŏw lĕngth | ălŏng.

The second of these two lines is, of course, the alexandrine. In the passage quoted from Coleridge iambic tetrameter alternates with iambic trimeter:

Hĕ prăy | ĕth bĕst, || .whŏ lŏv | ĕth bĕst
Ăll thĭngs || bŏth grĕat | ănd smăll;
Fŏr thĕ | dĕar Gŏd || whŏ lŏv | ĕth ŭs,
Hĕ măde || ănd lŏv | ĕth ăll.

How does one go about scanning a poem as these lines have been scanned? The procedure is much simpler than, say, that of bidding a hand of contract bridge.

STEPS IN SCANSION

1. Mark the syllables in the line to be scanned. A student beginning the study of scansion should pronounce the words aloud because the ear rather than the eye determines the number of syllables. Avoid distortion; a word should be pronounced in poetry as in prose. Remember that accent and lack of accent are relative rather than absolute. Notice the words *but, to, their, how, they,* and *of* in the following scansion:

Bŭt whĕn | tŏ mĭs | chĭef mŏr | tăls bĕnd | thĕir wĭll
Hŏw sŏon | thĕy fĭnd | fĭt ĭn | strŭmĕnts | ŏf ĭll.

2. Examine the marks over the syllables to discover which of the four main kinds of feet predominates. One kind of foot *will* predominate, but do not expect every foot in a line—let alone in a whole poem—to be like every other foot. Having determined the dominant kind of foot (and to be perfectly certain you should mark the syllables in more than one line), you are ready to put in the vertical marks that indicate the end of one foot and the beginning of another. Notice, in the examples

already given, that the vertical marks do not necessarily come before or after a word, but that they may, and frequently do, divide a word, especially in lines containing polysyllabic words. Here, with scansion, is such a line from *Paradise Lost:*

$$\text{Immŭ} \mid \text{táblĕ,} \mid\mid \text{ĭmmór} \mid \text{tăl,} \mid\mid \text{ĭn} \mid \text{fĭnĭte.}$$

3. Discover, by reading the line aloud, whether there is a pause, or **caesura,** and if there is, indicate its position by marking in a double vertical line or another single vertical line if the pause coincides with the end of a foot. The line just quoted from *Paradise Lost* is unusual in having two caesuras: one after the second foot, and one in the middle of the fourth foot. Caesuras are not necessarily accompanied by punctuation marks, as they are here, nor are they invariably in any one place in all the lines of a given poem. One of the ways by which a poet achieves variety is to shift the position of the caesura from line to line (look back at the quotation from the "Ancient Mariner"). In addition to achieving variety, the skillful poet will make his caesuras coincide with his units of thought. The effect of the caesura is not unlike the sense of lift that comes at the end of a musical phrase. Another pause may occur at the end of a line. A line with a pause at the end is said to be **end-stopped.**

> Sigh no more, ladies, sigh no more!
>   Men were deceivers ever;
> One foot in sea, and one on shore,
>   To one thing constant never.

WILLIAM SHAKESPEARE
(from *Much Ado About Nothing*)

In contrast, a line without a pause at the end is called a **run-on** line. The practice of running on the line to the next line is sometimes called **enjambment.**

> Roll on, thou deep and dark blue Ocean—roll!
> Ten thousand fleets sweep over thee in vain;
> Man marks the earth with ruin—his control
> Stops with the shore. . . .

GEORGE GORDON, LORD BYRON
(from *Childe Harold's Pilgrimage*)

The effect of the run-on third line is quite different from that of the end-stopped first.

4. Count the number of feet to determine the appropriate label for the line. Frequently one kind of line will alternate with another, as in the "Ancient Mariner."

5. It is a gross error to suppose that if the feet are not all alike, the poet must have made a mistake. Meter is not a straitjacket into which a poet must force his words. If it were, poets would be so limited in choosing their words that they would almost never be able to say what they wanted to. Meter is made for the poem, not the poem for meter. Another good reason why meter is seldom strictly "regular" is that poems in which the kind of foot is never varied are likely to become as monotonous as the ticking of a watch. Once the poet has established his meter, he will vary it according to the effects he wishes to create. These lines, for instance, occur in an iambic context:

> Thĭs á | gĕd Prínce, || nŏw flóur | ĭshíng | ĭn péace,
> Ănd blést | wĭth ĭs | sŭe || ŏf | ă lárge | ĭncréase,
> Wórn óut | wĭth bús | ĭness, || dĭd | ăt léngth | dĕbáte
> Tŏ sét | tlĕ thĕ | sŭccés | sĭon ŏf | thĕ státe.

> JOHN DRYDEN
> (from *Mac Flecknoe*)

Lines 1 and 3 have six accented syllables rather than the expected five. Consequently they move somewhat more slowly than the second, and much more slowly than the fourth, which contains two pyrrhic feet substituted for the expected iambs. An anapest substituted in a context that is primarily iambic also tends to hasten the movement, as in the fourth foot of this line:

> Kéen fít | fŭl gústs || ăre whís | pĕrĭng hére | ănd thére.

In practice almost any foot may be substituted for another. The most common substitutions are trochee or spondee for iamb (especially at the beginning of a line or directly after the caesura), iamb for anapest, and anapest for iamb.

Another way in which a poet can vary the meter of a line is to drop an unaccented syllable or two. Carets are inserted to replace the missing syllables:

> Take her up | tenderly,
>
> Lift her with | care; ∧ ∧
>
> Fashion'd so | slenderly,
>
> Young, and so | fair! ∧ ∧

THOMAS HOOD
(from "The Bridge of Sighs")

The omitted syllables create moments of silence.

6. Try to discover the meter in the poem instead of imposing on the poem your own notion of what the metrical pattern should be. Before putting in the foot marks, decide whether the poem is in **rising meter** (iambic and anapestic) or **falling meter** (trochaic and dactylic). In falling meter the voice is first up, and then it goes down:

> Greedy | hawk must | gorge its | prey. ∧
>
> Pious | priest must | have his | pay. ∧

In rising meter the voice is first down, and then it goes up:

> With hon | or and glo | ry through trou | ble and dan | ger.

The extra unaccented syllable at the end is called a **feminine ending.**

7. Avoid scansions that may be mechanically "correct" but that do not show how the voice moves in reading:

> ∧ ∧ With | honor and | glory through | trouble and | danger.

Here a falling meter has been imposed on a rising meter.

8. Since you must rely on your own ear, and since no two ears are exactly alike, there may be legitimate—but usually slight—differences between your scansion and another person's. The thing to avoid is a scansion that, like the following, could satisfy *nobody's* ear:

> With hon | or and | glory | through trou | ble and | danger.

To read the line in this fashion is to mangle English pronunciation beyond recognition.

Here is a summary of the steps to take in scanning a poem:

1. Mark the syllables. (Read the poem at this and each succeeding step.)
2. Mark the feet.
3. Mark the caesuras.
4. Expect to encounter variations, but do not consider them in naming the basic meter.
5. Check your scansion to make sure that it reflects the poem rather than a preconceived notion of your own.

EXERCISE 37

Scan the following poems and name the basic meter of each.

On a Fly Drinking out of His Cup

Busy, curious, thirsty fly!
Drink with me and drink as I:
Freely welcome to my cup,
Couldst thou sip and sip it up:
Make the most of life you may,   5
Life is short and wears away.
Both alike are mine and thine
Hastening quick to their decline:
Thine's a summer, mine's no more,
Though repeated to threescore.   10
Threescore summers, when they're gone,
Will appear as short as one!

WILLIAM OLDYS

Concord Hymn

By the rude bridge that arched the flood,
  Their flag to April's breeze unfurled,
Here once the embattled farmers stood,
  And fired the shot heard round the world.

The foe long since in silence slept;   5
   Alike the conqueror silent sleeps;
And Time the ruined bridge has swept
   Down the dark stream which seaward creeps.

On this green bank, by this soft stream,
   We set to-day a votive stone;   10
That memory may their deed redeem,
   When, like our sires, our sons are gone.

Spirit, that made those heroes dare
   To die, and leave their children free,
Bid Time and Nature gently spare   15
   The shaft we raise to them and thee.

RALPH WALDO EMERSON

once (3): April 19, 1775. to-day (10): July 4, 1837.

Limericks

There were three young women of Birmingham,
And I know a sad story concerning 'em:
    They stuck needles and pins
    In the reverend shins
Of the Bishop engaged in confirming 'em.   5

A lady there was of Antigua,
Who said to her spouse, "What a pig you are!"
    He answered, "My queen,
    Is it manners you mean,
Or do you refer to my figure?"   5

There was a young girl of Lahore,
With the same shape behind as before.
    As no one knew where
    To offer a chair,
She had to sit down on the floor.   5

COSMO MONKHOUSE

The Watch

I wakened on my hot, hard bed,
Upon the pillow lay my head;
Beneath the pillow I could hear
My little watch was ticking clear.
I thought the throbbing of it went   5
Like my continual discontent.
I thought it said in every tick:
I am so sick, so sick, so sick.
O death, come quick, come quick, come quick,
Come quick, come quick, come quick, come quick!   10

FRANCES CORNFORD

DISCUSSION OF METER

Some people regard scansion as a dull, mechanical sort of activity, having no usefulness to anyone except perhaps to the professional student or to poets. This view would be correct if scansion were an end in itself. But it is not. Scansion is, rather, a means whereby the reader understands and appreciates a poem more fully than he would if he had not scanned it. Marking the syllables and the feet and identifying the kind of meter present are useless activities unless they are followed by an analytical discussion. Discussions of meter usually contain answers to questions like these:

1. *Is the meter appropriate to the poem?* This question has to be asked about each individual poem, for none of the kinds of meter has built-in features that make it uniquely and automatically appropriate for a given subject. Occasionally a poem seems to be in a very inappropriate meter. In these lines from Christina Rossetti's "Next of Kin," an elderly person is addressing a younger one and telling him that he too will die eventually.

> Yet when your day is over, as mine is nearly done,
> And when your race is finished, as mine is almost run,
> You, like me, shall cross your hands and bow your graceful head:
> Yea, we twain shall sleep together in an equal bed.

The rapid, jogging effect of this meter is certainly inappropriate to such a doleful subject.

2. *Is the meter monotonous and unvaried?* If so, is there a discoverable reason for the monotony other than the poet's lack of skill?

3. *What does the meter contribute to the total effect of the poem?* In some poems the meter makes no easily definable contribution; in others, it does. The meter of Browning's "How They Brought the Good News from Ghent to Aix," for instance, reinforces the words in such a way that rapid and vigorous action is suggested. The poem begins like this:

> I sprang to the stirrup, and Joris, and he;
> I galloped, Dirck galloped, we galloped all three;
> "Good speed!" cried the watch, as the gate-bolts undrew;
> "Speed!" echoed the wall to us galloping through.

The meter, of course, does not gallop, but working with the words of the poem it creates the effect of galloping.

4. *Why has the poet varied his basic meter in certain places?* This is the most important question that arises in discussions of meter. Pay special attention to omitted syllables and substituted feet. They deserve comment because they control emphasis by accelerating or retarding a line. Try to discover why the poet apparently wished to change the speed of the line. The poet also varies his meter to call attention to important words. Take these two lines, for example:

> The drunkard now supinely snores,
> His load of ale sweats through his pores.

The meter is basically iambic. Yet in the third foot of the second line the poet has substituted a trochee for an expected iamb, has thereby singled out the word *sweats* for special attention, and can rely on the connotation of *sweats* to create the desired feeling of disgust in the reader.

A more savory example showing how a poet can use metrical variation to reinforce his meaning and direct his reader's response occurs in these lines from John Donne's sixteenth elegy, a poem in which a man is saying farewell to a girl with whom he is having a secret love affair and telling her how to behave while he is away traveling on the Continent.

> When I am gone, dream me some happiness,
> Nor let thy looks **our** long-hid love confess;

> Nor praise nor dispraise me; nor bless nor curse
> Openly love's force; nor in bed fright thy nurse
> With midnight startings, crying out, "Oh! Oh!
> Nurse, oh my love is slain! I saw him go
> O'er the white Alps alone, I saw him, I,
> Assailed, fight, taken, stabbed, bleed, fall, and die!"

The first four lines of this passage are dominantly iambic. Two of them are run-on to give the effect of talk. Then, at the end of line five, when the poet arrives at a moment of emotional stress, the meter becomes wildly different from the basic meter. A climax is reached with the loud spondees in the last line. They imitate the cries of the girl, frightened by a nightmare in which she sees her lover cut down by bandits. Notice, too, that the substituted spondee of *white Alps* in the seventh line emphasizes *white* and helps the reader picture the cold and desolate place where the bloody deed occurs.

5. *Is there more than one defensible way of scanning a line or a foot?* A discussion of the scansion of a poem should always avoid dogmatism. Defend the scansion that you have made, but by all means mention the possibility of alternative scansions. Even the most carefully worked-out scansion can show only approximately the metrical phenomena in a poem. At its best scansion is merely a compromise between the strictly regular meter that is, so to speak, at the back of the poet's mind as he writes and the reader's as he reads, and the many subtle variations on the basic meter that the poet incorporates for the skillful reader to discover.

EXERCISE 38

Discuss the use of meter in the following poems. Make scansions when they are necessary to support your statements.

Bermudas

> Where the remote Bermudas ride
> In th' ocean's bosom unespied,
> From a small boat that rowed along,
> The list'ning winds received this song:

What should we do but sing his praise   5
That led us through the wat'ry maze
Unto an isle so long unknown,
And yet far kinder than our own?
Where he the huge sea-monsters wracks,
That lift the deep upon their backs,   10
He lands us on a grassy stage,
Safe from the storms and prelates' rage.
He gave us this eternal spring
Which here enamels everything,
And sends the fowls to us in care,   15
On daily visits through the air.
He hangs in shades the orange bright,
Like golden lamps in a green night;
And does in the pomegranates close
Jewels more rich than Ormus shows.   20
He makes the figs our mouths to meet
And throws the melons at our feet,
But apples plants of such a price,
No tree could ever bear them twice.
With cedars, chosen by his hand,   25
From Lebanon, he stores the land,
And makes the hollow seas that roar
Proclaim the ambergris on shore.
He cast, of which we rather boast,
The Gospel's pearl upon our coast,   30
And in these rocks for us did frame
A temple, where to sound his name.
Oh, let our voice his praise exalt,
Till it arrive at heaven's vault;
Which thence, perhaps, rebounding, may   35
Echo beyond the Mexic Bay.
    Thus sung they in the English boat
An holy and a cheerful note,
And all the way, to guide their chime,
With falling oars they kept the time.   40

ANDREW MARVELL

Title: Some of the early settlers of these islands left England to
escape religious persecution. **apples** (23): pineapples. **pearl**
(30): see Matthew xiii:46.

1. What is the effect of the variation in meter in line 3? In line 12? In line 36?
2. Why are the apostrophes used in lines 2 (th'), 4, and 6?
3. Does the caesura regularly come in a particular place in Marvell's line? Study any ten lines to determine Marvell's practice.
4. Are there relatively many or relatively few variations in the meter?
5. Can you discover anything particularly appropriate or inappropriate about the meter?

Verses

*Supposed to Be Written by
Alexander Selkirk, during
His Solitary Abode in the
Island of Juan Fernandez*

I am monarch of all I survey,
  My right there is none to dispute;
From the centre all round to the sea,
  I am lord of the fowl and the brute.
Oh, solitude! where are the charms   5
  That sages have seen in thy face?
Better dwell in the midst of alarms,
  Than reign in this horrible place.

I am out of humanity's reach,
  I must finish my journey alone,   10
Never hear the sweet sound of speech;
  I start at the sound of my own.
The beasts, that roam over the plain,
  My form with indifference see;
They are so unacquainted with man,   15
  Their tameness is shocking to me.

Society, friendship, and love,
  Divinely bestow'd upon man,
Oh, had I the wings of a dove,
  How soon would I taste you again!   20
My sorrows I then might assuage
  In the ways of religion and truth,
Might learn from the wisdom of age,
  And be cheer'd by the sallies of youth.

Religion! what treasure untold   25
   Resides in that heavenly word!
More precious than silver and gold,
   Or all that this earth can afford.
But the sound of the church-going bell
   These vallies and rocks never heard,   30
Ne'er sigh'd at the sound of a knell,
   Or smil'd when a sabbath appear'd.

Ye winds, that have made me your sport,
   Convey to this desolate shore
Some cordial endearing report   35
   Of a land I shall visit no more.
My friends, do they now and then send
   A wish or a thought after me?
O tell them I yet have a friend,
   Though a friend I am never to see.   40

How fleet is a glance of the mind!
   Compar'd with the speed of its flight,
The tempest itself lags behind,
   And the swift wing'd arrows of light.
When I think of my own native land,   45
   In a moment I seem to be there;
But alas! recollection at hand
   Soon hurries me back to despair.

But the sea-fowl is gone to her nest,
   The beast is laid down in his lair,   50
Ev'n here is a season or rest,
   And I to my cabin repair.
There is mercy in every place;
   And mercy, encouraging thought!
Gives even affliction a grace,   55
   And reconciles man to his lot.

WILLIAM COWPER

Selkirk (Title): Often said to be an original for Defoe's Robinson Crusoe.

FREE VERSE

Granted that much more than meter is needed for a poem—and what that "much more" consists of is the subject of this book—does it follow that a poem must have meter? A large number of poets, especially in the early years of the twentieth century, answered this question negatively. Their poems, written in rhythmical language but not in the traditional meters, are called **free verse**. Nonmetrical poetry is called "free" because the poet has freed himself from conforming to the set metrical patterns.

Once I Pass'd through a Populous City

Once I pass'd through a populous city imprinting my brain for future use
    with its shows, architecture, customs, traditions,
Yet now of all that city I remember only a woman I casually met there
    who detain'd me for love of me,
Day by day and night by night we were together—all else has long been
    forgotten by me,
I remember I say only that woman who passionately clung to me,
Again we wander, we love, we separate again,   5
Again she holds me by the hand, I must not go,
I see her close beside me with silent lips sad and tremulous.

WALT WHITMAN

This piece of writing resembles metrical poetry in having capitals at the start of each line; but unlike metrical lines, these are not composed of recurring feet of the same kind and number. Whitman has relied on other devices (some of which will be discussed in the next chapter) to organize his poem. These devices would not be found in such number and frequency in ordinary prose. It might be well to look at the whole matter like this: prose is rhythmical; free verse is more rhythmical than prose; metered poetry is so highly rhythmical that the rhythm conforms to a measurable pattern.

A poet who chooses to write free rather than metered verse sacrifices certain things and gains others. One thing that he gives up is the primitive appeal to the nervous system that meter makes. Thus his poems will probably not reach so deeply into his audience's minds, and they will be somewhat difficult to memorize. An advantage of free verse is that the poet owes no allegiance to a metrical pattern that may take over the actual composition and force him to write like his predecessors who used that meter.

EXERCISE 39

Consider whether the imposition of meter on this ancient Hebrew song has resulted in improving it as a poem.

Psalm 23

The Lord is my shepherd;
I shall not want.
He maketh me to lie down in green pastures;
He leadeth me beside the still waters;
He restoreth my soul.   5
He leadeth me in the paths of righteousness for his name's sake.
Yea, though I walk through the valley of the shadow of death,
I will fear no evil, for thou art with me.
Thy rod and thy staff they comfort me.
Thou preparest a table before me in the presence of mine enemies;   10
Thou anointest my head with oil;
My cup runneth over.
Surely goodness and mercy shall follow me all the days of my life,
And I will dwell in the house of the Lord for ever.

THE BIBLE, KING JAMES VERSION

A Psalm of David

The Lord to me a shepherd is; want therefore shall not I.
He in the folds of tender grass doth cause me down to lie.
To waters calm me gently leads, restore my soul doth he;
He doth in paths of righteousness for his name's sake lead me.
Yea, though in valley of death's shade I walk, none ill I'll fear   5
Because thou art with me; thy rod and staff my comfort are.
For me a table thou hast spread in presence of my foes;

Thou dost anoint my head with oil; my cup it overflows.
Goodness and mercy surely shall all my days follow me,
And in the Lord's house I shall dwell so long as days shall be.   10

THE WHOLE BOOK OF PSALMS FAITHFULLY TRANSLATED
INTO ENGLISH METER (the "Bay Psalm-Book")

BLANK VERSE

Free verse must not be confused with **blank verse,** which is the
customary label for iambic pentameter without rhyme (see page 189).
Unlike free verse, blank verse has a regular metrical pattern. The
characters in Shakespeare's plays sometimes speak in prose, but more
often in unrhymed iambic pentameter verse. For instance, the Duke in
As You Like It makes this comment on having to live in a forest:

> Sweet are the uses of adversity,
> Which, like the toad, ugly and venomous,
> Wears yet a precious jewel in his head;
> And this our life, exempt from public haunt,
> Finds tongues in trees, books in the running brooks,
> Sermons in stones, and good in everything.

The ideas in these lines are not made more "poetic" by the addition of
rhyme:

> The man to solitude accustom'd long
> Perceives in ev'ry thing that lives a tongue;
> Not animals alone, but shrubs and trees,
> Have speech for him, and understood with ease.

WILLIAM COWPER
(from "The Needless Alarm")

The greatest dramatic (*Hamlet, King Lear*) and epic (*Paradise Lost*)
poems in English are in blank verse.

THE FUNCTIONS OF METER AND RHYTHM

Meter and rhythm have two main functions. First, they make a
poem pleasurable because they themselves are intrinsically delightful.
Like dancing and playing games, reading and writing poems are

among the rhythmical activities of mankind. These activities are everywhere apparent: children chant rhythmically, and so do certain kinds of insane people; boys enjoy passing a ball regularly back and forth; a smoothly running automobile motor is music to many an adult ear. Just why rhythm should affect people so powerfully and in so many different ways is far from clear; perhaps it has something to do with the in and out of their breathing, the come and go of their pulses.

In addition to making a poem enjoyable, meter and rhythm make it more meaningful. They are a part of the total meaning—a part that cannot always be described in words, but can always be felt and is always lost when a poem is paraphrased or when it is translated from one language to another.

The Hourglass

> Do but consider this small dust,
> Here running in the glass,
>   By atoms moved;
> Could you believe that this
> The body was   5
>   Of one that loved?
> And in his Mistress' flame, playing like a fly,
>   Turned to cinders by her eye?
>   Yes; and in death, as life, unblest,
>   To have't expressed,   10
> Even ashes of lovers find no rest.

BEN JONSON

Here the meter is very much a part of the meaning. The poem moves somewhat unsteadily, by fits and starts, as though the speaker were thinking of what he should say as he goes along. Spondees make line 1 slow and thoughtful:

$$\text{Dó bút } | \text{ cŏnsíd } | \text{ ĕr } || \text{ thís } | \text{ smáll dúst,}$$

Line 2, in contrast, is fast, its unaccented syllables and shorter length reinforcing the action of the running sand:

Here rún | ning || in | the glàss,

Line 3, a parenthesis, is appropriately shorter still. Then line 4, which marks the next step in the argument, is like line 1, the first step, except that it is a foot shorter—perhaps because the speaker is becoming more and more unwilling to give out information:

Could you | believe || that this

Lines 4 and 5 are run-on; yet there is bound to be a slight pause at the end of each, a pause that would be lessened if the lines were printed continuously. The pause seems to be functional. The speaker is in no hurry to give away the surprise in line 6: the sand in the glass is a man's ashes. Having divulged this much, as though reluctantly, he blurts out his next surprising question in two lines that resemble metrically no others in the poem:

And in | his Mist | ress' fláme, || playing | like a fly,

Turned to | cinders || by her | eye? ∧

To emphasize this surprise, he has shifted from the expected iambs to quite unexpected trochees. Although his rhetorical questions require no answer, he gives a resounding affirmative:

Yés; || and | in death, || as life, || unblest,

The omitted syllable at the end of line 8 and the strong caesura after the semicolon isolate the *yes*. The speaker now has a third point to make, and he makes it by means of another new metrical arrangement:

To have't | expressed,

Even | ashes | of lov | ers || find | no rest.

Shifting from iambs to trochees and then back to iambs forces the voice to linger on *lovers*. Thus the final point is made emphatically and at the same time reluctantly—as though the speaker knew that nobody would take his remarks for literal truth.

The meter enables the reader to participate in the sequence of thoughts, to experience the surprises in the poem. Since the experience of any poem is a large part of its meaning, the poem has a different meaning when put into a different meter, because it then conveys a different experience.

The Hour-Glass

> O think, fair maid! these sands that pass
> In slender threads adown this glass,
> Were once the body of some swain,
> Who lov'd too well and lov'd in vain,
> And let one soft sigh heave thy breast,   5
> That not in life alone unblest
> E'en lovers' ashes find no rest.

SAMUEL TAYLOR COLERIDGE

Coleridge omits the part about the lover who burns in the flames of his mistress' eye; he is not interested in such macabre details. Instead, his speaker wishes to emphasize the pathos of the situation and to communicate that pathos to a girl. The meter therefore moves with stately regularity throughout. It is notably varied only in line 5:

$$\breve{A}nd\ l\acute{e}t\ |\ \acute{o}ne\ s\acute{o}ft\ |\ s\acute{i}gh\ ||\ h\acute{e}ave\ |\ th\breve{y}\ br\acute{e}ast,$$

Coleridge has not only added the idea in this line, but he has emphasized it because it is an important part of his meaning. His poem seems to be a more finished performance than Jonson's; actually it is not, because Jonson distorted his meter intentionally. Coleridge avoided surprise and drama: these would be incompatible with tender feelings. His easy smoothness is as much a part of his meaning as Jonson's contrived roughness is part of *his*.

EXERCISE 40

Carefully scan the following poem; then explain how the poet has used rhythm structurally to reinforce feeling and meaning.

Song

Sweetest love, I do not go
  For weariness of thee,
Nor in the hope the world can show
  A fitter love for me;
    But since that I   5
Must die at last, 'tis best
To use myself in jest
    Thus by feigned deaths to die.

Yesternight the sun went hence,
  And yet is here today;   10
He hath no desire nor sense,
  Nor half so short a way:
    Then fear not me,
But believe that I shall make
Speedier journeys, since I take   15
    More wings and spurs than he.

O how feeble is man's power,
  That if good fortune fall,
Cannot add another hour,
  Nor a lost hour recall!   20
    But come bad chance,
And we join to it our strength,
And we teach it art and length,
    Itself o'er us to advance.

When thou sigh'st thou sigh'st not wind,   25
  But sigh'st my soul away;
When thou weep'st, unkindly kind,
  My life's blood doth decay.
    It cannot be
That thou lov'st me, as thou say'st,   30
If in thine my life thou waste,
  Thou art the best of me.

Let not thy divining heart
  Forethink me any ill;
Destiny may take thy part,   35
  And may thy fears fulfill;

> But think that we
> Are but turned aside to sleep;
> They who one another keep
> Alive, ne'er parted be.   40

JOHN DONNE

Show how meter (or rhythm) is a part of the meaning of these poems.

The Unawkward Singers

> Self-praise is a wonderful thing!
> It causes all the birds to sing:
> The sparrow's brag, thrush's conceit,
> They make the whole world cheerly repeat
> Cheerly repeat their praise.   5
>
> For any lark there is no other,
> No father, mother, sister, brother,
> No sweet wife, nor no dear love;
> The dove's the pool in which the dove,
> Loving, admires his ways.   10
>
> Wind out of the swan's throat
> His final operatic note:
> Impassioned on himself he dies,
> Knowing the world is him, is his
> By his self-celebration.   15
>
> Master man cannot so please
> Himself with eloquence like these;
> Thus clumsily his song is sung,
> Thick praise by a thick tongue
> For its own limitation.   20

DAVID FERRY

The Day

The day was a year at first
When children ran in the garden;
The day shrank down to a month
When the boys played ball.

The day was a week thereafter   5
When young men walked in the garden;
The day was itself a day
When love grew tall.

The day shrank down to an hour
When old men limped in the garden;   10
The day will last forever
When it is nothing at all.

THEODORE SPENCER

The Hill

Where are Elmer, Herman, Bert, Tom and Charley,
The weak of will, the strong of arm, the clown, the boozer, the fighter?
All, all, are sleeping on the hill.

One passed in a fever,
One was burned in a mine,   5
One was killed in a brawl,
One died in a jail,
One fell from a bridge toiling for children and wife—
All, all are sleeping, sleeping, sleeping on the hill.

Where are Ella, Kate, Mag, Lizzie and Edith,   10
The tender heart, the simple soul, the loud, the proud, the happy one?—
All, all, are sleeping on the hill.

One died in shameful child-birth,
One of a thwarted love,
One at the hands of a brute in a brothel,   15

One of a broken pride, in the search for heart's desire,
One after life in far-away London and Paris
Was brought to her little space by Ella and Kate and Mag—
All, all are sleeping, sleeping, sleeping on the hill.

Where are Uncle Isaac and Aunt Emily, 20
And old Towny Kincaid and Sevigne Houghton,
And Major Walker who had talked
With venerable men of the revolution?—
All, all, are sleeping on the hill.

They brought them dead sons from the war, 25
And daughters whom life had crushed,
And their children fatherless, crying—
All, all are sleeping, sleeping, sleeping on the hill.

Where is old Fiddler Jones
Who played with life all his ninety years, 30
Braving the sleet with bared breast,
Drinking, rioting, thinking neither of wife nor kin,
Nor gold, nor love, nor heaven?

Lo! he babbles of the fish-frys of long ago,
Of the horse-races of long ago at Clary's Grove, 35
Of what Abe Lincoln said
One time at Springfield.

EDGAR LEE MASTERS

Love Is a Sickness

Love is a sickness full of woes,
    All remedies refusing;
A plant that with most cutting grows,
    Most barren with best using.
        Why so? 5
    More we enjoy it, more it dies;
If not enjoyed it sighing cries,
        Hey ho.

Love is a torment of the mind,
   A tempest everlasting;   10
And Jove hath made it of a kind
   Not well, nor full, nor fasting.
     Why so?
   More we enjoy it, more it dies;
If not enjoyed it sighing cries,   15
   Hey ho.

SAMUEL   DANIEL
(from *Hymen's Triumph*)

8

THE SOUND
OF A POEM

Poems, unlike children, should be heard as well as seen. Poetry is a much older activity than printing or even writing; it began when words were merely sound waves in the air, not black marks on paper. Like so-called primitive people today, ancient man chanted or sang his poems from memory. The invention of writing weakened, but never entirely dissolved, the connection between poetry and oral recitation. A student of poetry must, therefore, learn to use his ears as well as his eyes if he is to understand and enjoy poems.

The almost universal appeal of music suggests that human ears delight in sounds that are arranged in patterns and in patterns of sound that are repeated. Many poems make a similar appeal, though poetry and music are fundamentally different. Music is an arrangement of sounds; poetry, an arrangement of words. To speak of a poem as "verbal music" is misleading because it blurs a distinction between the arts. Each art has its characteristic patterns of sound. The sound pat-

185

terns of poems may be classified under three heads: alliteration, assonance, and rhyme.

ALLITERATION

Alliteration is the repetition of identical or similar consonantal sounds, usually but not necessarily at the beginnings of words: *p*retty *p*ink *p*ills for *p*ale *p*eople. Alliteration does not depend on spelling: *ph*antom alliterates with *f*lower but not with *pn*eumonia; *c*ease with *sc*issors but not with *ch*ime. Colloquial English is strewn with alliterative tags like *might and main, hide nor hair, fit as a fiddle, bold as brass,* and so is advertising of the kind commonly considered "catchy." Since about 1400, however, alliteration has not been an important technical device in English poetry, although before that time it was used as an organizing principle in many poems. *Piers Plowman* is typical of the old system of versification according to which a word in the first part of every line alliterates with a word in the second:

> And now is *r*eligion a *r*ider, a *r*oamer by the streets,
> And *l*eader of *l*ove days, and a *l*and buyer.

Since the fourteenth century most poets have used alliteration sparingly, and only for special effects. It can, for instance, underline a contrast, as when Pope writes, "The strength he *g*ains is from the embrace he *g*ives." Or it can emphasize a connection between ideas, as when Dryden begins his poem "To the Memory of Mr. Oldham" with the line "Farewell, too *l*ittle and too *l*ately known." Byron's "Waterloo" describes a soldier who "rushed into the *f*ield, and, *f*oremost *f*ighting, *f*ell." Alliteration in this line helps the words convey to the reader an image of a single, sudden action. When used to create a connection or a contrast between ideas or events, alliteration is a legitimate device, but when used for its own sake it may be tiresome or even laughable. The person who reads a poem primarily for what it says rather than for how it sounds may think that there is an excessive amount of alliteration in this excerpt from Swinburne's *Atalanta in Calydon:*

> When the hounds of spring are on winter's traces,
>   The mother of months in meadow or plain
> Fills the shadows and windy places
>   With lisp of leaves and ripple·of rain. . . .

> For winter's rains and ruins are over,
>   And all the season of snows and sins;
> The days dividing lover and lover,
>   The light that loses the night that wins.

This is ingenious, but it raises a question. Has the poet sacrificed sense for sound? In line 6, for example, winter is said to be a season of sins. Is the word *sins* put in merely for alliterative effect? Here the device seems decorative rather than functional, since it makes little, if any, contribution to the meaning.

ASSONANCE

A second kind of repeated sound is **assonance,** or the repetition of similar or identical vowel sounds: "Thy kingdom come, thy will be done." The old proverb "A stitch in time saves nine" contains both alliteration and assonance. Other assonant pairs are *each, either; old, mouldy; lady, baby; deep, tree; gaunt, slaughter.* Because assonance depends on sound rather than on spelling, it can be detected only by the ear. Assonance is not used as deliberately and consciously as alliteration, but it has the same functions: to please the ear, to give emphasis, and to point up an antithesis.

EXERCISE 41

In the following poems, and in Auden's "O Where Are You Going" (page 153), locate all the instances of alliteration and assonance. Then try to explain whether they are decorative or whether they have some other function.

In Vitam Humanam

> The world's a bubble, and the life of man
>   Less than a span;
> In his conception wretched, and from the womb
>   So to the tomb;
> Curst from the cradle, and brought up to years   5
>   With cares and fears.
> Who, then, to frail mortality shall trust
> But limns the water, or but writes in dust.

Yet since with sorrow here we live oppressed,
    What life is best?   10
Courts are but only superficial schools
    To dandle fools;
The rural parts are turned into a den
    Of savage men;
And where's a city from all vice so free   15
But may be termed the worst of all the three?

Domestic cares afflict the husband's bed
    Or pains his head;
Those that live single take it for a curse,
    Or do things worse;   20
Some would have children; those that have them moan
    Or wish them gone;
What is it, then, to have or have no wife
But single thraldom or a double strife?

Our own affections still at home to please   25
    Is a disease;
To cross the sea to any foreign soil,
    Perils and toil;
Wars with their noise affright us; when they cease
    We're worse in peace.   30
What then remains, but that we still should cry
Not to be born, or being born, to die?

SIR FRANCIS BACON

Title: "On Human Life."

On a Venerable Beau

Still hovering round the fair at sixty-four,
Unfit to love, unable to give o'er;
A flesh-fly, that just flutters on the wing,
Awake to buzz, but not alive to sting;
Brisk where he cannot, backward where he can—   5
The teasing ghost of the departed man.

DAVID MALLET

Dark House, by Which Once More I Stand

Dark house, by which once more I stand
    Here in the long unlovely street,
    Doors, where my heart was used to beat
So quickly, waiting for a hand,

A hand that can be clasp'd no more—   5
    Behold me, for I cannot sleep,
    And like a guilty thing I creep
At earliest morning to the door.

He is not here; but far away
    The noise of life begins again,
    And ghastly thro' the drizzling rain
On the bald street breaks the blank day.

ALFRED, LORD TENNYSON
(from *In Memoriam*)

RHYME

A third kind of repeated sound is rhyme, perhaps the most commonly known of all the devices a poem may employ—though only a very naïve reader expects every poem to employ it. **Rhyme** may be defined as the repetition of both vowel and consonantal sounds at the ends of words. It is easily distinguished from the other two kinds of repeated sound: while *tool* alliterates with *toad,* and *toad* is assonant with *foam, foam* rhymes with *home.* Rhymes like *home* and *foam* are arbitrarily called **masculine rhymes**—a term that signifies no more than correspondence in sound between stressed syllables. The rhymes in the following bit of doggerel are masculine:

If all be true that I do think,
There are five reasons we should drink:
Good wine, a friend, or being dry,
Or lest we should be by and by,
Or any other reason why.

HENRY ALDRICH

Feminine rhyme is the term given to the correspondence in sound between words that do not end in an accented syllable: *mournfully, scornfully; leaping, creeping.*

> What is fame? An empty bubble.
> Gold? A transient, shining trouble.
>
> JAMES GRAINGER

The following epitaph may also be said to employ feminine rhymes because the lines end with the extra unaccented syllable known as a feminine ending (see page 165):

> Life is a jest, and all things show it;
> I thought so once, but now I know it.
>
> JOHN GAY

Feminine rhymes are well suited to light and humorous verse.

> Oh! ye immortal Gods! what is theogony?
>   Oh! thou, too, mortal man! what is philanthrophy?
> Oh! world, which was and is, what is cosmogony?
>   Some people have accused me of misanthrophy;
> And yet I know no more than the mahogany
>   That forms this desk, of what they mean; *lykanthrophy*
> I comprehend, for without transformation
> Men become wolves on any slight occasion.
>
> GEORGE GORDON, LORD BYRON
> (from *Don Juan*)

Although rhyme usually appears at the ends of lines, it may also occur within lines, especially in songs and ballads, and then it is called **internal rhyme.**

> I cannot eat but little meat,
>   My stomach is not good;
> But sure I think that I can drink
>   With him that wears a hood.
> Though I go bare, take ye no care,
>   I am nothing a-cold;
> I stuff my skin so full within
>   Of jolly good ale and old.
>
> ANONYMOUS
> (from *Gammer Gurton's Needle*)

Rhyme is capable of many subtle variations. **Rich rhymes** are made up of sounds identical in all respects: *bear, bare*. **Sight rhymes** (sometimes called eye rhymes) are based on correspondence in spelling, as in *dew, sew;* such rhymes as *find, wind* in older poems are now sight rhymes because of pronunciation changes. **Partial rhymes** do not have the correspondence in both vowel and consonant that rhyme proper has. Partial rhyme, which is known by several other names (slant rhyme, pararhyme, consonantal rhyme, near rhyme), makes use of both assonance and alliteration: *dear, dare; fear, rare; actress, mattress*. It is not so important to know the technical names of the different kinds of rhymes as to realize that rhyme does not have to be perfect and that the poet who uses an inexact rhyme has not necessarily made a "mistake."

EXERCISE 42

Identify the kinds of rhyme in the following poems.

Expectation

Chide, chide no more away
The fleeting daughters of the day,
Nor with impatient thoughts outrun
    The lazy Sun,
Or think the hours do move too slow;   5
    Delay is kind,
    And we too soon shall find
That which we seek, yet fear to know.

The mystic dark decrees
Unfold not of the Destinies,   10
Nor boldly seek to antedate
    The laws of Fate.
Thy anxious search awhile forbear,
    Suppress thy haste,
    And know that Time at last   15
Will crown thy hope, or fix thy fear.

THOMAS STANLEY

Song

The feathers of the willow
Are half of them grown yellow
   Above the swelling stream;
And ragged are the bushes,
And rusty now the rushes,   5
   And wild the clouded gleam.

The thistle now is older,
His stalk begins to moulder,
   His head is white as snow;
The branches all are barer,   10
The linnet's song is rarer,
   The robin pipeth now.

RICHARD WATSON DIXON

Charm

The owl is abroad, the bat, and the toad,
   And so is the catamountain;
The ant and the mole sit both in a hole,
   And frog peeps out o' the fountain;
The dogs they do bay, and the timbrels play;   5
   The spindle is now a-turning;
The moon it is red, and the stars are fled,
   But all the sky is a-burning.

BEN JONSON
(from *The Masque of Queens*)

When a Man Has Married a Wife

When a Man has Married a Wife
   he finds out whether
Her Knees and elbows are only
   glued together

WILLIAM BLAKE

THE FUNCTIONS OF RHYME

Down through the centuries poets and critics have debated whether rhyme is necessary or even desirable. The enemies of rhyme have cited Homer, Virgil, and other great Greek and Latin poets who did not use it. They have pointed out that cultivated readers do not respond to crude, jingling sounds, and that the necessity of finding a rhyme can, and often does, force a poet into saying things that he does not wish to say. The first of these arguments would carry weight only in an age that had an exaggerated respect for antiquity. The other two commit the fallacy of arguing against a practice by citing abuses of that practice. Rhyming can, of course, force an unskillful poet into triteness and absurdity, as Pope demonstrates in his *Essay on Criticism*.

> Where'er you find "the cooling western breeze,"
> In the next line, it "whispers through the trees."
> If crystal streams "with pleasing murmurs creep,"
> The reader's threaten'd (not in vain) with "sleep."

But the need to find a rhyme can also be a source of inspiration. An epitaph said to be on a tombstone in Leeds, England, provides a trivial but clear-cut example.

> Here lies my wife.
> Here lies she.
> Hallelujah!
> Hallelujee!

Needing a rhyme for *she,* this versifier coined a new exclamation that exactly expresses his ecstatic feelings on being released from bondage. The degree of skill that a poet possesses will determine whether rhyme is his servant or his master. A rhyming dictionary may help a would-be poet overcome one of the natural barriers of our language, the relative scarcity of rhyme words in English compared with the large number in, say, Italian. It may help him write verses for greeting cards, but it will never make him a poet because rhyme is only one of the elements in a poem.

A poet who can rhyme easily does, however, have certain advantages over one who cannot. Rhyme pleases most readers because it alternately creates an expectation and satisfies that expectation. The listener hears a sound which experience tells him will soon be repeated, with some slight differences. When he hears the repeated sound, he is pleased because he is no longer in suspense and because he feels that a difficulty has been overcome. We all enjoy difficulties if they can be quickly overcome, and we all like two sensations that are similar yet slightly different. Rhyme, then, is interesting and pleasing in itself.

A second advantage is the appeal of rhyme to the reader's memory. Most rhymed poems are in meter, and meter is also an aid to memorization. These facts, which hardly need explanation or illustration, account for the prevalence of rhymed folk-sayings about the weather and so on, for versified advertisements, and for mnemonic crutches like this one for bad spellers.

> *I* before *e*,
> Except after *c*;
> Or when sounded as *a*,
> As in *neighbor* or *weigh*.

Finally, and most important, end-rhyme cooperates with meter in giving shape and unity to a poet's ideas. It does so in two ways. First, the rhyming word plainly indicates the end of a line; it thus rounds off one of the main structural units of a poem. In this respect a rhymed poem is very different from prose because the lines of the poem stop at an expected time and in an expected way. Prose lines, which obey no such arbitrary rules, lack this kind of shape. Second, the rhymes at the ends of lines are arranged in a kind of pattern that is usually repeated over and over again for the entire length of the poem.

RHYME SCHEMES

A pattern of rhymes is known as a **rhyme scheme,** and a group of lines bound together by a rhyme scheme and by metrical devices (see Chapter 10) is called a stanza. Here is a stanza from *In Memoriam:*

> Behold, we know not anything;
>   I can but trust that good shall fall
>   At last—far off—at last, to all,
> And every winter change to spring.

Notice that according to the rhyme scheme Tennyson has adopted, the last words of lines 1 and 4 rhyme, as do those of lines 2 and 3. Rhyme schemes are customarily indicated by italicized lower-case letters: here *a b b a*. *In Memoriam* consists of hundreds of stanzas rhyming *a b b a;* a group of these would be marked *a b b a, c d d c, e f f e,* etc. There are many other possible rhyme schemes and stanzaic forms in English (see Chapter 10). Although rhyme is only one of the formal elements that a poet may use, it is a powerful one.

EXERCISE 43

Examine the sound patterns of this poem to determine what sound predominates; then explain why this sound is appropriate.

On the Late Massacre in Piedmont

Avenge, O Lord, thy slaughtered saints, whose bones
   Lie scattered on the Alpine mountains cold;
   Even them who kept thy truth so pure of old
   When all our fathers worshipped stocks and stones,
Forget not; in thy book record their groans
   Who were thy sheep and in their ancient fold
   Slain by the bloody Piedmontese that rolled
   Mother with infant down the rocks. Their moans
The vales redoubled to the hills, and they
   To heaven. Their martyred blood and ashes sow   10
   O'er all the Italian fields where still doth sway
The triple tyrant: that from these may grow
   A hundredfold, who having learned thy way
   Early may fly the Babylonian woe.

JOHN MILTON

Title: In 1655 the Catholic Duke of Savoy sent troops against a Protestant community living in the Piedmont. **triple tyrant** (12): the Pope. **Babylonian woe** (14): see Revelation xviii:2. The Protestants applied this verse to Rome.

OTHER REPEATED SOUNDS

In addition to assonance, alliteration, and rhyme, another kind of repeated sound is common in some kinds of poetry, especially in ballads and songs: the repetition of words, phrases, entire lines, or entire groups of lines. When these elements recur at regular intervals, they compose what is known as a **refrain.** Refrains usually appear at the ends of stanzas, but there is no rule saying that they must. In the following song, which Feste sings at the end of Shakespeare's *Twelfth Night,* every other line is a refrain.

> When that I was and a little tiny boy,
>   With hey, ho, the wind and the rain,
> A foolish thing was but a toy,
>   For the rain it raineth every day.
>
> But when I came to man's estate,   5
>   With hey, ho, the wind and the rain,
> 'Gainst knaves and thieves men shut their gate,
>   For the rain it raineth every day.
>
> But when I came, alas, to wive,
>   With hey, ho, the wind and the rain,   10
> By swaggering could I never thrive,
>   For the rain it raineth every day.
>
> But when I came unto my beds,
>   With hey, ho, the wind and the rain,
> With tosspots still had drunken heads,   15
>   For the rain it raineth every day.
>
> A great while ago the world begun,
>   With hey, ho, the wind and the rain,
> But that's all one, our play is done,
>   And we'll strive to please you every day.   20

A great many of the refrains in older lyrics and ballads (as in modern popular songs) defy rational analysis. Collections of nonsense syllables ("Hey nonny nonny," "Down derry down," "Fa la la") please the tongue and the ear, and nobody expects them to have much logical connection with the song proper. Easily learned and easily remembered, such refrains may have been first used during communal performances in which the audience joined with the soloist in singing the refrains. Yet despite their slender intellectual content, nonsense refrains can evoke feeling. In merry songs, they increase the merriment; in sad songs, they provide contrast.

Not every repeated word, phrase, or sentence in a poem is a refrain. Poets use the device of repetition for rhetorical as well as for musical effect. Like prose writers, they deliberately repeat ideas in order to emphasize them and to make them more persuasive. Repetition is one of the means by which a poet achieves urgency and intensity. The following passage, for instance, builds to an effective climax merely by repeating a formula.

> I know my body's of so frail a kind
>   As force without, fevers within, can kill;
>   I know the heavenly nature of my mind,
>   But 'tis corrupted both in wit and will;
>
> I know my soul hath power to know all things,   5
>   Yet is she blind and ignorant in all;
>   I know I am one of nature's little kings,
>   Yet to the least and vilest things am thrall.
>
> I know my life's a pain and but a span,
>   I know my sense is mocked with everything;   10
>   And to conclude, I know myself a man,
>   Which is a proud and yet a wretched thing.

SIR JOHN DAVIES
(from *Nosce Teipsum*)

ONOMATOPOEIA

One other sound device remains to be mentioned: **onomatopoeia,** which is the use of words whose sound suggests their meaning. Onomatopoeic words in English include *bleat, buzz, clink, clank, crash, quack, hiss, rattle, sneeze, snort, squeak,* and so on. A word of this kind obviously does not reproduce an actual sound as a phonograph record does; rather, it suggests the actual sound. A reader will not encounter onomatopoeia very often in poems because its usefulness is strictly limited. Extended onomatopoeic effects, as in Poe's famous "Bells" or Southey's "Cataract of Lodore," are mechanically ingenious, but they are likely to become tiresome upon repeated hearings. Used with restraint, onomatopoeia can help create appropriate auditory images (see Chapter 3).

And brushing ankle-deep in flowers,
We heard behind the woodbine veil
The milk that bubbled in the pail,
And buzzings of the honied hours.

ALFRED, LORD TENNYSON
(from *In Memoriam*)

Notice here how the other sound devices—for instance, alliteration and assonance—reinforce onomatopoeia.

EXERCISE 44

How does sound contribute to meaning in the following poems?

The Human Being Is a Lonely Creature

It is borne in upon me that pain
Is essential. The bones refuse to act.
Recalcitrancy is life's fine flower.
The human being is a lonely creature.

Fear is of the essence. You do not fear?   5
I say you lie. Fear is the truth of time.
If it is not now, it will come hereafter.
Death is waiting for the human creature.

Praise to harmony and love.
They are best, all else is false.   10
Yet even in love and harmony
The human being is a lonely creature.

The old sloughed off, the new new-born,
What fate and what high hazards join
As life tries out the soul's enterprise.
Time is waiting for the human creature.   15

Life is daring all our human stature.
Death looks, and waits for each bright eye.
Love and harmony are our best nurture.
The human being is a lonely creature.

RICHARD EBERHART

Jabberwocky

'Twas brillig, and the slithy toves
    Did gyre and gimble in the wabe:
All mimsy were the borogoves,
    And the mome raths outgrabe.

"Beware the Jabberwock, my son!   5
    The jaws that bite, the claws that catch!
Beware the Jubjub bird, and shun
    The frumious Bandersnatch!"

He took his vorpal sword in hand;
    Long time the manxome foe he sought—   10
So rested he by the Tumtum tree,
    And stood awhile in thought.

And, as in uffish thought he stood,
    The Jabberwock, with eyes of flame,
Came whiffling through the tulgey wood,   15
    And burbled as it came!

One, two! One, two! And through and through
    The vorpal blade went snicker-snack!
He left it dead, and with its head
    He went galumphing back.   20

"And hast thou slain the Jabberwock?
    Come to my arms, my beamish boy!
O frabjous day! Callooh; Callay!"
    He chortled in his joy.

'Twas brillig, and the slithy toves   25
    Did gyre and gimble in the wabe:
All mimsy were the borogoves,
    And the mome raths outgrabe.

LEWIS CARROLL

EUPHONY AND CACOPHONY

A poet may wish to give the general effect of **euphony**, or pleasant and sweet sound. Euphonious combinations of words can be spoken without sudden changes in the position of the lips, tongue, and jaw, and they are therefore easy to say.

> A thing of beauty is a joy for ever:
> Its loveliness increases; it will never
> Pass into nothingness; but still will keep
> A bower quiet for us, and a sleep
> Full of sweet dreams, and health, and quiet breathing.   5
>
> JOHN KEATS
> (from *Endymion*)

These lines almost say themselves. In addition to the end-rhymes, partial rhymes mark the caesuras in lines 2, 3, 4: *increases, nothingness, us*. This same consonantal sound occurs in *Pass* and *loveliness*. Line 3 has internal rhyme: *still, will*. The long *e* sound of the second rhyme (*keep, sleep*) is repeated in four other words: *increases, sweet, dreams, breathing*. The passage is euphonious because it contains sounds that harmonize.

Certain clusters of consonants are tongue-twisters:

> Irks care the crop-full bird? Frets doubt the maw-crammed beast?

This line, from Browning's "Rabbi Ben Ezra," gives the effect of **cacophony:** discord, harshness of sound. Cacophonous lines are not necessarily proof that a poet lacks skill; they can be intentional. In good poems both concord and discord are used functionally.

Government Injunction
Restraining Harlem Cosmetic Co.

They say La Jac Brite Pink Skin Bleach avails not,
They say its Orange Beauty Glow does not glow,
Nor the face grow five shades lighter nor the heart
Five shades lighter. They say no.

They deny good luck, love, power, romance, and inspiration   5
From La Jac Brite ointment and incense of all kinds,
And condemn in writing skin brightening and whitening
And whitening of minds.

There is upon the federal trade commission a burden of glory
So to defend the fact, so to impel   10
The plucking of hope from the hand, honor from the complexion,
Sprite from the spell.

                              JOSEPHINE MILES

Throughout this poem various sound devices are used to help communicate a rather complex attitude. The name of the product, for instance, cannot be pronounced without effort: "La Jac Brite Pink Skin Bleach." While his tongue struggles with these clusters of consonants, the reader has time to savor the absurdity of the name. But the poet's intention is not to ridicule this obviously phony cosmetic or the kinds of people who use it. Her barbs aim elsewhere.

In addition to the cacophony of line 1, the first stanza contains several other sound devices, all of them significant. The repetition of "They say" (lines 1, 2, 4) emphasizes the impersonality of the government, its anonymity. "They" have condemned this cosmetic because it does not do what the manufacturers claim it will do. "Their" negative attitude is stressed in every line: *not, not, nor, nor, no.* (Compare the effect of ending line 1 with "does not work" instead of "avails not.") The sound of *glow* (line 2) is echoed in *grow* (line 3), thus bringing together the two claims for the product that brought on the injunction: it lightens the skin, and it makes the skin glow pinkly. But the most skillful repetition is *lighter* (lines 3, 4). In its first use it means "lighter in color"; in its second, "lighter in weight." The F.T.C., which Miss Miles refuses (line 9) to dignify with capitals, has not, of course, said anything about lightening the hearts of the people who use La Jac; nor has the Harlem Cosmetic Co. But the poet, who is much more interested in hearts than in skins, knows that certain "colored" people use so-called skin bleach for the same reason that certain "white" people hopefully smear on various substitutes for sun tan: it makes them feel better inside.

The second stanza develops this idea. Line 5 lists some of the dreams that the injunction shatters, and lines 7 and 8 repeat the device of lines 3 and 4: *whitening* is first used literally, then metaphorically. Then, in stanza 3, the poet calls on the F.T.C. to defend the claims of fact against the claims of dream, if it wishes any glory from its action. The complex alliteration of lines 10–12

> . . . so to im*pel*
> The *pl*ucking of *h*ope from the *h*and, honor from the com*pl*exion,. . . .
> *Sp*rite from the *sp*ell

emphasizes the absurdity of the action: the F.T.C. has taken the
"sprite" (that is, the indwelling spirit) out of a "spell" (a magic rite).
"They" are so dedicated to facts that nothing else counts; "they" have
been so literal-minded as to issue an injunction against a dream.

EXERCISE 45

Read both of these poems aloud and then contrast the general effect
that they make. Identify the devices that contribute to the effect, and
decide whether each poem as a whole has an appropriate sound.

The Twilight Turns from Amethyst

The twilight turns from amethyst
  To deep and deeper blue,
The lamp fills with a pale green glow
  The trees of the avenue.

The old piano plays an air,   5
  Sedate and slow and gay;
She bends upon the yellow keys,
  Her head inclines this way.

Shy thoughts and grave wide eyes and hands
  That wander as they list—   10
The twilight turns to darker blue
  With lights of amethyst.

JAMES JOYCE

Twilight

Dusk comes early in the shaft,
An hour before the whistles and the first
Radios have laughed
Enticingly of cigarettes and soup,

And supper cans have burst   5
Condensed and desiccated food for Jim,
Home from work in time to hear the worst
Tiny tragedies his wife will tell to him
Of gas-pipe leaks and Mrs. Bailey's first.
With sunset, night   10
Flattens its black face on the windowpane,
Staring and waiting for the moment when
A switch is pulled, to throttle out the light,
To leap against the throats of tired men,
To stretch them on the bed, subdue the brain,   15
And drag its shapeless body through the house,
Driving its shadows with a dark disdain
Until it rests, triumphant over every part,
And takes a ticking clock for heart.

PAUL ENGLE

shaft (1): airshaft of a tenement.

SOUND AND MEANING

The last word on the relationship between sound and meaning is
often said to be contained in these lines.

True ease in writing comes from Art, not Chance,
As those move easiest who have learn'd to dance.
'Tis not enough no harshness gives offence;
The sound must seem an echo to the sense.
Soft is the strain when zephyr gently blows,   5
And the smooth stream in smoother numbers flows;
But when loud surges lash the sounding shore,
The hoarse rough verse should like the torrent roar.
When Ajax strives some rock's vast weight to throw,
The line, too, labours, and the words move slow: 10
Not so when swift Camilla scours the plain,
Flies o'er th' unbending corn, and skims along the main.

ALEXANDER POPE
(from *An Essay on Criticism*)

Camilla (11): a swift-footed maiden in the *Aeneid*.

Pope's advice to poets is excellent, but his illustrations are not very helpful because they are too obvious; there are few occasions when a poet must match sound and sense as mechanically as they are matched here. Usually they correspond in a way that is much more difficult to explain.

Upon Julia's Clothes

Whenas in silks my Julia goes,
Then, then, methinks, how sweetly flows
That liquefaction of her clothes.

Next, when I cast mine eyes and see
That brave vibration each way free,   5
O how that glittering taketh me!

ROBERT HERRICK

Since Herrick wishes to communicate a pleasant experience, he has chosen euphonious rather than cacophonous sounds. Julia is easy on the eyes; the poem is easy on the ears. Any harshness that might spoil the effect has been excluded from the poem.

All readers should be aware of one particular kind of absurdity that sometimes occurs in discussions of poetic sounds. It goes like this: "Every line of the first stanza of Herrick's 'Julia' contains an *l* sound, the same sound that appears in *lady, lullaby, lily, languor, lawn,* and other lovely and pleasant-sounding words. Therefore the musical smoothness of the poem is caused by the prevalence of the liquid *l* sound." But the liquid *l* sound also occurs in such expressions as "loathsome leaking lavatory," "leather leggings," and "lewd lithographs," and no reader who understands them will maintain that they are especially pleasant and musical. The fact of the matter is that words are pleasant according to their meaning just as much as according to their sound. If sound alone determined our reactions to words, we should find *coronary thrombosis* as pleasant as *yellow ambrosia.* Since letters and syllables are meaningless unless they have been incorporated into words, it is impossible to say that they have any particular effect apart from the words in which they appear. There are no happy vowels, irritable consonants, or sad syllables.

Something more can, however, be said about the contribution that sound makes to such a poem as Herrick's "Julia." One way to isolate this contribution is to compare a prose paraphrase with the poem:

When my Julia walks about dressed in silk, it seems to me that her clothes flow around her body as though they had turned to liquid. I find her very attractive because she walks so that her dress seems to vibrate and glitter.

This paraphrase hardly does justice to the sense of the poem, let alone to the sound. Lacking rhyme and meter, it does not please the ear as the poem does; it has neither shape nor structure, nor does it convey any of the dramatic excitement of the poem.

EXERCISE 46

Compare the following poem with Herrick's. Does it say what Herrick's poem says? Is the sound as well adapted to the sense? Does it communicate the same experience?

Herrick's Julia Improved

When all in silk my Julia's dressed,
She flows along, be it confessed,
As if her clothes had deliquesced.

Next, if and when I her behold,
Her oscillations are so bold,   5
She glistens like a lump of gold.

READING ALOUD

Students should read poems aloud in order to discover how sound reinforces sense and thereby increases understanding and enjoyment. Here are some suggestions:

1. Always read a poem much more slowly than you would read a prose selection.

2. Read the poem several times, trying a different way each time. If, for instance, the poem has a regular meter, try reading it first in almost a sing-song manner, and then in subsequent readings decrease the emphasis on the accented syllables.

3. Settle finally on the way to read the poem that seems best to you, and make your own private markings in the poem to remind you of how you think it is best read. The best reading is the one that will enable a person who is not looking at a copy of the poem to understand it and be aware of the meter without being distracted by it.

4. Read naturally; avoid pompous tones and affected speech mannerisms. A great many poems are available on records. You will find it interesting to compare your reading with that of a professional.

5. Look up the pronunciation as well as the meaning of all unfamiliar words. All the words should be given a modern pronunciation (unless, of course, you are reading a very old poet like Chaucer), even though you have to sacrifice a rhyme. In Pope's couplet

> Good nature and good sense must ever join;
> To err is human, to forgive divine.

the words *join* and *divine* are no longer exact rhymes as they were in the eighteenth century. You will occasionally encounter a situation like this when you are reading poetry more than two hundred years old, and when you do, you should always give each of the rhyme words its modern pronunciation. Sound is important, but it is less important than sense.

EXERCISE 47

Show how sound is "an echo of the sense" in these poems.

Slow, Slow, Fresh Fount

> Slow, slow, fresh fount, keep time with my salt tears;
>   Yet slower yet, oh faintly, gentle springs;
> List to the heavy part the music bears,
>   Woe weeps out her division when she sings.
>   Droop herbs and flowers,   5
>   Fall grief in showers;

Our beauties are not ours;
   Oh, I could still,
Like melting snow upon some craggy hill,
   Drop, drop, drop, drop,
Since nature's pride is now a withered daffodil.

BEN JONSON
(from *Cynthia's Revels*)

division (4): a harmonizing melody. **nature's pride** (11): Narcissus.

A Glass of Beer

The lanky hank of a she in the inn over there
Nearly killed me for asking the loan of a glass of beer;
May the devil grip the whey-faced slut by the hair,
And beat bad manners out of her skin for a year.

That parboiled ape, with the toughest jaw you will see   5
On virtue's path, and a voice that would rasp the dead,
Came roaring and raging the minute she looked at me,
And threw me out of the house on the back of my head!

If I asked her master he'd give me a cask a day;
But she, with the beer at hand, not a gill would arrange!   10
May she marry a ghost and bear him a kitten, and may
The High King of Glory permit her to get the mange.

JAMES STEPHENS

Now Sleeps the Crimson Petal

Now sleeps the crimson petal, now the white;
Nor waves the cypress in the palace walk;
Nor winks the gold fin in the porphyry font:
The fire-fly wakens: waken thou with me.

Now droops the milkwhite peacock like a ghost,   5
And like a ghost she glimmers on to me.

Now lies the Earth all Danaë to the stars,
And all thy heart lies open unto me.

Now slides the silent meteor on, and leaves
A shining furrow, as thy thoughts in me.   10

Now folds the lily all her sweetness up,
And slips into the bosom of the lake:
So fold thyself, my dearest, thou, and slip
Into my bosom and be lost in me.

ALFRED, LORD TENNYSON
(from *The Princess*)

A Dirge

Rough wind, that moanest loud
    Grief too sad for song;
Wild wind, when sullen cloud
    Knells all the night long;
Sad storm, whose tears are vain.   5
Bare woods, whose branches strain,
Deep caves and dreary main,
    Wail, for the world's wrong!

PERCY BYSSHE SHELLEY

The Jungle

It is not the still weight
of the tree, the
breathless interior of the wood,
tangled with wrist-thick

vines, the flies, reptiles,   5
the forever fearful monkeys
screaming and running
in the branches—

but

a girl waiting,
shy, brown, soft-eyed—
to guide you
          Upstairs, sir.

WILLIAM CARLOS WILLIAMS

Lucifer in Starlight

On a starred night Prince Lucifer uprose.
Tired of his dark dominion swung the fiend
Above the rolling ball in cloud part screened,
Where sinners hugged their spectre of repose.
Poor prey to his hot fit of pride were those.   5
And now upon his western wing he leaned,
Now his huge bulk o'er Afric's sands careened,
Now the black planet shadowed Arctic snows.
Soaring through wider zones that prickcd his scars
With memory of the old revolt from Awe,   10
He reached the middle height, and at the stars,
Which are the brain of heaven, he looked, and sank.
Around the ancient track marched, rank on rank,
The army of unalterable law.

GEORGE MEREDITH

1. Discuss the effect on the poem of making these changes in its diction: *black hell hole* for *dark dominion* (line 2); *earth* for *ball* (line 3); *kissed their phantom* for *hugged their spectre* (line 4); *bait* for *prey* (line 5); *big devil* for *black planet* (line 8); and *upper skies* for *wider zones* (line 9).
2. How do sound devices help the poet characterize Lucifer and describe his actions?
3. What keeps Lucifer from entering heaven? What sound device does the poet use to emphasize the *one* thing that keeps him out?

9

THE TONE
OF A POEM

In everyday life the tone of a speaker's voice frequently conveys as much meaning as his actual words. A father can say to his son, "Yes, you may borrow the car," in such a way that the son is as aware of his father's reluctance as if he had said, "No, you may not borrow the car." The father's tone has communicated more of his real meaning than his words have. The human voice can convey hundreds of different feelings and combinations of feelings that subtly modify the spoken words. It can even convey a meaning exactly opposite to the meaning of the words, as when a husband says to his wife, who has just run his car into a tree, "That was a brilliant thing to do." A woman selling fish once struck a well-known English author across the face with a mackerel because he had said to her, in a coy and flirtatious manner, "You are an isosceles triangle!"

TONE IN LITERATURE

The word *tone* in literary discussion is borrowed from the expression *tone of voice*. **Tone** is the manner in which a poet makes his statement;

210

it reflects his attitude toward his subject. Since printed poems lack the intonations of spoken words, the reader must learn to "hear" their tones with his mind's ear, or he may misunderstand them. Tone cannot be heard in one particular place, as rhymes are heard at the ends of lines; since it reflects a general attitude, it pervades the whole poem. Nor can a reader be certain that a poem will have the tone that he himself associates with a given subject. A great variety of tones is possible: irreverent, familiar, cryptic, reasonable, sweet, intense, patronizing, sneering, offhand, detached, mock-serious, tender, angry—in fact, there are as many tones as there are human attitudes or feelings.

Ode

How sleep the Brave, who sink to Rest,
By all their Country's Wishes blest!
When Spring, with dewy Fingers cold,
Returns to deck their hallow'd Mold,
She there shall dress a sweeter Sod,   5
Than Fancy's Feet have ever trod.

By Fairy Hands their Knell is rung,
By Forms unseen their Dirge is sung;
There Honour comes, a Pilgrim grey,
To bless the Turf that wraps their Clay,   10
And Freedom shall a-while repair,
To dwell a weeping Hermit there!

WILLIAM COLLINS

Fairy (7): supernatural.

Traveller's Curse after Misdirection

(*from the Welsh*)

May they stumble, stage by stage
On an endless pilgrimage,
Dawn and dusk, mile after mile,
At each and every step, a stile;
At each and every step withal   5
May they catch their feet and fall;

At each and every fall they take
May a bone within them break;
And may the bone that breaks within
Not be, for variation's sake,   10
Now rib, now thigh, now arm, now shin,
But always, without fail THE NECK.

ROBERT GRAVES

It is not difficult to detect the tone of either of these poems. The speaker of the first is making a confident public utterance; he is fanciful but serious. The speaker of the second is angry, frustrated, and comically vindictive. Graves's poem is an example of **light verse:** poems of unserious tone appealing primarily to a reader's sense of humor rather than to his mind and heart. Since light verse can be as skillfully written as serious poetry, there is always the danger that a beginning reader will treat it seriously, by searching it for symbols, hidden significances, and so on. Attention to tone can prevent this gross error. Good light verse is polished, not profound.

VERBAL IRONY

Arms and the Boy

Let the boy try along this bayonet-blade
How cold steel is, and keen with hunger of blood;
Blue with all malice, like a madman's flash;
And thinly drawn with famishing for flesh.

Lend him to stroke these blind, blunt bullet-heads   5
Which long to nuzzle in the hearts of lads,
Or give him cartridges of fine zinc teeth,
Sharp with the sharpness of grief and death.

For his teeth seem for laughing round an apple.
There lurk no claws behind his fingers supple;   10
And God will grow no talons at his heels,
Nor antlers through the thickness of his curls.

WILFRED OWEN

At first glance this poem seems to be fanatically militaristic. Let a young boy handle firearms, the speaker advises; make him familiar with bayonet blades, bullet heads, and cartridges. But does the speaker sincerely mean what he says? Does he really want the parents of young boys to take his advice literally? The images which describe the weapons suggest that he does not. These images personify the weapons, make them malicious and hungry for blood. They are images that a hater of war would use, not a lover of war. There is, then, a contradiction between what the speaker says literally and the way in which he says it—a contradiction that the third stanza resolves: God will not turn the boy into a monster with fangs, claws, talons, and horns, but man can do so by giving him arms and making him a soldier. If stanza 3 describes what happens when the boy is given arms, stanzas 1 and 2 must be ironical in tone.

A poem or any other work of literature contains **verbal irony** when it makes statements that mean the opposite of what they seem to mean on the surface. Failure to detect irony will cause a reader to understand just the opposite of what is intended—a very serious error indeed. There is, unfortunately, no magic formula for detecting verbal irony. If one existed, it would destroy the pleasure felt by an alert reader when he discovers that a writer is not saying what he means. This discovery always creates a bond between reader and writer something like the bond connecting two people who share a private joke. Recognition of verbal irony depends on the reader's mental alertness, his close attention to the words of a poem, and his quickness in responding to certain signals. Among these signals are inconsistencies like those in "Arms and the Boy," overstatement, and understatement (see Chapter 5).

Verbal irony must be carefully distinguished from mere **sarcasm.** According to *Webster's New Collegiate Dictionary,* the word *sarcasm* means "a keen or bitter taunt; a cutting gibe or rebuke." There is nothing ironical in such ordinary sarcasms as "Drop dead!" They say exactly what they mean. Even more elaborate insults are not necessarily ironical.

On Proclus's Great Nose

Thy nose no man can wipe, Proclus, unless
He have a hand as big as Hercules.
When thou dost sneeze, the sound thou dost not hear:
Thy nose is so far distant from thine ear.

ANONYMOUS
(*Seventeenth Century*)

These lines say what they mean, while an ironical poem on a large
nose would probably emphasize its smallness.

EXERCISE 48

Analyze the following poems. Determine which of them employs
verbal irony.

A Short Song of Congratulation

Long-expected one and twenty
Ling'ring year at last is flown,
Pomp and Pleasure, Pride and Plenty
Great Sir John, are all your own.

Loosen'd from the Minor's tether,   5
Free to mortgage or to sell,
Wild as wind, and light as feather
Bid the slaves of thrift farewell.

Call the Bettys, Kates, and Jennys
Ev'ry name that laughs at Care,   10
Lavish of your Grandsire's guineas,
Show the Spirit of an heir.

All that prey on vice and folly
Joy to see their quarry fly,
Here the Gamester light and jolly   15
There the Lender grave and sly.

Wealth, Sir John, was made to wander,
Let it wander as it will;
See the Jocky, see the Pander,
Bid them come, and take their fill.   20

When the bonny Blade carouses,
Pockets full, and Spirits high,
What are acres? What are houses?
Only dirt, or wet or dry.

If the Guardian or the Mother   25
Tell the woes of wilful waste,
Scorn their counsel and their pother,
You can hang or drown at last.

SAMUEL JOHNSON

1. Why is the year called "ling'ring" (line 2)?
2. What is the "Minor's tether" (line 5)?
3. What has Sir John done to deserve the epithet *great* (line 4)?
4. Who are those girls (line 9)?
5. For what is *acres* (line 23) a metonymy?
6. Does the speaker approve of the gamester (line 15), the jockey, and the pander (line 19)?

The Latest Decalogue

Thou shalt have one God only; who
Would be at the expense of two?
No graven images may be
Worshipped, except the currency:
Swear not at all; for for thy curse   5
Thine enemy is none the worse;
At church on Sunday to attend
Will serve to keep the world thy friend:
Honour thy parents; that is, all
From whom advancement may befall: 10
Thou shalt not kill; but needst not strive
Officiously to keep alive:
Do not adultery commit;
Advantage rarely comes of it:

Thou shalt not steal; an empty feat,   15
When it's so lucrative to cheat:
Bear not false witness; let the lie
Have time on its own wings to fly:
Thou shalt not covet; but tradition
Approves all forms of competition.   20
The sum of all is, thou shalt love,
If any body, God above:
At any rate shall never labour
More than thyself to love thy neighbour.

ARTHUR HUGH CLOUGH

to keep alive (12): to keep another man alive.

1. Why is biblical language used?
2. What does *two* (line 2) refer to? *all* (line 9)?
3. What are *graven images* (line 3)?
4. Explain the difference between the two parts of each couplet.
5. Locate every word associated with money. Why are there so many? What is the speaker's attitude toward money?
6. Is the speaker ridiculing the ten commandments? Explain your answer.
7. Most editors omit the last four lines. Does this omission improve the poem?

Epitaph on the Politician

Here richly, with ridiculous display,
The Politician's corpse was laid away.
While all of his acquaintance sneered and slanged
I wept: for I had longed to see him hanged.

HILAIRE BELLOC

slanged (3): used abusive language.

1. What is the speaker's motive in reporting the conduct of the dead man's friends?
2. What is ironical about the situation?

OTHER KINDS OF IRONY

Irony always involves two matters at variance with each other. In verbal irony, statement and meaning are at variance. In **irony of situa-**

tion, the variance exists between what should be and what is, or between what is expected to happen and what does happen. Ironical situations are common in literature, especially in fiction and drama, because they are common in life.

By Her Aunt's Grave

"Sixpence a week," says the girl to her lover,
"Aunt used to bring me, for she could confide
In me alone, she vowed. 'Twas to cover
The cost of her headstone when she died.
And that was a year ago last June;   5
I've not yet fixed it. But I must soon."

"And where is the money now, my dear?"
"O, snug in my purse . . . Aunt was *so* slow
In saving it—eighty weeks, or near." . . .
"Let's spend it," he hints. "For she won't know   10
There's a dance to-night at the Load of Hay."
She passively nods. And they go that way.

THOMAS HARDY

This situation is ironical because it is the opposite of what the aunt expected. The money that she had slowly saved for her tombstone is now going to be spent at a dance hall. Hardy does not condemn any of the three people: the short-sighted aunt, the weak niece, the insensitive young man. Instead of taking sides, he merely reports the ironical circumstances in an aloof and objective tone. Poems that describe or dramatize an ironical situation do not ordinarily contain verbal irony.

Irony of character is a device in which a discrepancy exists between what a character seems to be and what he is.

Miniver Cheevy

Miniver Cheevy, child of scorn,
    Grew lean while he assailed the seasons;
He wept that he was ever born,
    And he had reasons.

Miniver loved the days of old   5
    When swords were bright and steeds were prancing;
The vision of a warrior bold
    Would set him dancing.

Miniver sighed for what was not,
    And dreamed, and rested from his labors;   10
He dreamed of Thebes and Camelot,
    And Priam's neighbors.

Miniver mourned the ripe renown
    That made so many a name so fragrant;
He mourned Romance, now on the town,   15
    And Art, a vagrant.

Miniver loved the Medici,
    Albeit he had never seen one;
He would have sinned incessantly
    Could he have been one.   20

Miniver cursed the commonplace
    And eyed a khaki suit with loathing;
He missed the mediæval grace
    Of iron clothing.

Miniver scorned the gold he sought,   25
    But sore annoyed was he without it;
Miniver thought, and thought, and thought,
    And thought about it.

Miniver Cheevy, born too late,
    Scratched his head and kept on thinking;   30
Miniver coughed, and called it fate,
    And kept on drinking.

EDWIN ARLINGTON ROBINSON

on the town (15): impoverished.

Miniver is not what it seems to be. He thinks that he would have
been happy and successful had he lived in the glorious past rather than
in the dull present. Of course he is deluded: his sickness, his laziness,
and his addiction to drink would make him a miserable failure in any

age. Robinson uses verbal irony throughout the poem to convey his complex feelings about Miniver. He finds Miniver contemptible, pitiful, and ludicrous all at the same time and for the same reasons. Without irony, these contradictory feelings could not be expressed simultaneously.

A poet may employ irony of character by making the character the speaker (see "My Last Duchess," page 47). In such first-person poems irony of character is present whenever there is a discrepancy between what the character says about himself and what the poet wants the reader to think about him.

Next to of Course God

"next to of course god america i
love you land of the pilgrims' and so forth oh
say can you see by the dawn's early my
country 'tis of centuries come and go
and are no more what of it we should worry   5
in every language even deafanddumb
thy sons acclaim your glorious name by gorry
by jingo by gee by gosh by gum
why talk of beauty what could be more beautiful than these heroic happy dead   10
who rushed like lions to the roaring slaughter
they did not stop to think they died instead
then shall the voice of liberty be mute?"

He spoke. And drank rapidly a glass of water

E. E. CUMMINGS

Lines 1–13 appear to be a public speech, perhaps an oration celebrating Veterans' Day or the Fourth of July. In his opening remarks the speaker asserts that he loves America "next to of course god." Why does he say "of course"? Because his audience expects him to love God first, America second. But does he love God and America? There is nothing in the rest of his speech to suggest that he does. It consists entirely of odds and ends of patriotic songs, interspersed with nonsense and chauvinistic claptrap. It is a parody of a bad patriotic address, and a reader who feels admiration rather than contempt for the windbag who utters it totally misunderstands the poem. Cummings lets this man condemn himself by what comes out of his mouth.

EXERCISE 49

Identify and discuss the kinds of irony in these poems.

West London

Crouch'd on the pavement close by Belgrave Square
A tramp I saw, ill, moody, and tongue-tied;
A babe was in her arms, and at her side
A girl; their clothes were rags, their feet were bare.

Some labouring men, whose work lay somewhere there,   5
Pass'd opposite; she touch'd her girl, who hied
Across, and begg'd, and came back satisfied.
The rich she had let pass with frozen stare.

Thought I: Above her state this spirit towers;
She will not ask of aliens, but of friends,   10
Of sharers in a common human fate.

She turns from that cold succour, which attends
The unknown little from the unknowing great,
And points us to a better time than ours.

MATTHEW ARNOLD

Belgrave Square (1): a fashionable district.

1. Are lines 9–14 necessary? Explain your answer.
2. What "better time" does Arnold look forward to?

Ozymandias

I met a traveller from an antique land
Who said: Two vast and trunkless legs of stone
Stand in the desert. Near them, on the sand,
Half sunk, a shattered visage lies, whose frown,

And wrinkled lip, and sneer of cold command,   5
Tell that its sculptor well those passions read
Which yet survive, stamped on these lifeless things,
The hand that mocked them, and the heart that fed:
And on the pedestal these words appear:
"My name is Ozymandias, king of kings: 10
Look on my works, ye Mighty, and despair!"
Nothing beside remains. Round the decay
Of that colossal wreck, boundless and bare
The lone and level sands stretch far away.

PERCY BYSSHE SHELLEY

Title: a Pharaoh. survive (7): live longer than. hand (8):
the sculptor's. heart (8): the Pharaoh's heart, which fed
those passions.

Song

Go and catch a falling star,
    Get with child a mandrake root,
Tell me where all past years are,
    Or who cleft the devil's foot,
Teach me to hear mermaids singing,   5
Or to keep off envy's stinging,
        And find
        What wind
Serves to advance an honest mind.

If thou beest born to strange sights,   10
    Things invisible to see,
Ride ten thousand days and nights,
    Till age snow white hairs on thee.
Thou, when thou return'st, wilt tell me
All strange wonders that befell thee,   15
        And swear
        No where
Lives a woman true and fair.

If thou find'st one, let me know:
    Such a pilgrimage were sweet;   20
Yet do not; I would not go,
    Though at next door we might meet.

Though she were true when you met hcr,
And last till you write your letter,
        Yet she   25
        Will be
False, ere I come, to two or three.

JOHN DONNE

A Prayer for Old Age

God guard me from those thoughts men think
In the mind alone;
He that sings a lasting song
Thinks in a marrow-bone;

From all that makes a wise old man   5
That can be praised of all;
O what am I that I should not seem
For the song's sake a fool?

I pray—for fashion's word is out
And prayer comes round again—   10
That I may seem, though I die old,
A foolish, passionate man.

WILLIAM BUTLER YEATS

SATIRE

Cummings's poem on the political speaker is an example of **satire:** writing that exposes and discredits human vice and folly. Instead of holding up an ideal to the reader, the satirist holds up its opposite and invites the reader to join him in ridiculing it. Satirists sometimes make a direct attack on vice and folly; sometimes they attack indirectly by means of irony.

On Fabulla's Wig

The golden hair Fabulla wears
    Is hers. Who can deny it?
She swears 'tis hers, and true she swears,
    For I did see her buy it.

This epigram, paraphrased from the Latin poet Martial, is ironical because it pretends to defend Fabulla while actually attacking her. Fabulla is not satirized because she is old and bald, but because she goes about behaving as though she were young and attractive. A deformed or hideous person is not a proper butt for satire unless that person pretends to be sound and beautiful; a lame man is immune to satire until he claims to be a good dancer. Not all satire, of course, is personal. Customs, institutions, and organizations may also be objects of satire.

EXERCISE 50

Determine which of the following poems have a satirical tone and which do not.

The End of the World

Quite unexpectedly as Vasserot
The armless ambidextrian was lighting
A match between his great and second toe
And Ralph the lion was engaged in biting
The neck of Madame Sossman while the drum   5
Pointed, and Teeny was about to cough
In waltz-time swinging Jocko by the thumb—
Quite unexpectedly the top blew off:

And there, there overhead, there, there hung over
Those thousands of white faces, those dazed eyes,   10
There in the starless dark the poise, the hover,
There with vast wings across the canceled skies,
There in the sudden blackness the black pall
Of nothing, nothing, nothing—nothing at all.

ARCHIBALD MACLEISH

1. What is the *top* (line 8)?
2. What do the names of the performers suggest?
3. If the title were changed to "A Catastrophe," how would the meaning of the poem be altered?
4. If this is a satire, what is being satirized?

London

I wander thro' each charter'd street,
Near where the charter'd Thames does flow,
And mark in every face I meet
Marks of weakness, marks of woe.

In every cry of every Man,   5
In every Infant's cry of fear,
In every voice, in every ban,
The mind-forg'd manacles I hear.

How the Chimney-sweeper's cry
Every black'ning Church appalls;   10
And the hapless Soldier's sigh
Runs in blood down Palace walls.

But most thro' midnight streets I hear
How the youthful Harlot's curse
Blasts the new born Infant's tear,   15
And blights with plagues the Marriage hearse.

WILLIAM BLAKE

1. In an earlier version of the poem Blake used the adjective *dirty* rather than *charter'd* (line 2), a word that connotes legal restrictions of some sort. Is the earlier adjective preferable? Does the metaphor implied by *charter'd* occur elsewhere in the poem?

2. What is the effect of the repetition and parallel structure?

3. Why does Blake associate the chimney sweeper with the church? The soldier with the palace? What is the soldier's complaint?

4. Why does Blake mention a "youthful" (line 14) harlot rather than an old one?

5. *Blasts* (line 15) and *blights* (line 16) are metaphors drawn from gardening. Explain their appropriateness.

Peter

Peter hath lost his purse, but will conceal it
Lest she that stole it to his shame reveal it.

ANONYMOUS
(*Seventeenth Century*)

1. What is the thief's other occupation besides stealing?

The Fish

Although you hide in the ebb and flow
Of the pale tide when the moon has set,
The people of coming days will know
About the casting out of my net,
And how you have leaped times out of mind   5
Over the little silver cords,
And think that you were hard and unkind,
And blame you with many bitter words.

WILLIAM BUTLER YEATS

London, 1802

Milton! thou shouldst be living at this hour:
England hath need of thee: she is a fen
Of stagnant waters: altar, sword, and pen,
Fireside, the heroic wealth of hall and bower,
Have forfeited their ancient English dower   5
Of inward happiness. We are selfish men;
Oh! raise us up, return to us again;
And give us manners, virtue, freedom, power.
Thy soul was like a Star, and dwelt apart;
Thou hadst a voice whose sound was like the sea: 10
Pure as the naked heavens, majestic, free,
So didst thou travel on life's common way,
In cheerful godliness; and yet thy heart
The lowliest duties on herself did lay.

WILLIAM WORDSWORTH

Milton (1): Wordsworth is thinking of John Milton not only as
the great epic poet, but also as the great champion of freedom
and as the undersecretary of state for the Commonwealth.

1. Find some figures of language that reveal Wordsworth's attitude toward contemporary England and toward Milton. Identify the other figures and show how they are used.
2. Compare Wordsworth's description of the contemporary scene with Blake's in "London."

Bas-Relief

Five geese deploy mysteriously.
Onward proudly with flagstaffs,
Hearses with silver bugles,
Bushels of plum-blossoms dropping
For ten mystic web-feet—   5
Each his own drum-major,
Each charged with the honor
Of the ancient goose nation,
Each with a nose-length surpassing
The nose-lengths of rival nations.   10
Somberly, slowly, unimpeachably,
Five geese deploy mysteriously.

CARL SANDBURG

1. Where does the reader discover that the poet's subject is not geese?
2. What, literally, are the *plum-blossoms* (line 4)?

IRONY VERSUS SENTIMENTALITY

Satirists are not the only kinds of poets who may employ an ironical tone. Irony, in one form or another, is likely to be a device of any poet who wishes to suggest more than he says directly, or who wishes to avoid oversimplifying human experience.

To Hear an Oriole Sing

To hear an Oriole sing
May be a common thing—
Or only a divine.

It is not of the Bird
Who sings the same, unheard,   5
As unto Crowd—

The Fashion of the Ear
Attireth that it hear
In Dun, or fair—

So whether it be Rune,   10
Or whether it be none
Is of within.

The "Tune is in the Tree—"
The Skeptic—showeth me—
"No Sir! In Thee!"   15

EMILY DICKINSON

    The opening lines present a problem. Is the oriole's song a common thing or a divine thing? The remainder of the poem suggests that the answer to this question depends on the listener to the song. Whether it is divine (*rune*) or not depends on the inner response (the *within*) of the listener. To the speaker of the poem, the song is divine—but only divine. The word *only* (line 3) is ironical because it is unexpected; we should expect *only* to be applied to common rather than to divine things. Its use here implies the paradox that what is natural is more uncommon than what is divine. Irony has enabled the poet to be as hard-minded as the skeptic with whom she is arguing, and to express her sense of wonder without becoming sentimental.

    Sentimentality is the evocation of a greater amount of feeling or emotion than is justified by the subject. It must not be confused with *sentiment,* which is merely another name for feeling or emotion, and which lacks the bad connotations of *sentimentality.* Some students confuse these two nouns because the adjective *sentimental* seems to be derived from both. *Sentimental* goes with *sentimentality,* not with *sentiment.* The poet who adopts a sentimental tone becomes more tearful or more ecstatic over his subject than it deserves. The sentimentalist is addicted to worn-out baby shoes, gray-haired mothers, and small animals—subjects certain to evoke an automatic response in a particular kind of reader. But sentimentality is not so much a matter of subject as it is a matter of treatment.

Nestlings

O little bird! sing sweet among the leaves,
Safe hid from sight, beside thy downy nest;
The rain falls, murmuring to the drooping eaves
A low refrain, that suits thy music best.

Sing sweet, O bird! thy recompense draws nigh,—   5
Four callow nestlings 'neath the mother's wing.
So many flashing wings that by and by
Will cleave the sunny air. Oh, sing, bird, sing!

Sing, O my heart! Thy callow nestlings sleep,
Safe hidden 'neath a gracious folding wing,   10
Until the time when from their slumbers deep
They wake, and soar in beauty. Sing, heart, sing!

ANONYMOUS
(*Ninetenth Century*)

The difference in tone between this old piece of newspaper verse and Emily Dickinson's poem is readily apparent. The anonymous author is a sentimentalist; he has nothing fresh to say about his subject, nor any new experience to communicate. His poem seems to be mindless and phony. Perhaps he is sincere, but he has depended so heavily on clichés and stock responses and has so oversimplified the situation that a thoughtful reader finds him insincere and his poem dishonest.

WIT

When Emily Dickinson calls the oriole's song "only divine," she is being witty in a serious way. Her tone is playful and clever, yet the poem is perfectly serious and sincere. Only a naïve reader would assume that just because the poem is not long-faced and solemn, it is trivial. Serious poems as well as light verse may employ wit, or intellectual cleverness. The reader must determine whether a poem with a witty tone is serious or jocose.

There is, in literary history, a specialized use of the term *wit*. As applied to the writings of Donne, Herbert, Marvell, and other seventeenth-century English poets, **wit** signifies the ability to perceive and to express the complexities of experience. The poetry of wit contains metaphysical conceits (see page 98), paradoxes (see page 119), and irony.

The Mistress

An age in her embraces passed,
  Would seem a winter's day,
Where life and light, with envious haste,
  Are torn and snatched away.

But, oh! how slowly minutes roll,   5
  When absent from her eyes,
That feed my love, which is my soul;
  It languishes and dies.

For then no more a soul but shade,
  It mournfully does move,   10
And haunts my breast, by absence made
  The living tomb of love.

You wiser men despise me not,
  Whose love-sick fancy raves
On shades of souls, and Heaven knows what: 15
  Short ages live in graves.

Whene'er those wounding eyes, so full
  Of sweetness, you did see,
Had you not been profoundly dull,
  You had gone mad like me.   20

Nor censure us, you who perceive
  My best belov'd and me
Sigh and lament, complain and grieve;
  You think we disagree.

Alas! 'tis sacred jealousy,   25
  Love raised to an extreme,
The only proof 'twixt her and me,
  We love, and do not dream.

Fantastic fancies fondly move,
    And in frail joys believe,   30
Taking false pleasure for true love;
    But pain can ne'er deceive.

Kind jealous doubts, tormenting fears,
    And anxious cares, when past,
Prove our heart's treasure fixed and dear,   35
    And make us blest at last.

JOHN WILMOT, EARL OF ROCHESTER

Here a lover tells what his love means to him. He begins, surprisingly enough, by saying that a very long period of time spent in his lady's arms would be like a single winter's day. At first glance this comparison seems paradoxical, for how can love-making resemble winter? Lines 3 and 4 resolve the paradox; the lover is thinking of the shortness of a winter's day and of the intensity with which people who want "light and life" have to live in cold weather. He cannot spend an age with his mistress; the time that he can spend with her is much too short, like the time that the sun stays out in winter. He therefore is envious of time, and he takes his pleasures violently. Upon examination, then, the comparison does not seem far-fetched. But to be understood, it does require the reader to think rather than to form mental pictures. Many of the images in poems of serious wit cannot be visualized.

In stanzas 2 and 3 the lover explains what happens when he is away from the lady. In a very bold metaphor he says that his love is his soul—bold because a man's soul is his most precious possession, immaterial and immortal. Unless fed by the lady's eyes (an image that cannot be visualized), the soul dies and haunts the lover's breast, which paradoxically becomes a "living tomb" (line 12). The witty metaphor that extends through these two stanzas enables the lover to give the highest possible praises to his mistress.

Stanzas 4 and 5 show that the lover is aware of his excesses. He addresses some imaginary auditors, some men "wiser" than he, who may despise and mock him because he has said that his love is his soul. To defend himself, he says, "Short ages live in graves" (line 16): a cryptic remark, which may imply that his dead soul will revive shortly, when he sees the lady again. He must be ironical when he calls these listeners wise, because he later calls them "profoundly dull" (line 19) for not sharing his madness. Moreover, they do not understand the relationship between the lovers; they assume that the lovers disagree when they "sigh and lament, complain and grieve" (line 23).

In the last three stanzas the lover explains the nature of that relationship. Actually the two lovers are agreeing rather than disagreeing. They inflict pain on each other because pain is more real than pleasure. Without the pangs of "sacred jealousy" (line 25), their love would be so pleasant that it would seem a dream. Pleasure is deceptive; pain, on the other hand, "can ne'er deceive" (line 32). True love, he asserts, causes pain, and true lovers welcome that pain. This truth about love is profoundly paradoxical. The paradox was earlier suggested in the image of the winter's day, and it is finally resolved in the last stanza. Doubts and fears past, the lovers become "blest" (line 36), more "blest" than they would have been if they had never doubted and feared. They know that their love is "fixed" (line 35)—that is, firm—because it can survive such turmoil. The word *blest* ordinarily appears in a religious context; it reminds the reader that the lover has earlier spoken of his love as his soul and has called his jealousy sacred. Love, in short, is a kind of religion because it provides ultimate realities. Without love, life would not be real.

The tone of this poem is very different from the tone of a love poem like "A Red, Red Rose" by Robert Burns (see page 81). Both poems are hyperbolical, but Burns's hyperbolical figures appeal primarily to the reader's senses, Rochester's to both the intellect and the senses. Burns does not surprise the reader with witty paradoxes; his lover sings. Rochester's lover argues and explains, because he is more interested in defining the psychological state of being in love than in commending the beauty of his lady. Instead of addressing the lady, he addresses a public made up of dull men who cannot understand the religion of love. Hence his tone becomes satirical when he thinks of his public, intense and tender when he thinks of his mistress. The tone of Burns's lyric does not shift in this way. Rochester makes many more demands on the reader because the experience he is communicating is more complex than Burns's. The devices of serious wit have enabled him to communicate that experience.

BURLESQUE

As applied to literature, **burlesque** refers to an unserious work that contains grotesque and obvious distortions. Sometimes the author of a burlesque presents trivial matters as though they were important, sometimes important matters as though they were trivial.

The Nose

Ye souls unus'd to lofty verse
   Who sweep the earth with lowly wing,
Like sand before the blast disperse—
   A Nose! a mighty Nose I sing!
As erst Prometheus stole from heaven the fire   5
   To animate the wonder of his hand;
Thus with unhallow'd hands, O Muse, aspire,
   And from my subject snatch a burning brand!
So like the Nose I sing—my verse shall glow—
Like Phlegethon my verse in waves of fire shall flow!   10

SAMUEL TAYLOR COLERIDGE

The poem continues in this facetious way for several stanzas. The reader knows that its tone is not serious because of the gross discrepancy between the trivial subject and the grandiose treatment.

EXERCISE 51

Discuss the tone of these poems. Remember that all the elements in a poem contribute to its tone. Comment on any shifts of tone that you discover within a poem.

Song

Take, oh take those lips away,
   That so sweetly were forsworn,
And those eyes like break of day,
   Lights that do mislead the morn;
But my kisses bring again,   5
   Seals of love, though sealed in vain.

Hide, oh hide those hills of snow,
  Which thy frozen bosom bears,
On whose tops the pinks that grow
  Are of those that April wears;   10
But first set my poor heart free,
  Bound in those icy chains by thee.

JOHN FLETCHER
(from *The Bloody Brother*)

A Reasonable Affliction

Helen was just slipt into Bed:
  Her Eye-brows on the Toilet lay:
Away the Kitten with them fled,
  As Fees belonging to her Prey.

For this Misfortune careless Jane,   5
  Assure your self, was loudly rated:
And Madam getting up again,
  With her own Hand the Mouse-Trap baited.

On little Things, as Sages write,
  Depends our Human Joy, or Sorrow: 10
If We don't catch a Mouse To-night,
  Alas! no Eye-brows for To-morrow.

MATTHEW PRIOR

rated (6): berated.

Call for the Robin-Redbreast

Call for the robin-redbreast and the wren,
Since o'er shady groves they hover,
And with leaves and flowers to cover
The friendless bodies of unburied men.
  Call unto his funeral dole   5
  The ant, the field mouse, and the mole,
To rear him hillocks that shall keep him warm,
And, when gay tombs are robbed, sustain no harm;

But keep the wolf far thence, that's foe to men,
For with his nails he'll dig them up again.   10

JOHN WEBSTER
(from *The White Devil*)

cover (3): According to folklore, a robin will cover unburied
bodies. **gay** (8): elaborately adorned.

The Bustle in a House

The Bustle in a House
The Morning after Death
Is solemnest of industries
Enacted upon Earth—

The Sweeping up the Heart   5
And putting Love away
We shall not want to use again
Until Eternity.

EMILY DICKINSON

On Shooting Particles beyond the World

*"White Sands, N.M. Dec. 18 (UP). 'We first throw a little something
into the skies,' Zwicky said. 'Then a little more, then a shipload
of instruments—then ourselves.' "*

On this day man's disgust is known
Incipient before but now full blown
With minor wars of major consequence,
Duly building empirical delusions.

Now this little creature in a rage   5
Like new-born infant screaming compleat angler
Objects to the whole globe itself
And with a vicious lunge he throws

Metal particles beyond the orbit of mankind.
Beethoven shaking his first at death,   10
A giant dignity in human terms,
Is nothing to this imbecile fury.

The world is too much for him. The green
Of earth is not enough, love's deities,
Peaceful intercourse, happiness of nations,   15
The wild animal dazzled on the desert.

If the maniac would only realize
The comforts of his padded cell
He would have penetrated the
Impenetrability of the spiritual.   20

It is not intelligent to go too far.
How he frets that he can't go too!
But his particles would maim a star,
His free-floating bombards rock the moon.

Good Boy! We pat the baby to eructate,   25
We pat him then for eructation.
Good Boy Man! Your innards are put out,
From now all space will be your vomitorium.

The atom bomb accepted this world,
Its hatred of man blew death in his face.   30
But not content, he'll send slugs beyond,
His particles of intellect will spit on the sun.

Not God he'll catch, in the mystery of space.
He flaunts his own out-cast state
As he throws his imperfections outward bound,   35
And his shout that gives a hissing sound.

                        RICHARD EBERHART

Portrait d'une Femme

Your mind and you are our Sargasso Sea,
London has swept about you this score years
And bright ships left you this or that in fee:
Ideas, old gossip, oddments of all things,
Strange spars of knowledge and dimmed wares of price.   5
Great minds have sought you—lacking someone else.
You have been second always. Tragical?
No. You preferred it to the usual thing:

One dull man, dulling and uxorious,
One average mind—with one thought less, each year.   10
Oh, you are patient, I have seen you sit
Hours, where something might have floated up.
And now you pay one. Yes, you richly pay.
You are a person of some interest, one comes to you
And takes strange gain away: 15
Trophies fished up; some curious suggestion;
Fact that leads nowhere; and a tale or two,
Pregnant with mandrakes, or with something else
That might prove useful and yet never proves,
That never fits a corner or shows use,   20
Or finds its hour upon the loom of days:
The tarnished, gaudy, wonderful old work;
Idols and ambergris and rare inlays,
These are your riches, your great store; and yet
For all this sea-hoard of deciduous things,   25
Strange woods half sodden, and new brighter stuff:
In the slow float of differing light and deep,
No! there is nothing! In the whole and all,
Nothing that's quite your own.
                    Yet this is you.   30

                    EZRA POUND

Title: "Portrait of a Lady."

A Song

    Lord, when the sense of thy sweet grace
Sends up my soul to seek thy face,
Thy blessed eyes breed such desire,
I die in love's delicious fire.
    O love, I am thy sacrifice!   5
Be still triumphant, blessed eyes.
Still shine on me, fair suns, that I
Still may behold, though still I die.

    Though still I die, I live again,
Still longing so to be still slain;   10
So gainful is such loss of breath,
I die even in desire of death.

Still live in me this loving strife
Of living death and dying life;
For while thou sweetly slayest me,   15
Dead to myself, I live in thee.

RICHARD CRASHAW

Hippopotamothalamion

A hippopotamus had a bride
  Of rather singular beauty,
When he lay down at her side
  'Twas out of love, not duty—
  Hers was an exceptional beauty.   5
Take, oh take those lips away, etc.

He met her in Central Nigeria,
  While she was resident there,
Where life is distinctly superior
  And a hippo can take down her hair—   10
  And, God, but she was fair!
Take, oh take those lips away, etc.

She was coming up from her morning swim
  When first they chanced to meet:
He looked at her, she looked at him,   15
  And stood with reluctant feet
  Where mud and river meet.
Take, or take those lips away, etc.

Their eye-beams, twisted on one thread,
  Instantaneously did twine,   20
And he made up poetry out of his head,
  Such as: "Dear heart, be mine"—
  And he quoted, line for line,
"Hail to thee, blithe spirit," etc.

Now, hippopotamoid courtesy   25
  Is strangely meticulous—
A beautiful thing, you will agree,
  In a hippopotamus—
  And she answered, briefly, thus:
"Hail to thee, blithe spirit," etc.   30

Perhaps she was practicing the arts
    That grace old Hippo's daughter,
The coquetries that win all hearts,
    For even as he besought her
    She slid into the water.   35
Out, out, brief candle, etc.

Now on the borders of the wood,
    Whence love had drawn him hither,
He paces in an anguished mood,
    Darting hither and thither   40
    In a terrific dither.
Out, out, brief candle, etc.

The course of true love never yet
    Ran smooth, so we are told,
With thorns its pathway is beset   45
    And perils manifold,
    And has been from of old.
Out, out, brief candle, etc.

Yet soon a happier morning smiles,
    The marriage feast is spread—   50
The flower girls were crocodiles
    When hippopotamus led
    Hippopotamus, with firm tread
    A bride to the bridal bed.
Milton, thou should'st be living at this hour.   55

JOHN HALL WHEELOCK

Title: "A Nuptial Song for Hippopotamuses." Refrains: See
Shelley's "To a Skylark" and the poems on pages 232, 41, and
225. **eye-beams** (19): See page 352.

10

THE WHOLE
POEM

Like other works of art or finished creations, poems exist
within definite limits. They have a beginning and an end, and what
happens between those limits does not happen accidentally. A poem is
not a random assemblage of images and sounds, just as a piece of
music is not a random collection of noises. In a good poem all the
elements—diction, images, figures, meter, sound—are so organized that
they make up a unified whole. The whole poem is something different,
something more significant, than the sum of its parts, just as a house is
much more than a confused heap of bricks, boards, glass, nails, and so
on.

FORM

To give his material external shape, a poet may put it into one of the
fixed forms, which are combinations of lines that have been long established in English poetry. These are some of the most common forms:

239

Blank verse: unrhymed iambic pentameter lines (Tennyson, "Tears, Idle Tears").

Couplets: lines rhyming *a a b b c c,* etc. They are **closed** when the thought within the two lines is complete (Swift, "A Description of the Morning"), **open** when the thought runs past the two rhymed lines (Browning, "My Last Duchess"). Closed iambic pentameter couplets are called **heroic couplets** (Pope, *An Essay on Criticism*).

Stanzas: successive groups of the same number of lines held together by meter and rhyme scheme, printed as a unit, and separated by a space from similar units in a poem. Some poems are broken into **verse paragraphs** (Arnold, "Dover Beach"), units of thought of varying length.

The most common stanzas (couplets are occasionally printed as stanzas) are these:

Triplets or **tercets:** three lines rhyming *a a a* followed by three rhyming *b b b,* etc. (Tennyson, "The Eagle"). Triplets are sometimes inserted among couplets (Hopkins, "Spring and Fall").

Terza rima: a series of iambic pentameter lines rhyming *a b a* followed by three rhyming *b c b, c d c,* etc. (Shelley, "Ode to the West Wind").

Quatrains: stanzas of four lines with a fixed pattern of rhyme and meter. There are numerous possible arrangements, but the most common are these: pentameter rhyming *a b a b* (Housman, "The Chestnut Casts His Flambeaux"), *a b b a* (Arnold, "West London"), or *a a b b* (Herrick, "Upon Julia's Voice"); tetrameter rhyming *a b a b* (Swift, "The Progress of Beauty"), *a b b a* (Tennyson, "In Memoriam"), or *a a b b* (Housman, "To an Athlete Dying Young"); and alternating tetrameter and trimeter lines rhyming *a b a b* (Wordsworth, "Strange Fits of Passion Have I Known"). The last-mentioned arrangement comprises one of the quatrains called **ballad quatrains,** from their frequent use in **folk ballads** (page 250); a ballad quatrain may also rhyme *x a x a* ("Get Up and Bar the Door"), the symbol *x* indicating a nonrhyming line. Less common, probably because of their sing-song effect, are trimeter and dimeter quatrains (Frost, "Neither Out Far Nor in Deep" and "Dust of Snow").

Longer stanzas, of which there are a great variety, are analyzed and described in the same way as quatrains, by determining (1) the kind and number of feet in a line—all the lines will not necessarily be of equal length; (2) the number of lines in the stanza; and (3) the rhyme scheme. Three of the longer stanzaic forms have names: **rhyme royal**— seven iambic pentameter lines rhyming *a b a b b c c*—a form used by

Chaucer in *Troilus and Criseyde* and by Shakespeare in *Lucrece* (Wyatt, "They Flee from Me"); **ottava rima**—eight iambic pentameter lines rhyming *a b a b a b c c*—used by Byron in *Don Juan;* and the **Spenserian stanza**—nine lines, eight of them iambic pentameter and the ninth an alexandrine, rhyming *a b a b b c b c c*—used by Spenser in *The Faerie Queene* and by Keats in "The Eve of St. Agnes." In addition to the fixed stanzaic forms, there are also fixed forms for entire poems. By far the most important of these is the sonnet, which is treated below.

Knowing the names of the fixed forms and being able to describe them accurately will not necessarily increase a reader's understanding or enjoyment of poems. This knowledge is primarily useful in the way that any technical nomenclature is useful: it is a short cut. For instance, a reader who knows the terminology has a briefer way of saying, "In the poem 'The Ocean' Byron's stanzas, containing eight iambic pentameter lines followed by an alexandrine (iambic hexameter) and rhyming *a b a b b c b c c,* are livelier than Thomson's stanzas in *The Castle of Indolence,* which have the same form." The terminology enables one to say, "Byron writes a more lively Spenserian stanza than Thomson."

EXERCISE 52

Describe the stanzaic form in each of these poems:

1. Rochester, "The Mistress" (page 229).
2. Collins, "Ode" (page 211).
3. Donne, "Song" (page 221).
4. Kennedy, "In a Prominent Bar" (page 43).

STRUCTURE

Structure is the arrangement of materials within the poem.

Epitaph Intended for Sir Isaac Newton

Nature, and Nature's Laws lay hid in Night.
God said, Let Newton be! and All was Light.

ALEXANDER POPE

In form this poem is a single heroic couplet. Its structure might be described as chronological, or narrative, for the materials within the couplet are arranged according to a time sequence: the pre-Newtonian darkness, the coming of Newton, the post-Newtonian light.

You Beat Your Pate

You beat your Pate, and fancy Wit will come:
Knock as you please, there's no body at home.

ALEXANDER POPE

This poem has the same form as the "Epitaph," but a different structure. Line 1 presents a situation; line 2, an explanatory comment.

On the Funeral of a Rich Miser

What num'rous lights this wretch's corpse attend,
Who, in his lifetime, saved a candle's end!

ANONYMOUS
(*Eighteenth Century*)

Still in couplet form, this poem has a third kind of structure: an ironical contrast between lines 1 and 2.

Pope's poem on Newton, as the title indicates, is a **verse epitaph:** a label given to a brief poem on a dead person, either real or fictitious. Verse epitaphs are not necessarily suitable for inscription on tombstones, nor are they invariably serious (see Belloc's "Epitaph on the Politician"; Gay's "Life is a jest"). There are no fixed forms or tones for the epitaph or for the **verse epigram,** which is a brief poem usually ending with a witty point (Donne's "A Lame Beggar"; Pope's "You Beat Your Pate"). Succinct expression is valued in an epigram; in a good one, every successive detail makes an advance toward the final point.

The three little poems in couplets illustrate the fact that there are many more kinds of inner structure than there are of outer form. The latter can be and have often been tabulated in literary handbooks; the former cannot be reduced to systems because each poem has its own inner structure, its own way of relating the parts to the whole poem. With each new poem, therefore, the reader must discover the structure anew.

One of the most efficient means for laying bare the structure of a poem is to ask and answer this question: "What are its main parts, and what is the relationship of the parts to each other?" Many poems have two main parts.

The Fall of Rome

The piers are pummelled by the waves;
In a lonely field the rain
Lashes an abandoned train;
Outlaws fill the mountain caves.

Fantastic grow the evening gowns; 5
Agents of the Fisc pursue
Absconding tax-defaulters through
The sewers of provincial towns.

Private rites of magic send
The temple prostitutes to sleep; 10
All the literati keep
An imaginary friend.

Cerebretonic Cato may
Extoll the Ancient Disciplines,
But the muscle-bound Marines 15
Mutiny for food and pay.

Caesar's double-bed is warm
As an unimportant clerk
Writes I DO NOT LIKE MY WORK
On a pink official form. 20

Unendowed with wealth or pity,
Little birds with scarlet legs,
Sitting on their speckled eggs,
Eye each flu-infected city.

Altogether elsewhere, vast   25
Herds of reindeer move across
Miles and miles of golden moss,
Silently and very fast.

W. H. AUDEN

Fisc (6): "Fiscal Agency," a British equivalent of "Internal Revenue Service." **prostitutes** (10): The state religion of ancient Rome maintained in the temples prostitutes whose duty it was to solace the worshipers as part of the religious (especially fertility) rites. **literati** (11): poets and writers in general. **Cerebretonic** (13): "brain-bound." **Cato** (13): Stoic philosopher.

Stanzas 1 through 5 contain a rapid succession of specific details drawn from one aspect or another of what is known as civilization: trains, evening gowns, taxes, Marines, temples, double beds, and so on. In contrast, the main details of stanzas 6 and 7 do not come from the world of man, but from nature: birds, eggs, reindeer, moss. The poem, apparently, has two main parts that are contrasted with each other; it juxtaposes civilization and nature.

Having identified the parts, a reader should next examine their interconnections. In this poem the two parts are first set against each other in stanza 1: waves (part of nature) pummel the piers (man-made); rain lashes the train. The words *pummelled* and *lashes* suggest active hostility. As for the outlaws, nature seems already to have triumphed over them: they are living like animals in caves. The train, however, has not necessarily been abandoned because of rainstorms. It is more likely meant as a symbol of failure within the system; perhaps an unimportant flunky, like the clerk in line 19, was malingering when he should have done something to keep the train running. The train might also be a symbol for the social bonds that should unite people with each other—bonds that have become lax in this society. But perhaps the most interesting thing about the train is that it appears in a poem with this title.

The train, along with such other details as the Fisc (line 6) and the Marines (line 15), suggests that Auden is concerned with something less specific than the mere historical phenomenon of Rome's fall. The most famous dead civilization, Rome, is a convenient symbol of all decaying civilizations. Auden mixes ancient and modern instances indiscriminately, and each instance connotes several kinds of excess and disintegration. The government is floundering, perhaps because the ruler overindulges in sex (line 17), perhaps because the ruling classes have too many mad parties (line 5), perhaps because the citizens have good reasons not to pay taxes (lines 6–8). It is impossible to differentiate the instances that cause disintegration from those that are its effects. Morale is low in the armed forces and the church (lines 15–16; 9–10), those two great bulwarks of the state. Some intellectuals, like Cato, preach the traditional virtues to deaf ears (lines 13–14); others are so out of touch with their fellow men that all their personal relations are imaginary (lines 11–12). The ordinary people are bored by their work, which seems to them meaningless red tape (lines 18–20). But meantime the winds and the waters, the birds and the animals, go on as though nothing were happening. They have no stake in civilization. The scarlet-legged birds (lines 22–24) could not be less concerned; the fast-moving reindeer are "altogether elsewhere" (lines 25–28).

Although Auden avoids overt moralizing, it is not difficult to detect where his sympathies lie, and they do not lie with this civilization. There is an important change in tone after stanza 6. Stanzas 1–6 are frivolously but desperately contemptuous; stanza 7 is respectful. The vast expanse of golden moss has no sewers and no flu-infected cities. It is quiet and beautiful. Auden has arranged his material in such a way that his meaning is clear.

In a successful poem the inner structure subtly harmonizes with the outer form. The interaction between the two can perhaps best be studied in the sonnet, because there it is dramatically clear—if the sonnet is a good one.

THE SONNET

Formally considered, a **sonnet** contains fourteen iambic pentameter lines rhyming according to one of two general schemes. The Italian (or Petrarchan) sonnet has an octave (eight lines) rhyming *a b b a a b b a* followed by a sestet (six lines) usually rhyming *c d e c d e.* The English (or Shakespearean) sonnet has three quatrains usually rhyming *a b a b c d c d e f e f* followed by a couplet rhyming *g g.* Both kinds of sonnet provide opportunities for breaks or turns in the thought: the Italian, after line 8; the English, after line 12. Each quatrain of an English sonnet usually develops different aspects of a single thought.

To Sleep

A flock of sheep that leisurely pass by,
One after one; the sound of rain, and bees
Murmuring; the fall of rivers, winds and seas,
Smooth fields, white sheets of water, and pure sky;
I have thought of all by turns, and yet do lie   5
Sleepless! and soon the small birds' melodies
Must hear, first uttered from my orchard trees;
And the first cuckoo's melancholy cry.
Even thus last night, and two nights more, I lay
And could not win thee, Sleep! by any stealth: 10
So do not let me wear to-night away:
Without thee, what is all the morning's wealth?
Come, blessed barrier between day and day,
Dear mother of fresh thoughts and joyous health!

WILLIAM WORDSWORTH

This is a successful Italian sonnet because its inner structure corresponds at each point with its outer form. The first quatrain presents a series of visual, auditory, and tactile images; the second explains the significance of those images. Together the two quatrains form the octave, which presents the problem: the speaker's sleeplessness on a particular night. The sestet does not solve the problem, but relates it to the larger problem of several consecutive sleepless nights. Thus the poem moves from particularity to generality. Another difference between the octave and the sestet is that in the latter sleep is personified and addressed in an apostrophe. The octave is a first-person poem; the sestet, a second. As the speaker tells why he wishes to go to sleep, his tone becomes more urgent. Yet despite these differences in parts, the sonnet treats only one subject: sleeplessness.

Sonnet 30

When to the sessions of sweet silent thought
I summon up remembrance of things past,
I sigh the lack of many a thing I sought,
And with old woes new wail my dear time's waste.

Then can I drown an eye, unused to flow,   5
For precious friends hid in death's dateless night,
And weep afresh love's long-since cancelled woe,
And moan the expense of many a vanished sight.
Then can I grieve at grievances foregone,
And heavily from woe to woe tell o'er   10
The sad account of fore-bemoaned moan,
Which I new pay as if not paid before.
    But if the while I think on thee, dear friend,
    All losses are restored, and sorrows end.

WILLIAM SHAKESPEARE

In this representative English sonnet each shift in rhyme scheme signals a new development of the thought. The first quatrain states the subject in general terms: the sadness of "things past" (line 2). The second (lines 5–8) amplifies the subject with specific details: dead friends, lost loves, vanished sights. The third, which runs parallel with the second (see lines 5 and 9), is also general like the first, but is somewhat more intense. The main break in thought occurs after line 12, when the speaker suddenly remembers and directly addresses a dear friend who is still living. The final incisive couplet is balanced against the preceding twelve lines in such a way that it seems to solve the problem completely. The break, however, does not seem unduly abrupt because the couplet continues a legal-business metaphor that has run through the three quatrains: *sessions* (line 1), *summon* (line 2), *expense* (line 8), *tell* (line 10, in the sense of "count"), *account* (line 11), *pay* (line 12), and *losses* (line 14). This extended metaphor is an important element in the structure of the poem.

Few of the thousands of sonnets in existence adhere as closely to the theoretically fixed forms as do these two by Wordsworth and Shakespeare. In practice poets take all sorts of interesting liberties with the rhyme schemes and with the position of the turn. Even so, the sonnet is a difficult and challenging kind of poem to write because its complex outer form requires a supporting inner structure of thought.

EXERCISE 53

In addition to the sonnets below, this book contains many others in which the correspondence between structure and form can be profit-

ably studied: Keats, "On First Looking into Chapman's Homer";
Meredith, "Lucifer in Starlight"; Cummings, "Next to of course god";
MacLeish, "The End of the World"; Hopkins, "The Windhover";
Shakespeare, "Sonnet 116," etc.

Sonnet

Bright star! would I were steadfast as thou art—
　　Not in lone splendour hung aloft the night
And watching, with eternal lids apart,
　　Like nature's patient, sleepless Eremite,
The moving waters at their priestlike task　　　　　5
　　Of pure ablution round earth's human shores,
Or gazing on the new soft fallen mask
　　Of snow upon the mountains and the moors—
No—yet still steadfast, still unchangeable,
　　Pillow'd upon my fair love's ripening breast,　　10
To feel for ever its soft fall and swell,
　　Awake for ever in a sweet unrest,
Still, still to hear her tender-taken breath,
And so live ever—or else swoon to death.

JOHN KEATS

1. In what respects does the speaker wish to resemble the star? To differ from it?
2. Is this an English or an Italian sonnet? Where does the main turn in thought come? How has Keats varied the meter to emphasize the turn?
3. Explain the metaphors implied by *eternal lids* (line 3) and *priestlike* (line 5).
4. Resolve the paradox implied by *sweet unrest* (line 12).
5. Describe the tone. Is it lewd? Sentimental?

On His Blindness

When I consider how my light is spent
Ere half my days in this dark world and wide,
And that one talent which is death to hide
Lodged with me useless, though my soul more bent
To serve therewith my Maker, and present　　　　5
My true account, lest he returning chide,
"Doth God exact day-labor, light denied?"

I fondly ask. But Patience, to prevent
That murmur, soon replies: "God doth not need
Either man's work or his own gifts. Who best   10
Bear his mild yoke, they serve him best. His state
Is kingly: thousands at his bidding speed
And post o'er land and ocean without rest;
They also serve who only stand and wait."

JOHN MILTON

talent (3): See Matthew xxv: 14–30.

1. The opening lines are somewhat difficult syntactically. Point out the ending of the adverbial clause beginning with *When* (line 1).

2. Which of the two main kinds of sonnet is this one? What liberty has the poet taken with the form? Does the inner structure justify taking that liberty?

3. For what is *light* (line 1) a symbol? *yoke* (line 11)?

4. Explain the pun in *talent* (line 3).

5. *Thousands* (line 12) refers to God's angels. To what does Milton liken God in lines 11–13?

6. Would line 14 be improved if *sit* were substituted for *stand?* How would this substitution alter the theme?

Since There's No Help

Since there's no help, come let us kiss and part.
Nay, I have done; you get no more of me.
And I am glad, yea, glad with all my heart
That thus so cleanly I myself can free.
Shake hands forever, cancel all our vows,   5
And when we meet at any time again,
Be it not seen in either of our brows
That we one jot of former love retain.
Now at the last gasp of love's latest breath,
When, his pulse failing, passion speechless lies,   10
When faith is kneeling by his bed of death,
And innocence is closing up his eyes,
    Now if thou wouldst, when all have given him over,
    From death to life thou mightst him yet recover.

MICHAEL DRAYTON

1. Who is the speaker of this poem? Whom is he speaking to? What sort of person is he?
2. For what is *brows* (line 7) a metonymy?
3. Is the lover dying? To whom does *him* (line 14) refer?
4. Describe the tone. Is it consistent throughout?

PROGRESSION

Since a poem, unlike some other kinds of art, is not static, a convenient way to think of poetic structure is to think of it as a progression. **Progression** is the means by which a poem reveals itself—the means by which it moves from its beginning to its end. There are four main types of progression: narrative, descriptive, argumentative, expository. Within these main types there are as many sub-types as there are poems, because every individual poem has a progression unique to itself. If a reader is to experience a whole poem, he must be aware of how and where it is moving.

NARRATIVE PROGRESSION

A poem whose details are organized chronologically has a **narrative progression** (Frost, "Out, Out"; Blake, "A Poison Tree"). Such a poem tells a story, and it may have all or some of the features of plotted fiction: a **rising action** (in which a conflict develops), a **climax** (in which the conflict takes a decisive turn), and a **falling action** (in which the conflict reaches a conclusion).

The most obvious examples of narrative progression occur in **folk** or **popular ballads** ("Get Up and Bar the Door"), anonymous narrative songs handed down orally from one generation to the next. Rarely, however, do folk ballads tell a completely developed story; they frequently begin at or near the climax, or they move spasmodically by leaping over some events and lingering on others, so that the modern reader has to use his imagination to fill in details that are apparently missing. Both folk ballads and their imitations, called **art** or **literary ballads** (Keats, "La Belle Dame sans Merci"), commonly have one or more of these features: stanzaic form; repetition of one kind or another, as in a refrain or in parallel structure of sentences; stories about violent, horrible, or supernatural events ("Captain Carpenter"). Humor, except for the grimmest kind of irony and understatement, is missing from most ballads. Frequently the ballad story is related dramatically, by means of a dialogue between two speakers ("The Twa Corbies," page 304). The reader of such a ballad, like the reader of a dramatic monologue, must piece together the story from what a speaker says.

Although any poem whose details are arranged in a time sequence has a narrative progression, the story interest in such a poem may be considerable, as in a ballad, or it may be slight.

On a Gentlewoman Walking in the Snow

I saw fair Cloris walk alone
Where feathered rain came softly down;
And Jove descended from his tower
To court her in a silver shower.
The wanton snow flew to her breast   5
Like little birds into their nest;
And overcome with whiteness there,
For grief it thawed into a tear,
Thence falling on her garment's hem,
To deck her, froze into a gem.   10

WILLIAM STRODE

This elaborately conceited poem exists to compliment a lady, not to tell a story about her. Yet it progresses chronologically: Cloris takes a walk; Jove looks down and sees her, and he courts her as he courted Danaë, in a shower; the snow finds Cloris so attractive that it flies to her breast; then it thaws, falls to her skirt, and reluctant to leave her, freezes into a jewel. One couplet follows another in time.

EXERCISE 54

Study the progressions in these poems.

Captain Carpenter

Captain Carpenter rose up in his prime
Put on his pistols and went riding out
But he got wellnigh nowhere at that time
Till he fell in with ladies in a rout.

It was a pretty lady and all her train   5
That played with him so sweetly but before
An hour she'd taken a sword with all her main
And twined him of his nose for evermore.

Captain Carpenter mounted up one day
And rode straightway into a stranger rogue   10
That looked unchristian but be that as it may
The Captain did not wait upon prologue.

But drew upon him out of his great heart
The other swung against him with a club
And cracked his two legs at the shinny part   15
And let him roll and stick like any tub.

Captain Carpenter rode many a time
From male and female took he sundry harms
He met the wife of Satan crying "I'm
The she-wolf bids you shall bear no more arms."   20

Their strokes and counters whistled in the wind
I wish he had delivered half his blows
But where she should have made off like a hind
The bitch bit off his arms at the elbows.

And Captain Carpenter parted with his ears   25
To a black devil that used him in this wise
O Jesus ere his threescore and ten years
Another had plucked out his sweet blue eyes.

Captain Carpenter got up on his roan
And sallied from the gate in hell's despite   30
I heard him asking in the grimmest tone
If any enemy yet there was to fight?

"To any adversary it is fame
If he risk to be wounded by my tongue
Or burnt in two beneath my red heart's flame   35
Such are the perils he is cast among.

"But if he can he has a pretty choice
From an anatomy with little to lose
Whether he cut my tongue and take my voice
Or whether it be my round red heart he choose."   40

It was the neatest knave that ever was seen
Stepping in perfume from his lady's bower
Who at this word put in his merry mien
And fell on Captain Carpenter like a tower.

I would not knock old fellows in the dust   45
But there lay Captain Carpenter on his back
His weapons were the old heart in his bust
And a blade shook between rotten teeth alack.

The rogue in scarlet and gray soon knew his mind
He wished to get his trophy and depart;   50
With gentle apology and touch refined.
He pierced him and produced the Captain's heart.

God's mercy rest on Captain Carpenter now
I thought him Sirs an honest gentleman
Citizen husband soldier and scholar enow   55
Let jangling kites eat of him if they can.

But God's deep curses follow after those
That shore him of his goodly nose and ears
His legs and strong arms at the two elbows
And eyes that had not watered seventy years.   60

The curse of hell upon the sleek upstart
Who got the Captain finally on his back
And took the red red vitals of his heart
And made the kites to whet their beaks clack clack.

JOHN CROWE RANSOM

twined him of (8): separated him from.

The Monster

I left my room at last, I walked
The streets of that decaying town,
I took the turn I had renounced
Where the carved cherub crumbled down.

Eager as to a granted wish   5
I hurried to the cul de sac.
Forestalled by whom? Before the house
I saw an unmoved waiting back.

How had she never vainly mentioned
This lover, too, unsatisfied?   10
Did she dismiss one every night?
I walked up slowly to his side.

Those eyes glazed like her windowpane,
That wide mouth ugly with despair,
Those arms held tight against the haunches,   15
Poised, but heavily staying there:

At once I knew him, gloating over
A grief defined and realized,
And living only for its sake.
It was myself I recognized.   20

I could not watch her window now,
Standing before this man of mine,
The constant one I had created
Lest the pure feeling should decline.

What if I were within the house,   25
Happier than the fact had been
—Would he, then, still be gazing here,
The man who never can get in?

Or would I, leaving at the dawn
A suppler love than he could guess,   30
Find him awake on my small bed,
Demanding still some bitterness?

                    THOM GUNN

A Slumber Did My Spirit Seal

A slumber did my spirit seal;
  I had no human fears:
She seemed a thing that could not feel
  The touch of earthly years.

No motion has she now, no force;   5
  She neither hears nor sees;
Rolled round in earth's diurnal course,
  With rocks, and stones, and trees.

WILLIAM WORDSWORTH

She (3): Lucy (see pages 106 and 134).

DESCRIPTIVE PROGRESSION

A **descriptive progression** is an arrangement of pictorial details. Although there are descriptive passages in many poems, there are few purely descriptive poems because of the very nature of poetry. Poetry is a temporal rather than a spatial art, and when it tries to compete with such a spatial art as painting the result is rather thin.

Symphony in Yellow

An omnibus across the bridge
  Crawls like a yellow butterfly,
  And, here and there, a passer-by
Shows like a little restless midge.

Big barges full of yellow hay   5
  Are moved against the shadowy wharf,
  And, like a yellow silken scarf,
The thick fog hangs along the quay.

The yellow leaves begin to fade
  And flutter from the Temple elms,
  And at my feet the pale green Thames
Lies like a rod of rippled jade.

OSCAR WILDE

Temple (10): district in London.

Unlike a painter, Wilde cannot present his picture all at once with each detail in its place; he has to present his details piecemeal—one at a time. To overcome this difficulty, which is inherent in all word-paintings, Wilde has chosen a title that suggests a musical rather than a pictorial analogy. He has selected and presented details from the landscape that blend harmoniously to give a dominant impression of greenish yellowness. Each successive detail contributes to that impression. Had Wilde gone on piling up yellow details through several more quatrains, he would have forfeited his readers' interest.

In most poems descriptive progressions are used in conjunction with some other kind of progression. In Keats's "To Autumn," for instance, there is a good deal of description, but the presence of narrative and expository progressions makes the poem something much more interesting than a mere series of autumnal vignettes would be.

ARGUMENTATIVE PROGRESSION

When a poet advances a proposition and then presents reasons in defense of it, he uses an **argumentative progression.** Donne's famous sonnet beginning "Death, be not proud" consists of a series of reasons why death should not be proud; his "Valediction Forbidding Mourning" similarly gives reasons why true lovers need not be sad when they are temporarily separated. Few poems, however, have only an argumentative progression because a person who merely wants to present an argument can do so more convincingly in prose than in verse.

Terence, This Is Stupid Stuff

'Terence, this is stupid stuff:
You eat your victuals fast enough;
There can't be much amiss, 'tis clear,
To see the rate you drink your beer.
But, oh, good Lord, the verse you make,　　　　5
It gives a chap the belly-ache.
The cow, the old cow, she is dead;
It sleeps well, the horned head:
We poor lads, 'tis our turn now
To hear such tunes as killed the cow.　　　　10

Pretty friendship 'tis to rhyme
Your friends to death before their time
Moping melancholy mad.
Come, pipe a tune to dance to, lad.'

   Why, if 'tis dancing you would be, 15
There's brisker pipes than poetry.
Say, for what were hop-yards meant,
Or why was Burton built on Trent?
Oh many a peer of England brews,
Livelier liquor than the Muse, 20
And malt does more than Milton can
To justfiy God's ways to man.
Ale, man, ale's the stuff to drink
For fellows whom it hurts to think:
Look into the pewter pot 25
To see the world as the world's not.
And faith, 'tis pleasant till 'tis past:
The mischief is that 'twill not last.
Oh I have been to Ludlow fair
And left my necktie God knows where, 30
And carried half-way home, or near,
Pints and quarts of Ludlow beer:
Then the world seemed none so bad,
And I myself a sterling lad;
And down in lovely muck I've lain, 35
Happy till I woke again.
Then I saw the morning sky:
Heigho, the tale was all a lie;
The world, it was the old world yet,
I was I, my things were wet, 40
And nothing now remained to do
But begin the game anew.

   Therefore, since the world has still
Much good, but much less good than ill,
And while the sun and moon endure 45
Luck's a chance, but trouble's sure,
I'd face it as a wise man would,
And train for ill and not for good.
'Tis true, the stuff I bring for sale
Is not so brisk a brew as ale; 50

Out of a stem that scored the hand
I wrung it in a weary land.
But take it: if the smack is sour,
The better for the embittered hour;
It should do good to heart and head   55
When your soul is in my soul's stead;
And I will friend you, if I may,
In the dark and cloudy day.

There was a king reigned in the East:
There, when kings will sit to feast,   60
They get their fill before they think
With poisoned meat and poisoned drink.
He gathered all that springs to birth
From the many-venomed earth;
First a little, thence to more,   65
He sampled all her killing store;
And easy, smiling, seasoned sound,
Sate the king when healths went round.
They put arsenic in his meat
And stared aghast to watch him eat;   70
They poured strychnine in his cup
And shook to see him drink it up:
They shook, they stared as white's their shirt:
Them it was their poison hurt.
—I tell the tale that I heard told.   75
Mithridates, he died old.

A. E. HOUSMAN

this (1): the poems of "Terence" (Housman's playful name for
himself?).   Burton (18): English brewery town on the River
Trent.   Milton (21): The stated purpose of *Paradise Lost* is "to
justify the ways of God to men."   Ludlow (29): English town
in Shropshire.   king (59): Mithridates, king of Pontus (132–63
B.C.).

The poem has two main parts, each containing an argument. In the
first part (lines 1–14) somebody advises Terence—whose poems, like
Housman's (see pages 83, 276, 345), are apparently somewhat morbid—
to write about happier subjects. Terence then replies (lines 15–76). He
argues first that beer is a better escape from life's troubles than poetry.
Then he points out that escape by way of beer is at best temporary.

Since life is what it is, trouble cannot be permanently avoided. And since trouble must be faced, poetry can help a man face it, especially if the poetry has a sour taste (line 53). Terence's conclusions follow logically from his premises. To clinch his argument that bitterness is desirable in poems, he concludes with an anecdote about Mithridates, who became venom-proof by eating a little poison every day.

EXPOSITORY PROGRESSION

Any arrangement by means of which a poet sets forth or exposes his ideas and feelings is an **expository progression**. Thus broadly defined, a progession of this kind must exist in every good poem.

At the beginning of Thom Gunn's "The Monster," the reader does not know who the monster is; at the end, he recognizes that the monster is the lover's "double," or alter ego that insists on suffering and perhaps even enjoys suffering. Such a discovery occurs in every poem, or some such question is answered. The attitude of the lover in Drayton's "Since There's No Help" is not evident when the sonnet opens; it becomes evident as the poem progresses. What will happen to Cloris, in Strode's poem, as she walks in the snow? What happened while a slumber sealed the spirit of a lover in Wordsworth's poem? Every poem raises and answers some sort of question. One kind of expository progression, then, is a movement from ignorance at the beginning of the poem to knowledge at the end. If a poem expresses a feeling, that feeling will be less vague at the end than at the beginning; if it expresses an idea, the idea will be clearer; if it describes a scene, the scene will be more vivid in the reader's mind.

There are many ways by which a poem may move from ignorance to knowledge, from vagueness to precision. The following poem accomplishes the movement by supporting a generalization with specific details.

Sonnet 66

Tired with all these, for restful death I cry:
As to behold desert a beggar born,
And needy nothing trimmed in jollity,
And purest faith unhappily forsworn,

And gilded honor shamefully misplaced,   5
And maiden virtue rudely strumpeted,
And right perfection wrongfully disgraced,
And strength by limping sway disabled,
And art made tongue-tied by authority,
And folly, doctor-like, controlling skill,   10
And simple truth miscalled simplicity,
And captive good attending captain ill:
    Tired with all these, from these would I be gone,
    Save that to die, I leave my love alone.

                    WILLIAM SHAKESPEARE

Contrast (Keats's sonnet beginning "Bright star!") and comparison (any poem with an extended metaphor) are other common expository devices. A succession of figurative comparisons (King's "Sic Vita") or precise images (Swift's "Description of the Morning") help to make the subject of a poem stand out distinctly as itself, and nothing else.

Another general kind of expository progression causes a poem to become more emotionally profound as it proceeds from beginning to end. This sort of progression is best studied in the **lyric,** a term originally applied to poems that were sung to the accompaniment of a lyre, but now applied to any short poem expressing personal thoughts and feelings rather than public events (see Herrick, "To Blossoms"; Byron, "She Walks in Beauty"; Roethke, "The Waking"; and many other poems in this book). A lyric is ordinarily stanzaic and euphonic; its speaker is not necessarily the poet.

Mother, I Cannot Mind My Wheel

Mother, I cannot mind my wheel;
    My fingers ache, my lips are dry:
Oh! if you felt the pain I feel!
    But Oh, who ever felt as I?

No longer could I doubt him true;   5
    All other men may use deceit:
He always said my eyes were blue,
    And often swore my lips were sweet.

              WALTER SAVAGE LANDOR

wheel (1): spinning wheel.

In this lyric, which Landor adapted from a fragment by Sappho, a girl complains to her mother. There is a kind of false emotional climax at line 4. At this point the girl's feelings seem to be deepest, but the reader is not yet emotionally involved because he needs more information. The reader's response is greater at line 8 than at line 4. Although the poem has no narrative progression, it does imply a story: a man has flattered the girl, gained her confidence, probably seduced her, and then certainly abandoned her. The poem has two expository progressions that function concurrently: as the reader becomes more mentally aware —that is, as his mind takes in what has happened—he becomes more emotionally involved.

Unlike a sentimentalist, who would pump emotion into the poem, Landor avoids any overt expression of feeling in the second quatrain. Here the girl is meditating aloud, remembering what has happened. "No longer could I doubt him true," she says, to justify herself for having given in to him. The irony in "All other men may use deceit" increases the pathos. This man was obviously a deceiver; if he had been faithful, the girl would now be happy. The word *swore* (line 8) suggests an oath to be faithful. It is ironical because it is modified by *often:* for a faithful person one oath is enough. The man often swore that her lips were sweet. He apparently knew very well just how sweet they were. By letting the situation speak for itself, so that the reader must share in creating the experience, Landor increases the emotional impact of the poem. He arranges the details in such a way that they make a progressively greater appeal to the heart.

The ode and the elegy, two varieties of lyric, ordinarily have more complex patterns of thought and feeling than those in a relatively simple song like Landor's, and they are ordinarily longer than "song" lyrics. Down through the ages the term **ode** has been applied to poems in many different forms, but most poems so designated have a serious tone and treat lofty subjects (Keats, "Ode on a Grecian Urn"). The term **elegy,** originally designating a poem in a particular Latin or Greek meter, now is given to poems of contemplative tone that treat death in general or mourn a dead person (Gray, "Elegy Written in a Country Church-Yard"; Milton, "Lycidas").

EXERCISE 55

Study the progressions of thought and feeling in these poems.

Rondeau

Jenny kissed me when we met,
  Jumping from the chair she sat in;
Time, you thief, who love to get
  Sweets into your list, put that in:
Say I'm weary, say I'm sad,   5
  Say that health and wealth have missed me,
Say I'm growing old, but add,
  Jenny kissed me.

LEIGH HUNT

1. The title announces that this poem imitates a French form. What can you infer about the rondeau from this poem?
2. What effect do the feminine rhymes have on the tone?
3. Comment on the shortness of line 8.

Ode to Leven-Water

On Leven's banks, while free to rove,
And tune the rural pipe to love;
I envied not the happiest swain
That ever trod the Arcadian plain.
    Pure stream! in whose transparent wave   5
My youthful limbs I wont to lave;
No torrents stain thy limpid source;
No rocks impede thy dimpling course,
That sweetly warbles o'er its bed,
With white, round, polish'd pebbles spread;   10
While, lightly pois'd, the scaly brood
In myriads cleave thy chrystal flood;
The springing trout in speckled pride;
The salmon, monarch of the tide;
The ruthless pike, intent on war;   15
The silver eel, and mottled par.
Devolving from thy parent lake,
A charming maze thy waters make,
By bowers of birch, and groves of pine,

And edges flower'd with eglantine.   20
  Still on thy banks so gayly green,
May num'rous herds and flocks be seen,
And lasses chanting o'er the pail,
And shepherds piping in the dale,
And ancient faith that knows no guile,   25
And industry imbrown'd with toil,
And hearts resolv'd, and hands prepar'd,
The blessings they enjoy to guard.

                           TOBIAS SMOLLETT

Leven-Water (title): Loch Leven in Scotland.   par (16): young
salmon.

1. Paraphrase lines 1–2 and line 23.
2. Why does the poem start in the past tense and then shift to the present?
3. Characterize the speaker. What features of country life does he ignore? What
   features does he emphasize?
4. Of what structural significance are the divisions into verse paragraphs?

The Lovers in the Graveyard

Sin is but the hope that is too precious to be found engaged in;
That we guard from becoming public property at the cost of private shame.
The lovers, cast out of the town by the threat they are
To the beauty that is kept in darkened rooms on second floors,
That cannot afford the permanency of marriage or the cost of its upkeep, 5
Take themselves to the place where the people are that it no longer dis-
    turbs—
Where, after centuries of being wound in a blanket of earth,
They are at last perhaps able to reach a bone to a bone; their touch
Is the honesty, after shame, that lives in the frankness of the last exposure.
Among the lovers here, that in their loss have come to meet again,   10
These lovers find at last a field which their presence does not embarrass;
In the burial ground that shows in the summer heat-lightning
The tombstones of their fathers' and mothers' loves,
His touch on her legs feels like freshly cut fingernails,
Her hair against his mouth like the sentences by which they have come
    to know themselves,   15
And her lips on his neck like a cool wind out of some distant land

That flows too over this earth on which they find themselves:
Where the flesh does not have to wait until doomsday to find its resurrec
tion in the grass.

In the short second that the moon comes out from behind the clouds,
The stones and vaults look like the houses of the town; in the moon-
light   20
The beauty here is the ghosts of bodies already covered by the earth;
The beauty that the living have to chase lest their own joys become com-
mon,
Here is the element in which they rest—within it live both the worm and
the root
That the living generations must pay for in care: the green sward of the
mother's heart
On which children tread bare places growing up—the tree of her life   25
Which gathers the shades to it and hangs them up like fruit in the foliage;
Beneath it the worm in the mouth, and the ant in the skull.
The young lovers have here created their house in their hearts, at night
In the graveyard, upon the grass of their needs and among the stones of
their touch:
The names of their own dead are inscribed upon the doors—those who
have died   30
That they might live, having reached through the rooms of shame
To create for them in the seclusion of a public death their private refuge;
Those who have given themselves up for the lovers, to preserve shame in
the housekeeping of marriage,
Lying beautiful on the hillside that has taken their nudity again to its
breast,
Where their fading lips are lit again by the smile of the sunrise in the
East,   35
And the other worlds their loves have lit are the stars that shine all night
in the dark.

THEODORE HOLMES

1. Explain the central paradox, suggested by the title, around which this poem is
   organized.
2. What other antinomies or opposites in the poem reinforce or reflect the main
   paradox?
3. What are the three different attitudes toward love that the poet attributes to
   people in the poem?
4. In what ways is the graveyard like the town?

5. What judgments does the speaker of the poem make or imply about the various people he mentions?

Ode to the West Wind

1

O wild West Wind, thou breath of Autumn's being,
Thou, from whose unseen presence the leaves dead
Are driven, like ghosts from an enchanter fleeing,

Yellow, and black, and pale, and hectic red,   5
Pestilence-stricken multitudes: O thou,
Who chariotest to their dark wintry bed

The wingèd seeds, where they lie cold and low,
Each like a corpse within its grave, until
Thine azure sister of the Spring shall blow

Her clarion o'er the dreaming earth, and fill   10
(Driving sweet buds like flocks to feed in air)
With living hues and odours plain and hill:

Wild Spirit, which art moving everywhere;
Destroyer and preserver; hear, oh, hear!

2

Thou on whose stream, 'mid the steep sky's commotion,   15
Loose clouds like earth's decaying leaves are shed,
Shook from the tangled boughs of Heaven and Ocean,

Angels of rain and lightning: there are spread
On the blue surface of thine airy surge,
Like the bright hair uplifted from the head   20

Of some fierce Mænad, even from the dim verge
Of the horizon to the zenith's height
The locks of the approaching storm. Thou dirge

Of the dying Year, to which this closing night
Will be the dome of a vast sepulchre,   25
Vaulted with all thy congregated might

Of vapours, from whose solid atmosphere
Black rain, and fire, and hail will burst: oh, hear!

3

Thou who didst waken from his summer dreams
The blue Mediterranean, where he lay,   30
Lulled by the coil of his crystàlline streams,

Beside a pumice isle in Baiæ's bay,
And saw in sleep old palaces and towers
Quivering within the wave's intenser day,

All overgrown with azure moss and flowers   35
So sweet, the sense faints picturing them! Thou
For whose path the Atlantic's level powers

Cleave themselves into chasms, while far below
The sea-blooms and the oozy woods which wear
The sapless foliage of the ocean, know   40

Thy voice, and suddenly grow gray with fear,
And tremble and despoil themselves: oh, hear!

4

If I were a dead leaf thou mightest bear;
If I were a swift cloud to fly with thee;
A wave to pant beneath thy power, and share   45

The impulse of thy strength, only less free
Than thou, O uncontrollable! If even
I were as in my boyhood, and could be

The comrade of thy wanderings over Heaven,
As then, when to outstrip thy skiey speed   50
Scarce seemed a vision; I would ne'er have striven

As thus with thee in prayer in my sore need.
Oh, lift me as a wave, a leaf, a cloud!
I fall upon the thorns of life! I bleed!

A heavy weight of hours has chained and bowed   55
One too like thee: tameless, and swift, and proud.

5

Make me thy lyre, even as the forest is:
What if my leaves are falling like its own!
The tumult of thy mighty harmonies

Will take from both a deep, autumnal tone,   60
Sweet though in sadness. Be thou, Spirit fierce,
My spirit! Be thou me, impetuous one!

Drive my dead thoughts over the universe
Like withered leaves to quicken a new birth!
And, by the incantation of this verse,   65

Scatter, as from an unextinguished hearth
Ashes and sparks, my words among mankind!
Be through my lips to unawakened Earth

The trumpet of a prophecy! O Wind,
If Winter comes, can Spring be far behind?   70

PERCY BYSSHE SHELLEY

Baiæ (32): village near Naples, Italy.

1. Where does the first sentence in the poem end? The second? The third? Comment on the effect produced.

2. How can the wind be both "destroyer and preserver" (line 14)?

3. The scene is different in each of the first three sections. Where and what is the wind blowing in section 1? Where and what in 2? In 3?

4. Analyze these implicit metaphors: *boughs* (line 17); *dirge* (line 23); *sleep* (line 33). Are there extended metaphors?

5. Into what two main parts may the poem be divided? How are the parts related?

6. What is the speaker's sore need (line 52)? Does he wish that his troubles were gone with the wind, or does he have some other need?

7. Explain why it is necessary to understand sections 1–4 in order to know the full import of these words in section 5: *leaves* (line 58); *universe* (line 63); *new birth* (line 64).

8. What is the speaker's prophecy (line 69)?

9. What is the full answer to the question with which the ode ends? Could this ode be regarded as propaganda for a revolution? Can any good come from the scattered sparks of a fire (lines 66–67)?

10. How does Shelley's notions of what constitutes an ode differ from Smollett's?

Song

Go, lovely rose!
Tell her that wastes her time and me
That now she knows,

When I resemble her to thee
How sweet and fair she seems to be.   5

Tell her that's young
And shuns to have her graces spied,
That hadst thou sprung
In deserts where no men abide,
Thou must have uncommended died.   10

Small is the worth
Of beauty from the light retired;
Bid her come forth,
Suffer herself to be desired,
And not blush so to be admired.   15

Then die, that she
The common fate of all things rare
May read in thee;
How small a part of time they share
That are so wondrous sweet and fair!   20

EDMUND WALLER

1. Paraphrase line 2 and give synonyms for *resemble* (line 4), *deserts* (line 9), and *suffer* (line 14).

2. What does the speaker of the poem want? Trace the argumentative progression.

3. What is the theme? The tone?

CONVENTIONS AND TRADITIONS

Poems, like all other forms of art, have their **conventions**—artificial and sometimes unrealistic devices that are accepted by common agreement between the artist and his public. In the movies, for instance, the passage of time is sometimes indicated by a series of rapidly flashed pictures of newspaper headlines and easily recognized events. The audience may spend only a minute looking at the pictures, yet it agrees to accept that minute as equivalent to twenty-five years in the hero's life. Among the conventions of poems are rhyme, meter, fixed forms, symbols—in fact, any of the devices that make poems different from ordinary discourse. One kind of poem—necessarily excluded from this book because of its length—which makes elaborate use of conventions is the **epic:** a narrative poem of heroic action, such as Homer's *Iliad* and *Odyssey,* Virgil's *Aeneid,* Milton's *Paradise Lost.* Although the epic tells a story, it begins by convention in the middle; it employs extended similes, invokes the Muses, contains lists of things, traces the characters' genealogies, shows supernatural beings interfering in the affairs of men, depicts games.

A poem that uses conventions similar to those in other poems is said to be written in a **tradition.** Among the many traditions are the Petrarchan (see page 96) and the metaphysical (page 98). A theme may be traditional; there are, for instance, hundreds of poems on the *carpe diem* ("seize the day") theme (Marvell, "To His Coy Mistress"). One tradition that can baffle a reader unless he recognizes it is the pastoral, which is found in both prose and verse. The author of a work in the **pastoral tradition** depicts his characters as shepherds, who may fall in love with shepherdesses (Marlowe, "The Passionate Shepherd"), or who may lament a death (Milton, "Lycidas"—a pastoral elegy).

THE MEANING OF A WHOLE POEM

"What does this poem mean?" is a highly ambiguous question because how one answers it depends mainly on how one defines *mean.* Some definitions of *mean* are more useful than others. For instance, one not very useful definition is "mean in prose." Then the question becomes "What would this poem mean if it were written in prose?" and the answer is a prose paraphrase of the poem. This answer is unsatisfactory because translating the words of the poem into other words completely changes the poem. "Poetry," says Robert Frost, "is what gets lost in translation." A more useful definition of *mean* is "say about its subject." The answer to the question "What does this poem say about its subject?" is a statement of the theme. Yet the theme is not equivalent to the total meaning of the poem, because it is only one element. No one would read with any interest a book merely listing the themes of poems; one might as well read a book of rhyme schemes. Perhaps the best definition of *mean* is one that makes the question ask, "What does the poem say about its subject and how does it say it?" The answer to this question is a discussion of both the how (the manner) and the what (the matter) of the whole poem. Unlike the paraphrase, the discussion is not offered as a substitute for the poem. Nor can it be a substitute, because in the poem itself manner and matter are fused. The discussion separates them only for purposes of study.

There are two chief ways in which the discussion of a poem can go wrong. First, beginning readers are likely to concentrate more on the matter than on the manner of a poem. A reader who ignores tone, fails to recognize figurative statements, pays no need to the connotation of words—who uses only the mental equipment he uses on the sporting pages of a tabloid—will inevitably misinterpret a poem. Such a reader is ignoring the manner of the poem. Second, a reader who does not pay attention to the whole poem will also misinterpret it. This reader seizes on a part of the poem and allows that part unduly to influence his view of the whole. A discussion must accord with the whole poem.

Students are often surprised to discover that authorities on poetry, even expert critics, offer different interpretations of the same poem. As a result of this discovery they are tempted to conclude that a poem has any meaning that an individual reader may find in it. Told that his interpretation of a poem is wrong, a student may ask, "If a poem can have a number of meanings, who is to say which is the right one?"

This is a fair question, and it deserves an honest answer. First of all, no poem has a single "correct" interpretation in the way that a problem in arithmetic has a single right answer. The interpretations of different readers will differ as their individual sensibilities do. An interpretation will reflect the depth and breadth of the reader's experience, both in literature and in life. But the fact that a poem does not have a single "right" interpretation does not mean that it cannot be given a wrong one, or that a wrong one cannot be labeled as such. Who is to say what is wrong and what is right? The poem itself.

EXERCISE 56

This exercise is intended to demonstrate that a wrong interpretation can be revealed simply by using the poem itself as a criterion. Follow the directions step by step.

The Folly of Being Comforted

One that is ever kind said yesterday:
'Your well-belovèd's hair has threads of grey,
And little shadows come about her eyes;

Time can but make it easier to be wise
Though now it seems impossible, and so   5
All that you need is patience.'
                                        Heart cries, 'No,
I have not a crumb of comfort, not a grain.
Time can but make her beauty over again:
Because of that great nobleness of hers
The fire that stirs about her, when she stirs,   10
Burns but more clearly. O she had not these ways
When all the wild summer was in her gaze.'

O heart! O heart! if she'd but turn her head,
You'd know the folly of being comforted.

WILLIAM BUTLER YEATS

1. Frame in your own mind an interpretation of this poem by answering these
   questions:
   a. What is the motive of the "ever kind" person who makes the remarks in
      lines 2–6? What does he mean by *wise* (line 4)?
   b. What does the main speaker think of the advice he is given?
   c. What is the relationship between the speaker and the woman?

2. A distinguished critic has annotated this poem as follows:
   "The final couplet—in which the poet's rationalization that his beloved is
   really more beautiful now that she is older, is suddenly and devastatingly
   shattered by the physical reality—has an almost epigrammatic quality."[1]
   So far as you can judge from this note, what does his interpretation of the
   poem seem to be? How does it compare with yours?

3. Read the following interpretation, and then read the poem again:

The title of Yeats's poem is "The Folly of Being Comforted." So the
poet is in need of being comforted about something. There are two
possibilities. If the reader jumps to conclusions on the basis of lines
2–3, he will decide that the poet needs to be comforted about the fact
that his beloved is growing older. But if the fact that she is aging
disturbs him, "one that is ever kind" would neither be kind nor com-
forting by calling those cruel facts to his attention, and saying that time
and patience will remedy the situation. Time can make it only worse.
The only other possibility for the lover's unhappiness would be that his
love was unrequited. In this case the advice of "one who is ever kind"

[1] *Poems in English 1530–1940*, ed. David Daiches and William Charvat. Copyright
1950. The Ronald Press Company, New York, p. 731. Reprinted by permission.

makes rational sense. "Your beloved is growing older," the friend says; "time will take its toll; if only you have patience your love will die."

To this advice, however well-meant, the "heart" (line 6) can only answer, 'No!" The heart has reasons the mind knows nothing of. The heart refuses to take any consolation from the fact that its beloved is aging; the passing of time "can but make her beauty over again"—that is, re-create it and on a higher level. Because of her "nobleness" her beauty becomes more incandescent with age; her autumnal beauty is even more ravishing than the beauty of her youth, "When all the wild summer was in her gaze." Let her but "turn her head," and the poet becomes aware of the "fire that stirs about her when she stirs." She has merely to turn her face to him and the poet has shattering proof that the aging of the woman he loves will bring no end to the pangs of his unrequited love. She turns her head, he sees the effects of time, but it makes no difference. The fire "burns but more clearly." Thus the "folly" of being comforted, of taking idle comfort from the kind words of a friend. The proffered consolation is no consolation at all.

4. Have you changed your mind about what the poem means? In what ways?

11

JUDGING

A POEM

In two respects judging a poem is like judging anything else. All judges ask and answer such questions as these: Is it good? In what particular way is it good? Is it bad? In what particular way is it bad? All acts of judgment also presuppose a judge who thoroughly understands and genuinely likes the sort of thing he is judging. Without these qualifications no one can rightly make any judgments at all. A man who hates, or thinks he hates, all poems or all pies is not a proper judge of any particular poem or pie. Similarly, a man who neither understands motors nor knows how to drive is a very poor judge of automobiles.

LITERARY JUDGMENTS

In all other respects judging a poem differs greatly from judging an automobile or a pie. When a consumers' organization tests a car, it has preconceived notions about how the car should function, and it will condemn a model that is noisy, inefficient, or costly to repair and operate. A car critic has a set of standards that he can automatically apply. A critic of poems has no such ready-made scientific tests, despite the tons of ink that theorists have shed in the effort to reduce aesthetic judgments to a system. There are so many kinds of poems, and so many ways in which a poem can be good, that no single set of standards will work for all poems. Yet it would be wrong to conclude that there are no standards at all, that a poem must be good if somebody likes it. Liking is not judging, and a poem is not a pie. Judging a poem, then, is not expressing a preference, as for a certain kind of food. Nor is it testing the poem to see whether it says what an individual reader would like it to say.

VALUES

Ars Poetica

A poem should be palpable and mute
As a globed fruit,

Dumb
As old medallions to the thumb,

Silent as the sleeve-worn stone   5
Of casement ledges where the moss has grown—

A poem should be wordless
As the flight of birds.

*

A poem should be motionless in time
As the moon climbs,   10

Leaving, as the moon releases
Twig by twig the night-entangled trees,

Leaving, as the moon behind the winter leaves,
Memory by memory the mind—

A poem should be motionless in time   15
As the moon climbs.

*

A poem should be equal to:
Not true.

For all the history of grief
An empty doorway and a maple leaf.   20

For love
The leaning grasses and two lights above the sea—

A poem should not mean
But be.

ARCHIBALD MACLEISH

Title: "Poetic Art."

The repeated use of *should* (lines 1, 7, 9, 15, 17, 23) indicates that this poem is concerned with literary judgments. MacLeish would presumably value more highly a poem that did what he says poems should do than one that did not. *Palpable* (line 1) implies that a good poem is concrete, that like such real things as fruit, medallions, and ledges it makes an appeal to the senses. A good poem must therefore contain precise images. But what of *mute, dumb, silent,* and *wordless?* It is paradoxical to apply these adjectives to a poem, a structure of words. The truth behind the paradox is the special way that good poems use language. Although made of words, a poem does not use words to communicate factual information, but to communicate experience. Poems are also wordless in the sense that their words cannot be translated. Every word in a good poem seems to be the inevitably right one and in the inevitably right place. Although the words are organized into an organic unity, something like that of natural products like fruit, a poem is also something made, like a medallion. The words in a good poem are rich in connotation, as old objects are rich in associations. Finally, the words move in a progression, as birds fly.

In the second section MacLeish is concerned with the relationship between a poem and time. This relationship is also paradoxical. Although poetry is a temporal art, and although a particular poem is the product of a particular time, a good poem will seem independent of time. Like the moon, which is always "climbing" yet always appears static in the heavens, a poem at a given moment will be both static and dynamic—that is, moving yet standing still in such a way as to illuminate the mind.

Section three contains two paradoxes. First, it asserts that a poem is "not true," but, rather, is "equal to": that is, it is an equivalent of an experience that may or may not have actually happened. The statement that a poem is not true does not deny the validity of its experience but merely emphasizes the element of make-believe in all imaginative literature. The very language of a good poem is figurative, and therefore not literally true. Poems present concrete images as if they were "all the history of grief" or "love." By convention the reader accepts the object for the idea, the image for the emotion. Finally, in the most famous lines of the poem, MacLeish claims that a poem "should not mean/ But be." Here he is not necessarily saying that good poems lack meaning; his own poem is very meaningful. Rather, he is insisting that a poem exists in such a way that it has more meaning than can be set down in any verbal statement about it. The amount of meaning in a good poem is inexhaustible because the poem is what it is.

These, then, are among the values that MacLeish seems to admire: concreteness, concentration, exactness and inevitability in diction, structure, memorability, imaginative figures, and meaning coextensive with the poem itself.

EXERCISE 57

To what degree, and in what respects, do these poems exemplify the values set forth in "Ars Poetica"? Think about these poems, and about others that you have read, and then consider this question: Are there good poems that do not exemplify the values of "Ars Poetica," but some other values?

I Counsel You Beware

Good creatures, do you love your lives
And have you ears for sense?
Here is a knife like other knives,
That cost me eighteen pence.

I need but stick it in my heart
  And down will come the sky,
And earth's foundations will depart
  And all you folk will die.

A. E. HOUSMAN

Shall I Wasting in Despair

Shall I, wasting in despair,
Die because a woman's fair?
Or make pale my cheeks with care
'Cause another's rosy are?
Be she fairer than the day,   5
Or the flow'ry meads in May,
  If she be not so to me,
  What care I how fair she be?

Shall my heart be grieved or pined
'Cause I see a woman kind?   10
Or a well-disposèd nature
Joinèd with a lovely feature?
Be she meeker, kinder, than
Turtle-dove or pelican,
  If she be not so to me,   15
  What care I how kind she be?

Shall a woman's virtues move
Me to perish for her love?
Or her well-deserving known
Make me quite forget mine own?   20
Be she with that goodness blest
Which may gain her name of best,
  If she be not such to me,
  What care I how good she be?

'Cause her fortune seems too high,   25
Shall I play the fool and die?
Those that bear a noble mind,
Where they want of riches find,

Think what with them they would do
That without them dare to woo;   30
    And unless that mind I see,
    What care I how great she be?

Great, or good, or kind, or fair,
I will ne'er the more despair;
If she love me, this believe,   35
I will die ere she shall grieve;
If she slight me when I woo,
I can scorn and let her go;
    For if she be not for me,
    What care I for whom she be?   40

                    GEORGE WITHER

pelican (14): traditionally supposed to feed its own blood to its
young.

Now Winter Nights Enlarge

Now winter nights enlarge
    The number of their hours;
And clouds their storms discharge
    Upon the airy towers.
Let now the chimneys blaze   5
    And cups o'erflow with wine,
Let well-tuned words amaze
    With harmony divine.
Now yellow waxen lights
    Shall wait on honey love,   10
While youthful revels, masques, and courtly sights
    Sleep's leaden spells remove.

This time doth well dispense
    With lovers' long discourse;
Much speech hath some defense,   15
    Though beauty no remorse.
All do not all things well:
    Some measures comely tread;
Some knotted riddles tell;

Some poems smoothly read.
The summer hath his joys,
    And winter his delights;
Though love and all his pleasures are but toys,
    They shorten tedious nights.

THOMAS CAMPION

To ——

Music, when soft voices die,
Vibrates in the memory—
Odours, when sweet violets sicken,
Live within the sense they quicken.

Rose leaves, when the rose is dead,   5
Are heaped for the belovèd's bed;
And so thy thoughts, when thou art gone,
Love itself shall slumber on.

PERCY BYSSHE SHELLEY

Once by the Pacific

The shattered water made a misty din.
Great waves looked over others coming in,
And thought of doing something to the shore
That water never did to land before.
The clouds were low and hairy in the skies,   5
Like locks blown forward in the gleam of eyes.
You could not tell, and yet it looked as if
The shore was lucky in being backed by cliff,
The cliff in being backed by continent;
It looked as if a night of dark intent   10
Was coming, and not only a night, an age.
Someone had better be prepared for rage.
There would be more than ocean water broken
Before God's last *Put out the Light* was spoken.

ROBERT FROST

GOOD AND BAD POEMS

A good poem is one in which the various elements—rhythm, sound, diction, figurative language—collaborate successfully in presenting an experience. In contrast, the elements of a bad poem do not work together, but one or more of them either does not make its contribution to the experience, or actively detracts from it. The first step in judging a poem is to look closely at the poem to see whether it actually is what it purports to be—that is, to see whether the poet has made a structure of words that is equivalent to the experience he wishes to present.

What Does Little Birdie Say

What does little birdie say
In her nest at peep of day?
Let me fly, says little birdie,
Mother, let me fly away.
Birdie, rest a little longer,   5
Till the little wings are stronger.
So she rests a little longer,
Then she flies away.

What does little baby say,
In her bed at peep of day?   10
Baby says, like little birdie,
Let me rise and fly away.
Baby, sleep a little longer,
Till the little limbs are stronger.
If she sleeps a little longer,   15
Baby too shall fly away.

ALFRED, LORD TENNYSON
(from "Sea Dreams")

One wrong way to judge this poem would be to look at the signature and exclaim, "Ah, Tennyson! This must be a great poem because it's by a famous poet." A judgment founded merely on an author's name is no judgment at all, because it is a truism of literary history that even the greatest authors are not great all the time. If Homer sometimes nods and Shakespeare occasionally sleeps, Dryden, Wordsworth, and

Shelley frequently snore. An author's name is not necessarily a hall-mark.

Another procedure would be to look up the opinions of well-known literary critics and teachers and to accept their judgment as final. But this, too, is a wrong approach to the problem because critics and teachers are not infallible. Moreover, the sheep-like student who always accepts established opinions may earn good grades in certain kinds of literature courses, but he will never develop his own powers of discrimination.

Tennyson's poem itself must be examined to discover whether it actually is what it purports to be. A mother appears to be speaking, or perhaps singing, these words to a very small child. She is describing the experience of growing up by comparing the child to a little bird, which she calls a *birdie* because such baby talk is appropriate to the occasion. The simple diction and strictly regular meter are also appropriate because the listening child will understand the former and enjoy the latter. As a poem for a small child, this is a good one; if it were intended for adults, it would be insufferably bad because it oversimplifies and sentimentalizes the experience of growing up. But all the evidence suggests that Tennyson did not write the poem for adults, and therefore he was not trying to communicate an experience that would satisfy them.

The Night Has a Thousand Eyes

> The night has a thousand eyes,
>   And the day but one;
> Yet the light of the bright world dies
>   With the dying sun.
>
> The mind has a thousand eyes,   5
>   And the heart but one;
> Yet the light of a whole life dies
>   When love is done.

FRANCIS WILLIAM BOURDILLON

Although a reader can never know for certain what a poet's intentions were when he wrote a given poem, it seems likely that Bourdillon intended this poem for adults because it is about an adult experience: the end of a love affair. The questions to ask about this poem, then, are these: Does the poem communicate this experience? Does it tell, as exactly as words can tell, what falling out of love feels like? When love is done, the poet says, all light dies in a person's life. One could hardly object to this metaphorical overstatement except, perhaps, to say that it is trite. To support the metaphor, however, the poet develops an elaborate parallel between the way love goes out of a life and the way the sun goes out of the sky, leaving it dark for the stars. Look closely at this parallel. If seeing thousands of stars is a pleasant experience—and most people would find it so—the parallel is inappropriate because it contributes nothing to the unhappy experience that the poem is attempting to communicate. If the parallel is specious, the poem is a failure because it contains nothing except the parallel. Moreover, lines 5 and 6 seem to have no other function in the poem than to keep the parallel intact. Most readers, indeed, would prefer not to visualize a heart with an eye in it, even though the eye is about to go blind. This grotesquely anatomical image was apparently forced on the poet because he was determined to find something to correspond with the cliché *mind's eye*. When the devices of a poem assume control, as they do here, the result is invariably disastrous. This poem is bad because it does not do what it was designed to do: it fails to communicate an experience in such a way that the reader also has the experience.

At this point it might be well to forestall an objection that beginning readers sometimes make: "This poem may be bad, according to the strict standards of critical judgment, but it is so much better than any I could write that I admire it. Besides, I understand it." The first part of this remark confuses making and judging. Writing a good poem is indeed impossible for most people, but this fact does not justify a refusal to pass judgment. Only a very mad, or a very poor, or a very stingy man would say, "This egg may be rotten, but it's a better egg than I could lay, so I'll eat it and like it." As for understanding the poem, the reader who thinks that he does understand it has been deluded by its simple language. The individual words are clear enough, but they have been put together in such a way that they cannot be understood. An obscure poem is not necessarily profound; it may be merely confused.

EXERCISE 58

I Have a Rendezvous with Death

I have a rendezvous with Death
At some disputed barricade,
When Spring comes back with rustling shade
And apple-blossoms fill the air—
I have a rendezvous with Death   5
When Spring brings back blue days and fair.

It may be he shall take my hand
And lead me into his dark land
And close my eyes and quench my breath—
It may be I shall pass him still.   10
I have a rendezvous with Death
On some scarred slope of battered hill,
When Spring comes round again this year
And the first meadow-flowers appear.

God knows 'twere better to be deep   15
Pillowed in silk and scented down,
Where Love throbs out in blissful sleep,
Pulse nigh to pulse, and breath to breath,
Where hushed awakenings are dear . . .
But I've a rendezvous with Death   20
At midnight in some flaming town,
When Spring trips north again this year,
And I to my pledged word am true,
I shall not fail that rendezvous.

ALAN SEEGER

1. Identify the experience that the poet apparently is attempting to communicate.
2. How well does he communicate that experience? Do all the elements of the poem contribute to it? Specifically, what contribution is made by the descriptions of spring? By the scene in bed?
3. Are the details organized in such a way that the important parts of the experience are emphasized?

4. Is the fact that Seeger was killed in action on July 5, 1916, relevant to our judgment of the poem?

5. Compare the poem with the following. Does it present a more complete experience than Seeger's poem?

Death Stands above Me

Death stands above me, whispering low
I know not what into my ear:
Of his strange language all I know
Is, there is not a word of fear.

WALTER SAVAGE LANDOR

KINDS OF BAD POEMS

It is usually easier to say why a poem is bad than why a poem is good because every good poem is distinctly different from every other good one; bad poems, however, are likely to resemble each other in certain definite ways. In any bad poem the words are not equivalent to the experience. In sentimental poems, for instance, the words express more feeling than the experience warrants (see page 227). A second kind of badness results when a poet relies on another poet to furnish him with words, images, and structures. His poem, which uses an established set of conventions in a tame and unexciting way, is said to be **conventional.** Conventional poems are bad because they grow directly out of other poems rather than out of experiences. They abound because in every age a few poets use the conventions so supremely well that lesser poets cannot resist their influence. To detect this kind of badness, one needs considerable knowledge of literary history—unless the original poem and the derivative poem are juxtaposed. Then even the beginning reader can distinguish between the imitation and the original. A conventional poem is not the same as a **parody,** which imitates an original poem by applying its meter and language to a different—usually trivial or absurd—subject.

A third kind of bad poem simply fails to communicate an experience. There are many reasons for this kind of failure. A poem may, for instance, be excessively didactic and prosaic.

> Love virtue; avoid all temptations;
>   Be humble and meek and sincere;
> Walk upright in all situations;
>   To God then you'll always be dear.

This quatrain is too platitudinous and too general to convey any experience. However much a reader may agree with the advice it gives, he must call it a bad poem because advice of this sort is much better given in prose, in a sermon or an inspirational talk. A poem will also not communicate an experience if all or most of its images and figures are intelligible only to the poet himself and perhaps to a few of his friends and admirers.

> The fantods of the evening bilked the slipper?
> maribou. Maribou.   maribou rudesby
> Swash. out, exegete.
> Mephitic quadrumanes in mine rixa. . . . fap!

Obviously an extreme case of a poetaster mumbling to himself.

Finally, there are empty and windy poems in which the amount of experience is in inverse proportion to the number of words.

> The Sea!!   The Sea!! Sea! Sea! Sea!!!
> Water! Waves! Wind! Fish!
> Boats! Sun!
> Sea!

A reader should expect a poem to concentrate experience rather than dilute it.

EXERCISE 59

Among the following, distinguish the good poems from the bad. Explain in what particular way a given poem is bad.

Virtue

> Sweet day, so cool, so calm, so bright,
> The bridal of the earth and sky:
> The dew shall weep thy fall tonight,
>   For thou must die.

Sweet rose, whose hue, angry and brave,   5
Bids the rash gazer wipe his eye:
Thy root is ever in its grave,
    And thou must die.

Sweet spring, full of sweet days and roses,
A box where sweets compacted lie;   10
My music shows ye have your closes,
    And all must die

Only a sweet and virtuous soul,
Like seasoned timber, never gives;
But though the whole world turn to coal,   15
    Then chiefly lives.

GEORGE HERBERT

closes (11): cadences.

Thus Passeth

Oh Nature! World! Oh Life! Oh Time!
Why aren't you always in your prime?
Why doesn't summer always stay?
Why aren't the flowers always gay?
Why is love's song so short a tune?   5
Why isn't January June?
I sigh to see all young girls grow
Older and older, their hair like snow.
All things on earth thus pass away:
Nothing save virtue lasts for aye.   10

ANONYMOUS
(*Twentieth Century*)

Simple Nature

Be it not mine to steal the cultured flower
    From any garden of the rich and great,
Nor seek with care, through many a weary hour,
    Some novel form of wonder to create.

Enough for me the leafy woods to rove,   5
  And gather simple cups of morning dew,
Or, in the fields and meadows that I love,
  Find beauty in their bells of every hue.
Thus round my cottage floats a fragrant air,
  And though the rustic plot be humbly laid,   10
Yet, like the lilies gladly growing there,
  I have not toil'd, but take what God has made.
    My Lord Ambition pass'd, and smiled in scorn;
    I plucked a rose, and lo! it had no thorn.

GEORGE JOHN ROMANES

The World Is Too Much with Us

The world is too much with us; late and soon,
Getting and spending, we lay waste our powers:
Little we see in Nature that is ours;
We have given our hearts away, a sordid boon!
This Sea that bares her bosom to the moon;   5
The winds that will be howling at all hours,
And are up-gathered now like sleeping flowers;
For this, for everything, we are out of tune;
It moves us not.—Great God! I'd rather be
A Pagan suckled in a creed outworn;   10
So might I, standing on this pleasant lea,
Have glimpses that would make me less forlorn;
Have sight of Proteus rising from the sea;
Or hear old Triton blow his wreathèd horn.

WILLIAM WORDSWORTH

God's World

O world I cannot hold thee close enough!
  Thy winds, thy wide grey skies!
  Thy mists, that roll and rise!
Thy woods, this autumn day, that ache and sag
And all but cry with colour! That gaunt crag   5
To crush! To lift the lean of that black bluff!

World, World, I cannot get thee close enough!
Long have I known a glory in it all,
   But never knew I this:
   Here such a passion is   10
As stretcheth me apart,—Lord, I do fear
Thou'st made the world too beautiful this year;
My soul is all but out of me,—let fall
No burning leaf; prithee, let no bird call.

EDNA ST. VINCENT MILLAY

God's Grandeur

The world is charged with the grandeur of God.
   It will flame out, like shining from shook foil;
   It gathers to a greatness, like the ooze of oil
Crushed. Why do men then now not reck his rod?
Generations have trod, have trod, have trod;   5
   And all is seared with trade; bleared, smeared with toil;
   And wears man's smudge and shares man's smell: the soil
Is bare now, nor can foot feel, being shod.

And for all this, nature is never spent;
   There lives the dearest freshness deep down things;   10
And though the last lights off the black West went
   Oh, morning, at the brown brink eastward, springs—
Because the Holy Ghost over the bent
   World broods with warm breast and with ah! bright wings.

GERARD MANLEY HOPKINS

On a Faded Violet

The odour from the flower is gone
   Which like thy kisses breathed on me;
The colour from the flower is flown
   Which glowed on thee and only thee!

A shrivelled, lifeless, vacant form,   5
   It lies on my abandoned breast,
And mocks the heart which yet is warm,
   With cold and silent rest.

I weep,—my tears revive it not!
I sigh,—it breathes no more on me;   10
Its mute and uncomplaining lot
Is such as mine should be.

PERCY BYSSHE SHELLEY

LIKING AND JUDGING

Although a reader cannot reasonably expect a poem to corroborate his own personal view of life, he will be more likely to respond favorably to one that does than to one that does not. The former kind of poem will automatically seem better to him than the latter, but it is dangerous for him to assume that it *is* better. This assumption not only confuses liking and judging, but it misapplies to a poem the standards that are properly applied in judging persuasive writings—editorials, political talks, religious tracts, and the like. A judge who condemns a poem because he does not agree with its idea is not judging the poem as a poem. In fact, he is ignoring the poem and judging it as though it were a prose paraphrase of itself. Good poems communicate experience, not propaganda. Protestants can admire the *Divine Comedy,* Catholics *Paradise Lost,* and both the *Iliad.*

In judging a poem, it is well to ignore two questions at the outset: "Do I agree with the ideas?" "Do I like the poem?" The reader who attempts to answer these questions too early is likely to ignore the poem and to concentrate instead on himself and his own ideas. If he postpones answering these questions until he has fully considered the poem as a poem, he may find himself liking the poem and agreeing with its ideas because he understands it better than when he first read it. On the other hand, the analysis may confirm his dislike of the poem, and if it does, he must never pretend that he likes the poem merely because he thinks that he should like it, or because his teacher expects him to. Hypocritical admiration has no place in the study of poems or anything else because it circumvents the aim of all study, which is to cultivate genuine admiration of excellence. Whether or not a reader likes a poem frequently depends on the variety, number, and depth of his experiences in both literature and life. A student who dislikes a certain poem may, if he does not shut his mind against it, come to like it when he has lived longer and read more. On the other hand, he may never like the poem, because no one likes all poems, even all good poems.

EXERCISE 60

1. Judge these two poems as poems. Then decide which "philosophy of life" you prefer, and try to explain why.

Dover Beach

The sea is calm to-night.
The tide is full, the moon lies fair
Upon the straits;—on the French coast the light
Gleams and is gone; the cliffs of England stand,
Glimmering and vast, out in the tranquil bay.   5
Come to the window, sweet is the night-air!
Only, from the long line of spray
Where the sea meets the moon-blanch'd land,
Listen! you hear the grating roar
Of pebbles which the waves draw back, and fling,   10
At their return, up the high strand,
Begin, and cease, and then again begin,
With tremulous cadence slow, and bring
The eternal note of sadness in.

Sophocles long ago   15
Heard it on the Ægean, and it brought
Into his mind the turbid ebb and flow
Of human misery; we
Find also in the sound a thought,
Hearing it by this distant northern sea.   20

The Sea of Faith
Was once, too, at the full, and round earth's shore
Lay like the folds of a bright girdle furl'd.
But now I only hear
Its melancholy, long, withdrawing roar,   25
Retreating, to the breath
Of the night-wind, down the vast edges drear
And naked shingles of the world.

Ah, love, let us be true
To one another! for the world, which seems   30
To lie before us like a land of dreams,
So various, so beautiful, so new,

Hath really neither joy, nor love, nor light,
Nor certitude, nor peace, nor help for pain;
And we are here as on a darkling plain   35
Swept with confused alarms of struggle and flight,
Where ignorant armies clash by night.

MATTHEW ARNOLD

Say Not the Struggle Nought Availeth

Say not the struggle nought availeth,
   The labour and the wounds are vain,
The enemy faints not, nor faileth,
   And as things have been, things remain.

If hopes were dupes, fears may be liars;   5
   It may be, in yon smoke concealed,
Your comrades chase e'en now the fliers,
   And, but for you, possess the field.

For while the tired waves, vainly breaking,
   Seem here no painful inch to gain,   10
Far back through creeks and inlets making
   Came, silent, flooding in, the main,

And not by eastern windows only,
   When daylight comes, comes in the light,
In front the sun climbs slow, how slowly,   15
   But westward, look, the land is bright.

ARTHUR HUGH CLOUGH

2. Do the same for these two poems.

Dust of Snow

The way a crow
Shook down on me
The dust of snow
From a hemlock tree

Has given my heart   5
A change of mood
And saved some part
Of a day I had rued.

ROBERT FROST

In the Pauper's Turnip-Field

Crow, in pulpit lone and tall
Of yon charred hemlock, grimly dead,
Why on me in preachment call—
Me, by nearer preachment led
Here in homily of my hoe.   5
The hoe, the hoe,
My heavy hoe
That earthward bows me to foreshow
A mattock heavier than the hoe.

HERMAN MELVILLE

THE BEST POEMS

In every age bad poems are more numerous than good because the ability to write good ones is rare, and the demand for bad ones is high. Fortunately bad poems, like other consumer-goods, are perishable. The bits of verse that fill the odd corners of a newspaper are soon forgotten, along with the advertisements for shirts and cabbages and the lists of television programs. Good poems, in contrast, do not wear out; they are among the most enduring products of the human mind. A good poem lasts in two ways: for the individual reader, and for the whole reading public. The individual cannot exhaust it in one reading, or even in many readings. Throughout his life he can return to the poem and find new things in it. The echoes that it sets up in his mind will reverberate at the most unlikely times and places. It will change his way of looking at the world, because it will give him an experience that he might otherwise never have had. A good poem also outlives the individual reader, and it will last as long as its language is known or studied. Regardless of its age, a good poem has something to say because it focuses on what is permanent in human life. Time, then, is one of the best judges of a poem.

A good poem effectively renders an experience. The best poems, as distinct from the merely good ones, render a *significant* experience and render it fully. They give final form to an experience that really matters to human beings. They are likely to be somewhat complex, for they treat the most complex matter in the world: man—as a spiritual, physical, moral, and intellectual being. The best poems thus embody a kind of wisdom about the whole man that differs from the specialized knowledge available in treatises on psychology, religion, ethics, medicine, government, and so on. Since poets and other creators of literature look at man as a whole, they have one of the most important functions in life. By defining our experiences, they tell us what we are.

EXERCISE 61

Many discriminating readers have admired these poems. Analyze them to see whether you can discover why.

A Song

Ask me no more where Jove bestows,
When June is past, the fading rose:
For in your beauty's orient deep,
These flowers, as in their causes, sleep.

Ask me no more whither doth stray   5
The golden atoms of the day:
For in pure love heaven did prepare
Those powders to enrich your hair.

Ask me no more whither doth haste
The nightingale, when May is past: 10
For in your sweet dividing throat
She winters, and keeps warm her note.

Ask me no more where those stars light,
That downwards fall in dead of night:
For in your eyes they sit, and there   15
Fixèd become as in their sphere.

Ask me no more if east or west
The phoenix builds her spicy nest:
For unto you at last she flies,
And in your fragrant bosom dies.   20

THOMAS CAREW

causes (4): essence.   sweet dividing (11): melodiously trilling.

Sonnet 116

Let me not to the marriage of true minds
Admit impediments. Love is not love
Which alters when it alteration finds,
Or bends with the remover to remove.
O, no! it is an ever-fixèd mark,   5
That looks on tempests and is never shaken;
It is the star to every wandering bark,
Whose worth's unknown, although his height be taken.
Love's not Time's fool, though rosy lips and cheeks
Within his bending sickle's compass come;   10
Love alters not with his brief hours and weeks,
But bears it out even to the edge of doom.
    If this be error and upon me proved,
    I never writ, nor no man ever loved.

WILLIAM SHAKESPEARE

mark (5): beacon.   unknown (8): unknowable.   height (8):
altitude.   bears it out (12): endures.

Tithonus

The woods decay, the woods decay and fall,
The vapours weep their burthen to the ground,
Man comes and tills the field and lies beneath,
And after many a summer dies the swan.
Me only cruel immortality   5
Consumes: I wither slowly in thine arms,
Here at the quiet limit of the world,

A white-hair'd shadow roaming like a dream
The ever-silent spaces of the East,
Far-folded mists, and gleaming halls of morn.   10

    Alas! for this gray shadow, once a man—
So glorious in his beauty and thy choice,
Who madest him thy chosen, that he seem'd
To his great heart none other than a God!
I ask'd thee, "Give me immortality."   15
Then didst thou grant mine asking with a smile,
Like wealthy men who care not how they give.
But thy strong Hours indignant work'd their wills,
And beat me down and marr'd and wasted me,
And tho' they could not end me, left me maim'd   20
To dwell in presence of immortal youth,
Immortal age beside immortal youth,
And all I was, in ashes. Can thy love,
Thy beauty, make amends, tho' even now
Close over us, the silver star, thy guide,   25
Shines in those tremulous eyes that fill with tears
To hear me? Let me go: take back thy gift:
Why should a man desire in any way
To vary from the kindly race of men,
Or pass beyond the goal of ordinance   30
Where all should pause, as is most meet for all?

    A soft air fans the cloud apart: there comes
A glimpse of that dark world where I was born.
Once more the old mysterious glimmer steals
From thy pure brows, and from thy shoulders pure,   35
And bosom beating with a heart renew'd.
Thy cheek begins to redden thro' the gloom,
Thy sweet eyes brighten slowly close to mine,
Ere yet they blind the stars, and the wild team
Which love thee, yearning for thy yoke, arise,   40
And shake the darkness from their loosen'd manes,
And beat the twilight into flakes of fire.

    Lo! ever thus thou growest beautiful
In silence, then before thine answer given
Departest, and thy tears are on my cheek.   45

Why wilt thou ever scare me with thy tears,
And make me tremble lest a saying learnt,
In days far-off, on that dark earth, be true?
"The Gods themselves cannot recall their gifts."

Ay me! ay me! with what another heart   50
In days far-off, and with what other eyes
I used to watch—if I be he that watch'd—
The lucid outline forming round thee; saw
The dim curls kindle into sunny rings;
Changed with thy mystic change, and felt my blood   55
Glow with the glow that slowly crimson'd all
Thy presence and thy portals, while I lay,
Mouth, forehead, eyelids, growing dewy-warm
With kisses balmier than half-opening buds
Of April, and could hear the lips that kiss'd   60
Whispering I knew not what of wild and sweet,
Like that strange song I heard Apollo sing,
While Ilion like a mist rose into towers.

Yet hold me not for ever in thine East:
How can my nature longer mix with thine?   65
Coldly thy rosy shadows bathe me, cold
Are all thy lights, and cold my wrinkled feet
Upon thy glimmering thresholds, when the steam
Floats up from those dim fields about the homes
Of happy men that have the power to die,   70
And grassy barrows of the happier dead.
Release me, and restore me to the ground;
Thou seëst all things, thou wilt see my grave:
Thou wilt renew thy beauty morn by morn;
I earth in earth forget these empty courts,   75
And thee returning on thy silver wheels.

ALFRED, LORD TENNYSON

Title: In Greek mythology, Eos (Aurora, the dawn) so loved
Tithonus that she gave him immortality, but not eternal
youth. Here Tithonus speaks to Eos. star (25): the morning
star. kindly (29): natural. Ilion (63): Troy, whose walls
were built by Apollo's music.

The Death of a Toad

A toad the power mower caught,
Chewed and clipped of a leg, with a hobbling hop has got
  To the garden verge, and sanctuaried him
  Under the cineraria leaves, in the shade
    Of the ashen heartshaped leaves, in a dim,   5
      Low, and a final glade.

  The rare original heartsblood goes,
Spends on the earthen hide, in the folds and wizenings, flows
  In the gutters of the banked and staring eyes. He lies
  As still as if he would return to stone,   10
    And soundlessly attending, dies
      Toward some deep monotone,

  Toward misted and ebullient seas
And cooling shores, toward lost Amphibia's emperies.
  Day dwindles, drowning, and at length is gone   15
  In the wide and antique eyes, which still appear
    To watch, across the castrate lawn,
      The haggard daylight steer.

RICHARD WILBUR

So We'll Go No More A-Roving

So we'll go no more a-roving
  So late into the night,
Though the heart be still as loving,
  And the moon be still as bright.

For the sword outwears its sheath,   5
  And the soul wears out the breast,
And the heart must pause to breathe,
  And love itself have rest.

Though the night was made for loving,
  And the day returns too soon,   10
Yet we'll go no more a-roving
  By the light of the moon.

GEORGE GORDON, LORD BYRON

To a Friend Whose Work Has Come to Nothing

Now all the truth is out,
Be secret and take defeat
From any brazen throat,
For how can you compete,
Being honour bred, with one   5
Who, were it proved he lies,
Were neither shamed in his own
Nor in his neighbours' eyes?
Bred to a harder thing
Than Triumph, turn away   10
And like a laughing string
Whereon mad fingers play
Amid a place of stone,
Be secret and exult,
Because of all things known   15
That is most difficult.

WILLIAM BUTLER YEATS

The Onset

Always the same, when on a fated night
At last the gathered snow lets down as white
As may be in dark woods, and with a song
It shall not make again all winter long
Of hissing on the yet uncovered ground,   5
I almost stumble looking up and round,
As one who overtaken by the end
Gives up his errand, and lets death descend
Upon him where he is, with nothing done
To evil, no important triumph won,   10
More than if life had never been begun.

Yet all the precedent is on my side:
I know that winter death has never tried
The earth but it has failed: the snow may heap
In long storms an undrifted four feet deep   15
As measured against maple, birch, and oak,

It cannot check the peeper's silver croak;
And I shall see the snow all go down hill
In water of a slender April rill
That flashes tail through last year's withered brake   20
And dead weeds, like a disappearing snake.
Nothing will be left white but here a birch,
And there a clump of houses with a church.

ROBERT FROST

PART

TWO

POEMS

FOR

COMPARISON

GROUP 1

The Three Ravens

There were three ravens sat on a tree,
  Downe a downe, hay downe, hay downe.
There were three ravens sat on a tree,
  With a downe.
There were three ravens sat on a tree,   5
They were as blacke as they might be.
  With a downe derrie, derrie, derrrie,
    downe, downe.

The one of them said to his mate,
"Where shall we our breakefast take?"

"Downe in yonder greene field,   10
There lies a knight slain under his shield.

"His hounds they lie downe at his feete,
So well they can their master keepe.

"His haukes they flie so eagerly,
There's no fowle dare him come nie."   15

Downe there comes a fallow doe,
As great with yong as she might goe.

She lift up his bloudy hed,
And kist his wounds that were so red.

She got him up upon her backe,   20
And carried him to earthen lake.

She buried him before the prime,
She was dead herselfe ere even-song time.

God send every gentleman
Such haukes, such hounds, and such a leman.   25

ANONYMOUS

Downe, etc. (2): refrain, to be repeated in each stanza. **Nie**
(15): nigh. **yong** (17): young. **lake** (21): pit. **prime** (22):
6 A.M. **leman** (25): beloved lady.

The Twa Corbies

As I was walking all alane,
I heard twa corbies making a mane;
The tane unto the t'other say,
"Where sall we gang and dine to-day?"

"In behint yon auld fail dyke,   5
I wot there lies a new slain knight;
And naebody kens that he lies there,
But his hawk, his hound, and lady fair.

"His hound is to the hunting gane,
His hawk to fetch the wild-fowl hame,   10
His lady's ta'en another mate,
So we may mak our dinner sweet.

"Ye'll sit on his white hause-bane,
And I'll pike out his bonny blue een;
With ae lock o his gowden hair   15
We'll theek our nest when it grows bare.

"Mony a one for him makes mane,
But nane sall ken where he is gane;
O'er his white banes, when they are bare,
The wind sall blaw for evermair."   20

ANONYMOUS

Title: "The Two Ravens." **alane** (1): alone. **mane** (2):
moan. **tane** (3): one. **sall** (4): shall. **gang** (4): go. **auld
fail dyke** (5): old turf wall. **hause-bane** (13): neck bone.
pike (14): pick. **een** (14): eyes. **ae** (15): one. **gowden**
(15): golden. **theek** (16): thatch.

GROUP 2

Stopping by Woods on a Snowy Evening

Whose woods these are I think I know.
His house is in the village though;
He will not see me stopping here
To watch his woods fill up with snow.

My little horse must think it queer   5
To stop without a farmhouse near
Between the woods and frozen lake
The darkest evening of the year.

He gives his harness bells a shake
To ask if there is some mistake.   10
The only other sound's the sweep
Of easy wind and downy flake.

The woods are lovely, dark and deep.
But I have promises to keep,
And miles to go before I sleep,   15
And miles to go before I sleep.

                                ROBERT FROST

Loveliest of Trees

Loveliest of trees, the cherry now
Is hung with bloom along the bough,
And stands about the woodland ride
Wearing white for Eastertide.

Now, of my threescore years and ten,   5
Twenty will not come again,
And take from seventy springs a score,
It only leaves me fifty more.

And since to look at things in bloom
Fifty springs are little room,   10
About the woodlands I will go
To see the cherry hung with snow.

                        A. E. HOUSMAN

GROUP 3

The Passionate Shepherd to His Love

Come live with me and be my love,
And we will all the pleasures prove
That valleys, groves, hills, and fields,
Woods, or steepy mountain yields.

And we will sit upon the rocks,   5
Seeing the shepherds feed their flocks
By shallow rivers, to whose falls
Melodious birds sing madrigals.

And I will make thee beds of roses
And a thousand fragrant posies,   10
A cap of flowers and a kirtle
Embroidered all with leaves of myrtle;

A gown made of the finest wool
Which from our pretty lambs we pull;
Fair-linèd slippers for the cold,   15
With buckles of the purest gold;

A belt of straw and ivy buds,
With coral clasps and amber studs.
And if these pleasures may thee move,
Come live with me and be my love.   20

The shepherd swains shall dance and sing
For thy delight each May morning.
If these delights thy mind may move,
Then live with me and be my love.

CHRISTOPHER MARLOWE

The Nymph's Reply to the Shepherd

If all the world and love were young,
And truth in every shepherd's tongue,
These pretty pleasures might me move
To live with thee and be thy love.

Time drives the flocks from field to fold,   5
When rivers rage and rocks grow cold,
And Philomel becometh dumb;
The rest complains of cares to come.

The flowers do fade, and wanton fields
To wayward winter reckoning yields.   10
A honey tongue, a heart of gall,
Is fancy's spring, but sorrow's fall.

Thy gowns, thy shoes, thy beds of roses,
Thy cap, thy kirtle, and thy posies
Soon break, soon wither, soon forgotten: 15
In folly ripe, in reason rotten.

Thy belt of straw and ivy buds,
Thy coral clasps and amber studs,
All these in me no means can move
To come to thee and be thy love.   20

But could youth last and love still breed,
Had joys no date nor age no need,
Then these delights my mind might move
To live with thee and be thy love.

                              SIR WALTER RALEGH

Philomel (7): Philomela.

The Bait

Come live with me and be my love,
And we will some new pleasures prove,
Of golden sands and crystal brooks,
With silken lines and silver hooks.

There will the river whispering run,   5
Warmed by thy eyes more than the sun;
And there the enamored fish will stay,
Begging themselves they may betray.

When thou wilt swim in that live bath,
Each fish, which every channel hath,   10
Will amorously to thee swim,
Gladder to catch thee, than thou him.

If thou to be so seen beest loath,
By sun or moon, thou darkenest both;
And if myself have leave to see,   15
I need not their light, having thee.

Let others freeze with angling reeds,
And cut their legs with shells and weeds,
Or treacherously poor fish beset
With strangling snare or windowy net.   20

Let coarse bold hands from slimy nest
The bedded fish in banks out-wrest,
Or curious traitors, sleave-silk flies,
Bewitch poor fishes' wandering eyes.

For thee, thou need'st no such deceit,   25
For thou thyself art thine own bait;
That fish that is not catched thereby,
Alas, is wiser far than I.

JOHN DONNE

Love's Hopefulness

He stands outside the fast-barred door
In lowly patience evermore,
Crying and crying, "Shame my dear,
Thrice shame to keep me standing here;
For I can send a feathery fire   5
Straight to the heart of your desire;
Transfix your vacillating soul
And burn your will to make you whole."

"As seas conceal huge hidden treasures
So in your murky deeps lie pleasures.   10
You drive like some hot tempest wind
Through foaming seas my bobbing mind;
Uncharted shoals surround my bark,
I fear destruction in your dark;
You toss me over heaving slopes   15
And fire my will to drown my hopes."

"Then damn your tears and love me well:
Though lost we are, we'll love in hell.
We'll lie on banks of ember flowers,
And heap up coals in pretty bowers;   20
Around us sooty imps will wing,
The ghost of Orpheus will sing,
And I will bathe your burning thigh
In sluggish Lethe sliding by,
And devils themselves in hellish bliss   25
Will roast above our blazing kiss;
And hell and heaven will cease to war
If you will but unbar the door."

O. B. HARDISON, JR.

GROUP 4

La Belle Dame sans Merci

O what can ail thee, knight-at-arms,
    Alone and palely loitering?
The sedge has wither'd from the lake,
    And no birds sing.

O what can ail thee, knight-at-arms,   5
    So haggard and so woe-begone?
The squirrel's granary is full,
    And the harvest's done.

I see a lilly on thy brow,
    With anguish moist and fever dew,   10
And on thy cheeks a fading rose
    Fast withereth too.

I met a lady in the meads,
    Full beautiful—a faery's child,
Her hair was long, her foot was light,   15
    And her eyes were wild.

I made a garland for her head,
    And bracelets too, and fragrant zone;
She look'd at me as she did love,
    And made sweet moan.   20

I set her on my pacing steed,
    And nothing else saw all day long,
For sidelong would she bend, and sing
    A faery's song.

She found me roots of relish sweet,   25
    And honey wild, and manna dew,
And sure in language strange she said—
    'I love thee true.'

She took me to her elfin grot,
    And there she wept, and sigh'd full sore,   30
And there I shut her wild wild eyes
    With kisses four.

And there she lulled me asleep,
    And there I dream'd—Ah! woe betide!
The latest dream I ever dream'd   35
    On the cold hill side.

I saw pale kings and princes too,
   Pale warriors, death-pale were they all;
They cried—'La Belle Dame sans Merci
   Hath thee in thrall!'   40

I saw their starved lips in the gloam,
   With horrid warning gaped wide,
And I awoke and found me here,
   On the cold hill's side.

And this is why I sojourn here,   45
   Alone and palely loitering,
Though the sedge has wither'd from the lake,
   And no birds sing.

JOHN KEATS

Title: "The Beautiful, Pitiless Lady."

The Harlot's House

We caught the tread of dancing feet,
We loitered down the moonlit street,
And stopped beneath the harlot's house.

Inside, above the din and fray,
We heard the loud musicians play   5
The 'Treues Liebes Herz' of Strauss.

Like strange mechanical grotesques,
Making fantastic arabesques,
The shadows raced across the blind.

We watched the ghostly dancers spin   10
To sound of horn and violin,
Like black leaves wheeling in the wind.

Like wire-pulled automatons,
Slim silhouetted skeletons
Went sidling through the slow quadrille.   15

They took each other by the hand,
And danced a stately saraband;
Their laughter echoed thin and shrill.

Sometimes a clockwork puppet pressed
A phantom lover to her breast,   20
Sometimes they seemed to try to sing.

Sometimes a horrible marionette
Came out, and smoked its cigarette
Upon the steps like a live thing.

Then, turning to my love, I said,   25
"The dead are dancing with the dead,
The dust is whirling with the dust."

But she—she heard the violin,
And left my side, and entered in:
Love passed into the house of lust.   30

Then suddenly the tune went false,
The dancers wearied of the waltz,
The shadows ceased to wheel and whirl.

And down the long and silent street,
The dawn, with silver-sandalled feet,   35
Crept like a frightened girl.

OSCAR WILDE

Treues Liebes Herz (6): "True Love's Heart"

GROUP 5

To an Athlete Dying Young

The time you won your town the race
We chaired you through the market-place;
Man and boy stood cheering by,
And home we brought you shoulder-high.

To-day, the road all runners come,   5
Shoulder-high we bring you home,
And set you at your threshold down,
Townsman of a stiller town.

Smart lad, to slip betimes away
From fields where glory does not stay   .   10
And early though the laurel grows
It withers quicker than the rose.

Eyes the shady night has shut
Cannot see the record cut,
And silence sounds no worse than cheers   15
After earth has stopped the ears:

Now you will not swell the rout
Of lads that wore their honours out,
Runners whom renown outran
And the name died before the man.   20

So set, before its echoes fade,
The fleet foot on the sill of shade,
And hold to the low lintel up
The still-defended challenge-cup.

And round that early-laurelled head   25
Will flock to gaze the strengthless dead.
And find unwithered on its curls
The garland briefer than a girl's.

A. E. HOUSMAN

Some Wretched Creature, Savior, Take

Some Wretched creature, savior take
Who would exult to die
And leave for thy sweet mercy's sake
Another Hour to me

EMILY DICKINSON

GROUP 6

During Wind and Rain

They sing their dearest songs—
He, she, all of them—yea,
Treble and tenor and bass,
   And one to play;
With the candles mooning each face. . . .   5
   Ah, no; the years O!
How the sick leaves reel down in throngs!

They clear the creeping moss—
Elders and juniors—aye,
Making the pathways neat   10
   And the garden gay;
And they build a shady seat. . . .
   Ah, no; the years, the years;
See, the white storm-birds wing across!

They are blithely breakfasting all—   15
Men and maidens—yea,
Under the summer tree,
   With a glimpse of the bay,
While pet fowl come to the knee. . . .
   Ah, no; the years O!   20
And the rotten rose is ript from the wall.

They change to a high new house,
He, she, all of them—aye,
Clocks and carpets and chairs
   On the lawn all day,   25
And brightest things that are theirs. . . .
   Ah, no; the years, the years;
Down their carved names the rain-drop ploughs.

THOMAS HARDY

The Tide Rises, the Tide Falls

The tide rises, the tide falls,
The twilight darkens, the curlew calls;
Along the sea-sands damp and brown
The traveller hastens toward the town,
   And the tide rises, the tide falls.   5

Darkness settles on roofs and walls,
But the sea, the sea in the darkness calls;
The little waves, with their soft, white hands,
Efface the footprints in the sands,
   And the tide rises, the tide falls.   10

The morning breaks; the steeds in their stalls
Stamp and neigh, as the hostler calls;
The day returns, but nevermore
Returns the traveller to the shore,
   And the tide rises, the tide falls.   15

HENRY WADSWORTH LONGFELLOW

GROUP 7

Meeting at Night

The gray sea and the long black land;
And the yellow half-moon large and low;
And the startled little waves that leap
In fiery ringlets from their sleep,
As I gain the cove with pushing prow,   5
And quench its speed i' the slushy sand.

Then a mile of warm sea-scented beach;
Three fields to cross till a farm appears;
A tap at the pane, the quick sharp scratch
And blue spurt of a lighted match,   10
And a voice less loud, through its joys and fears,
Than the two hearts beating each to each!

ROBERT BROWNING

Parting at Morning

Round the cape of a sudden came the sea,
And the sun looked over the mountain's rim:
And straight was a path of gold for him,
And the need of a world of men for me.

ROBERT BROWNING

GROUP 8

The Two Deserts

    Not greatly moved with awe am I
To learn that we may spy
Five thousand firmaments beyond our own.
The best that's known
Of the heavenly bodies does them credit small.   5
View'd close, the Moon's fair ball
Is of ill objects worst,
A corpse in Night's highway, naked, fire-scarr'd, accurst;
And now they tell
That the Sun is plainly seen to boil and burst   10
Too horribly for hell.
So, judging from these two,
As we must do,
The Universe, outside our living Earth,
Was all conceiv'd in the Creator's mirth,   15
Forecasting at the time Man's spirit deep,
To make dirt cheap.

Put by the Telescope!
Better without it man may see,
Stretch'd awful in the hush'd midnight,   20
The ghost of his eternity.
Give me the nobler glass that swells to the eye
The things which near us lie,
Till Science rapturously hails,
In the minutest water-drop,   25
A torment of innumerable tails.
These at the least do live.
But rather give
A mind not much to pry
Beyond our royal-fair estate   30
Betwixt these deserts blank of small and great.
Wonder and beauty our own courtiers are,
Pressing to catch our gaze,
And out of obvious ways
Ne'er wandering far.   35

COVENTRY PATMORE

Desert Places

Snow falling and night falling fast oh fast
In a field I looked into going past,
And the ground almost covered smooth in snow,
But a few weeds and stubble showing last.

The woods around it have it—it is theirs.   5
All animals are smothered in their lairs.
I am too absent-spirited to count;
The loneliness includes me unawares.

And lonely as it is that loneliness
Will be more lonely ere it will be less—   10
A blanker whiteness of benighted snow
With no expression, nothing to express.

They cannot scare me with their empty spaces
Between stars—on stars where no human race is.
I have it in me so much nearer home   15
To scare myself with my own desert places.

                              ROBERT FROST

GROUP 9

Days

Daughters of Time, the hypocritic Days,
Muffled and dumb like barefoot dervishes,
And marching single in an endless file,
Bring diadems and fagots in their hands.
To each they offer gifts after his will,   5
Bread, kingdoms, stars, and sky that holds them all.
I, in my pleached garden, watched the pomp,
Forgot my morning wishes, hastily
Took a few herbs and apples, and the Day
Turned and departed silent. I, too late,   10
Under her solemn fillet saw the scorn.

RALPH WALDO EMERSON

hypocritic (1): playing a part.   pleached (7): with boughs in-
tertwined.

Today

So here hath been dawning
Another blue Day:
Think wilt thou let it
Slip useless away.

Out of Eternity   5
This new Day is born;
Into Eternity,
At night, will return.

Behold it aforetime
No eye ever did: 10
So soon it forever
From all eyes is hid.

Here hath been dawning
Another blue Day:
Think wilt thou let it   15
Slip useless away.

THOMAS CARLYLE

GROUP 10

Sonnet 129

The expense of spirit in a waste of shame
Is lust in action; and, till action, lust
Is perjured, murderous, bloody, full of blame,
Savage, extreme, rude, cruel, not to trust;
Enjoyed no sooner but despisèd straight;   5
Past reason hunted, and no sooner had,
Past reason hated, as a swallowed bait
On purpose laid to make the taker mad;
Mad in pursuit, and in possession so;
Had, having, and in quest to have, extreme;   10
A bliss in proof—and proved, a very woe;
Before, a joy proposed; behind, a dream.
    All this the world well knows; yet none knows well
    To shun the heaven that leads men to this hell.

WILLIAM SHAKESPEARE

spirit (1): vitality.   to trust (4) to be trusted.

Abstinence Sows Sand All Over

Abstinence sows sand all over
The ruddy limbs and flaming hair,
But Desire Gratified
Plants fruits of life and beauty there.

WILLIAM BLAKE

Doing a Filthy Pleasure Is

Doing a filthy pleasure is, and short;
And done, we straight repent us of the sport.
Let us not, then, rush blindly on unto it
Like lustful beasts, that only know to do it,
For lust will languish, and that heat decay.   5
But thus, thus, keeping endless holiday,
Let us together closely lie, and kiss;
There is no labor, nor no shame in this.
This hath pleased, doth please, and long will please; never
Can this decay, but is beginning ever.   10

BEN JONSON

GROUP 11

Plot Improbable, Character Unsympathetic

I was born in a bad slum
Where no one had to die
To show his skeleton.
The wind came through the walls,
A three-legged rat and I   5
Fought all day for swill.
My father was crazed, my mother cruel
My brothers chopped the stairs for fuel,
I tumbled my sisters in a broken bed
And jiggled them till all were dead.   10
Then I ran away and lived with my lice
On my wits, a knife, and a pair of dice,
Slept like a rat in the river reeds,
Got converted fifty times
To fifty different creeds   15
For bowls of mission broth,
Till I killed the grocer and his wife
With a stove-poker and a butcher-knife.
The mayor said, Hang him high,
The merchants said, He won't buy or sell,   20
The bishop said, He won't pay to pray.
They flung me into a jail,
But I, I broke out,
Beat my bars to a bell,
Ran all around the town   25
Dingling my sweet bell,
And the mayor wanted it for his hall,
The merchants wanted to buy it,
The bishop wanted it for his church,
But I broke my bell in two,   30
Of one half a huge bullet made,
Of the other an enormous gun,
Took all the people of all the world
And rolled them into one,

And when the World went by   35
With a monocle in his eye,
With a silk hat on his head,
Took aim and shot him dead.

                          ELDER OLSON

Infant Sorrow

My mother groan'd, my father wept;
Into the dangerous world I leapt,
Helpless, naked, piping loud,
Like a fiend hid in a cloud.

Struggling in my father's hands   5
Striving against my swaddling bands,
Bound & weary, I thought best
To sulk upon my mother's breast.

When I saw that rage was vain,
And to sulk would nothing gain,   10
Turning many a trick & wile,
I began to soothe & smile.

And I sooth'd day after day
Till upon the ground I stray;
And I smil'd night after night,   15
Seeking only for delight.

And I saw before me shine
Clusters of the wand'ring vine,
And many a lovely flower & tree
Stretch'd their blossoms out to me.   20

My father then with holy look,
In his hand a holy book,
Pronounc'd curses on my head
And bound me in a mirtle shade.

Why should I be bound to thee,   25
O my lovely mirtle tree?
Love, free love, cannot be bound
To any tree that grows on ground.

O, how sick & weary I
Underneath my mirtle lie,   30
Like to dung upon the ground
Underneath my mirtle bound.

Oft my mirtle sigh'd in vain
To behold my heavy chain;
Oft my father saw us sigh,   35
And laugh'd at our simplicity.

So I smote him & his gore
Stained the roots my mirtle bore.
But the time of youth is fled,
And grey hairs are on my head.   40

WILLIAM BLAKE

mirtle (24): The myrtle, sacred to Venus, is a symbol of Love.

GROUP 12

The Berg
(*A Dream*)

I saw a ship of martial build
(Her standards set, her brave apparel on)
Directed as by madness mere
Against a stolid iceberg steer,
Nor budge it, though the infatuate ship went down.   5
The impact made huge ice-cubes fall
Sullen, in tons that crashed the deck;
But that one avalanche was all—
No other movement save the foundering wreck.

Along the spurs of ridges pale,   10
Not any slenderest shaft and frail,
A prism over glass-green gorges lone,
Toppled; or lace of traceries fine,
Nor pendant drops in grot or mine
Were jarred, when the stunned ship went down.   15
Nor sole the gulls in cloud that wheeled
Circling one snow-flanked peak afar,
But nearer fowl the floes that skimmed
And crystal beaches, felt no jar.
No thrill transmitted stirred the lock   20
Of jack-straw needle-ice at base;
Towers undermined by waves—the block
Atilt impending—kept their place.
Seals, dozing sleek on sliddery ledges
Slipt never, when by loftier edges   25
Through very inertia overthrown,
The impetuous ship in bafflement went down.

Hard Berg (methought), so cold, so vast,
With mortal damps self-overcast;
Exhaling still thy dankish breath—   30
Adrift dissolving, bound for death;
Though lumpish thou, a lumbering one—
A lumbering lubbard loitering slow,
Impingers rue thee and go down,
Sounding thy precipice below,   35
Nor stir the slimy slug that sprawls
Along thy dead indifference of walls.

                                        HERMAN MELVILLE
sliddery (24): slippery.

The Convergence of the Twain
(Lines on the loss of the "Titanic")

In a solitude of the sea
Deep from human vanity,
And the Pride of Life that planned her, stilly couches she.

Steel chambers, late the pyres
Of her salamandrine fires,   5
Cold currents thrid, and turn to rhythmic tidal lyres.

Over the mirrors meant
To glass the opulent
The sea-worm crawls—grotesque, slimed, dumb, indifferent.

Jewels in joy designed   10
To ravish the sensuous mind
Lie lightless, all their sparkles bleared and black and blind.

Dim moon-eyed fishes near
Gaze at the gilded gear
And query: "What does this vaingloriousness down here?" . . .   15

Well: while was fashioning
This creature of cleaving wing,
The Immanent Will that stirs and urges everything

Prepared a sinister mate
For her—so gaily great—   20
A Shape of Ice, for the time far and dissociate.

And as the smart ship grew,
In stature, grace, and hue,
In shadowy silent distance grew the Iceberg too.

Alien they seemed to be: 25
No mortal eye could see
The intimate welding of their later history.

Or sign that they were bent
By paths coincident
On being anon twin halves of one august event.   30

Till the Spinner of the Years
Said "Now!" And each one hears,
And consummation comes, and jars two hemispheres.

THOMAS HARDY

thrid (6): thread.

The Imaginary Iceberg

We'd rather have the iceberg than the ship,
although it meant the end of travel.
Although it stood stock-still like cloudy rock
and all the sea were moving marble.
We'd rather have the iceberg than the ship;   5
we'd rather own this breathing plain of snow
though the ships' sails were laid upon the sea
as the snow lies undissolved upon the water.
O solemn, floating field,
are you aware an iceberg takes repose   10
with you, and when it wakes may pasture on your snows?

This is a scene a sailor'd give his eyes for.
The ship's ignored. The iceberg rises
and sinks again; its glassy pinnacles
correct elliptics in the sky.   15
This is a scene where he who treads the boards
is artlessly rhetorical. The curtain
is light enough to rise on finest ropes
that airy twists of snow provide.
The wits of these white peaks   20
spar with the sun. Its weight the iceberg dares
upon a shifting stage and stands and stares.

The iceberg cuts its facets from within.
Like jewelry from a grave
it saves itself perpetually and adorns   25
only itself, perhaps the snows
which so surprise us lying on the sea.
Good-bye, we say, good-bye, the ship steers off
where waves give in to one another's waves
and clouds run in a warmer sky.   30
Icebergs behoove the soul
(Both being self-made from elements least visible)
to see them so: fleshed, fair, erected indivisible.

ELIZABETH BISHOP

GROUP 13

Musée des Beaux Arts

About suffering they were never wrong,
The Old Masters: how well they understood
Its human position; how it takes place
While someone else is eating or opening a window or just walking dully
    along;
How, when the aged are reverently, passionately waiting   5
For the miraculous birth, there always must be
Children who did not specially want it to happen, skating
On a pond at the edge of the wood:
They never forgot
That even the dreadful martyrdom must run its course   10
Anyhow in a corner, some untidy spot
Where the dogs go on with their doggy life and the torturer's horse
Scratches its innocent behind on a tree.
In Brueghel's *Icarus,* for instance: how everything turns away
Quite leisurely from the disaster; the ploughman may   15
Have heard the splash, the forsaken cry,
But for him it was not an important failure; the sun shone
As it had to on the white legs disappearing into the green
Water; and the expensive delicate ship that must have seen
Something amazing, a boy falling out of the sky,   20
Had somewhere to get to and sailed calmly on.

W. H. AUDEN

Title: "Fine-Arts Museum." **Icarus** (14): painting by Pieter
Brueghel the Elder (1520?–69).

Love Winged My Hopes

Love winged my hopes and taught me how to fly
Far from base earth, but not to mount too high:
    For true pleasure
    Lives in measure,
    Which if men forsake,   5
Blinded, they into folly run, and grief for pleasure take.

But my vain hopes, proud of their new-taught flight,
Enamored, sought to woo the sun's fair light,
    Whose rich brightness
    Moved their lightness   10
    To aspire so high
That, all scorched and consumed with fire, now drowned
    in woe they lie.

And none but Love their woeful hap did rue,
For Love did know that their desires were true;
    Though Fate frownèd,   15
    And now drownèd
    They in sorrow dwell;
It was the purest light of heaven for whose fair love they
    fell.

ANONYMOUS
(*Seventeenth Century*)

Fall of Icarus: Brueghel

Flashing through falling sunlight
A frantic leg late plunging from its strange
Communicating moment
Flutters in shadowy waves.

Close by those shattered waters—   5
The spray, no doubt, struck shore—
One dreamless shepherd and his old sheep dog
Define outrageous patience
Propped on staff and haunches,
Intent on nothing, backs bowed against the sea,   10
While the slow flocks of sheep gnaw on the grass-thin coast.
Crouched in crimson homespun an indifferent peasant
Guides his blunt plow through gravelled ground,
Cutting flat furrows hugging this hump of land.
One partridge sits immobile on its bough   15
Watching a Flemish fisherman pursue
Fish in the darkening bay;
Their stillness mocks rude ripples rising and circling in.

Yet that was a stunning greeting
For any old angler, peasant, or the grand ship's captain,   20
Though sent by a mere boy
Bewildered in the gravitational air,
Flashing his wild white arms at the impassive sea-drowned sun.

Now only coastal winds
Ruffle the partridge feathers,   25
Muting the soft ripping of sheep cropping,
The heavy whisper
Of furrows falling, ship cleaving,
Water lapping.

Lulled in the loose furl and hum of infamous folly,   30
Darkly, how silently, the cold sea suckles him.

JOSEPH LANGLAND

GROUP 14

Sonnet 1

Loving in truth, and fain in verse my love to show,
That she, dear she, might take some pleasure of my pain,
Pleasure might cause her read, reading might make her know,
Knowledge might pity win, and pity grace obtain,
I sought fit words to paint the blackest face of woe;   5
Studying inventions fine, her wits to entertain,
Oft turning others' leaves to see if thence would flow
Some fresh and fruitful showers upon my sunburned brain.
But words came halting forth, wanting invention's stay;
Invention, nature's child, fled stepdame Study's blows,   10
And others' feet still seemed but strangers in my way.
Thus, great with child to speak, and helpless in my throes,
Biting my truant pen, beating myself for spite,
"Fool," said my muse to me, "look in thy heart and write."

                                          SIR PHILIP SIDNEY

In My Craft or Sullen Art

In my craft or sullen art
Exercised in the still night
When only the moon rages
And the lovers lie abed
With all their griefs in their arms,   5
I labour by singing light
Not for ambition or bread
Or the strut and trade of charms
On the ivory stages
But for the common wages   10
Of their most secret heart.

Not for the proud man apart
From the raging moon I write
On these spindrift pages
Nor for the towering dead   15
With their nightingales and psalms
But for the lovers, their arms
Round the griefs of the ages,
Who pay no praise or wages
Nor heed my craft or art.   20

                                          DYLAN THOMAS

GROUP 15

Cupid Mistaken

As after Noon, one Summer's Day,
   Venus stood bathing in a River;
Cupid a-shooting went that Way,
   New strung his Bow, new fill'd his Quiver.

With Skill He chose his sharpest Dart: 5
   With all his Might his Bow He drew:
Swift to His beauteous Parent's Heart
   The too well-guided Arrow flew.

I faint! I die! the Goddess cry'd:
   O cruel, could'st Thou find none other,   10
To wreck thy Spleen on? Parricide!
   Like Nero, Thou has slain thy Mother.

Poor Cupid sobbing scarce could speak;
   Indeed, Mamma, I did not know Ye:
Alas! how easie my Mistake?   15
   I took you for your Likeness, Cloe.

              MATTHEW PRIOR

Chloe Divine

Chloe's a Nymph in flowery groves,
   A Nereid in the streams;
Saint-like she in the temple moves,
   A woman in my dreams.

Love steals artillery from her eyes,   5
   The Graces point her charms;
Orpheus is rivall'd in her voice,
   And Venus in her arms.

Never so happily in one
   Did heaven and earth combine;   10
And yet 'tis flesh and blood alone
   That makes her so divine.

            THOMAS D'URFEY

GROUP 16

To One in Paradise

Thou wast all that to me, love
  For which my soul did pine—
A green isle in the sea, love,
  A fountain and a shrine,
All wreathed with fairy fruits and flowers,   5
And all the flowers were mine.

Now all my days are trances,
  And all my nightly dreams
Are where thy grey eye glances,
  And where thy footstep gleams—   10
In what ethereal dances,
  By what eternal streams!

EDGAR ALLAN POE

Tears, Idle Tears

Tears, idle tears, I know not what they mean,
Tears from the depth of some divine despair
Rise in the heart, and gather to the eyes,
In looking on the happy Autumn-fields,
And thinking of the days that are no more.   5

Fresh as the first beam glittering on a sail,
That brings our friends up from the underworld,
Sad as the last which reddens over one
That sinks with all we love below the verge;
So sad, so fresh, the days that are no more.   10

Ah, sad and strange as in dark summer dawns
The earliest pipe of half-awaken'd birds
To dying ears, when unto dying eyes
The casement slowly grows a glimmering square;
So sad, so strange, the days that are no more.   15

Dear as remember'd kisses after death,
And sweet as those by hopeless fancy feign'd
On lips that are for others; deep as love,
Deep as first love, and wild with all regret;
O Death in Life, the days that are no more.   20

ALFRED, LORD TENNYSON
(from *The Princess*)

Song

Come, my Celia, let us prove,
While we can, the sports of love;
Time will not be ours forever:
He at length our good will sever.
Spend not, then, his gifts in vain; · · · 5
Suns that set may rise again,
But if once we lose this light,
'Tis with us perpetual night.
Why should we defer our joys?
Fame and rumor are but toys. · · · 10
Cannot we delude the eyes
Of a few poor household spies?
Or his easier ears beguile,
Thus removèd by our wile?
'Tis no sin love's fruits to steal; · · · 15
But the sweet thefts to reveal,
To be taken, to be seen,
These have crimes accounted been.

BEN JONSON
(from *Volpone*)

Come, Lesbia, Let Us Live and Love

Come, Lesbia, let us live and love,
nor give a damn what sour old men say.
The sun that sets may rise again
but when our light has sunk into the earth,
it is gone forever. · · · 5
Give me a thousand kisses,
then a hundred, another thousand,
another hundred
and in one breath
still kiss another thousand, · · · 10
another hundred.
O then with lips and bodies joined
many deep thousands;
confuse
their number,
so that poor fools and cuckolds (envious · · · 15
even now) shall never
learn our wealth and curse us
with their evil eyes.

CATULLUS
(translated by Horace Gregory)

To the Virgins, to Make Much of Time

Gather ye rosebuds while ye may:
  Old Time is still a-flying,
And this same flower that smiles today
  Tomorrow will be dying.

The glorious lamp of heaven, the sun,   5
  The higher he's a-getting,
The sooner will his race be run,
  And nearer he's to setting.

That age is best which is the first,
  When youth and blood are warmer;   10
But being spent, the worse and worst
  Times still succeed the former.

Then be not coy, but use your time;
  And while ye may, go marry:
For having lost but once your prime,   15
  You may forever tarry.

ROBERT HERRICK

To His Coy Mistress

Had we but world enough and time,
This coyness, lady, were no crime.
We would sit down and think which way
To walk, and pass our long love's day;
Thou by the Indian Ganges' side   5
Shouldst rubies find; I by the tide
Of Humber would complain. I would
Love you ten years before the Flood;
And you should, if you please, refuse
Till the conversion of the Jews.   10

My vegetable love should grow
Vaster than empires, and more slow.
An hundred years should go to praise
Thine eyes, and on thy forehead gaze;
Two hundred to adore each breast,   15
But thirty thousand to the rest;
An age at least to every part,
And the last age should show your heart.
For, lady, you deserve this state,
Nor would I love at lower rate.   20
   But at my back I always hear
Time's wingèd chariot hurrying near;
And yonder all before us lie
Deserts of vast eternity.
Thy beauty shall no more be found,   25
Nor in thy marble vault shall sound
My echoing song; then worms shall try
That long preserved virginity,
And your quaint honor turn to dust,
And into ashes all my lust.   30
The grave's a fine and private place,
But none, I think, do there embrace.
   Now therefore, while the youthful hue
Sits on thy skin like morning dew,
And while thy willing soul transpires   35
At every pore with instant fires,
Now let us sport us while we may;
And now, like amorous birds of prey,
Rather at once our time devour,
Than languish in his slow-chapped power.   40
Let us roll all our strength, and all
Our sweetness, up into one ball;
And tear our pleasures with rough strife
Thorough the iron gates of life.
Thus, though we cannot make our sun   45
Stand still, yet we will make him run.

ANDREW MARVELL

Coy (title): cold, disdainful. **Mistress** (title): lady, without
the modern connotation. **conversion of the Jews** (10): symbol
of the end of the world. **vegetable** (11): having great powers
of growth. **chapped** (40): devouring. **thorough** (44):
through.

GROUP 18

The Last Night

The last Night that She lived
It was a Common Night
Except the Dying—this to Us
Made Nature different

We noticed smallest things—   5
Things overlooked before
By this great light upon our Mind
Italicized—as 'twere.

As We went out and in
Between Her final Room   10
And Rooms where Those to be alive
Tomorrow were, a Blame

That Others could exist
While She must finish quite
A Jealousy for Her arose   15
So nearly infinite—

We waited while She passed—
It was a narrow time—
Too jostled were Our Souls to speak
At length the notice came.   20

She mentioned, and forgot—
Then lightly as a Reed
Bent to the Water, struggled scarce—
Consented, and was dead—

And We—We placed the Hair—   25
And drew the Head erect—
And then an awful leisure was
Belief to regulate—

EMILY DICKINSON

I Heard a Fly Buzz

I heard a Fly buzz—when I died—
The Stillness in the Room
Was like the Stillness in the Air—
Between the Heaves of Storm—

The Eyes around—had wrung them dry—   5
And Breaths were gathering firm
For that last Onset—when the King
Be witnessed—in the Room—

I willed my Keepsakes—Signed away
What portion of me be   10
Assignable—and then it was
There interposed a Fly—

With Blue—uncertain stumbling Buzz—
Between the light—and me—
And then the Windows failed—and then   15
I could not see to see—

EMILY DICKINSON

GROUP 19

Leda and the Swan

Though her Mother told her
    Not to go a-bathing,
Leda loved the river
    And she could not keep away;
Wading in its freshets   5
    When the noon was heavy;
Walking by the water
    At the close of day.

Where between its waterfalls,
    Underneath the beeches,   10
Gently flows a broader
    Hardly moving stream,
And the balanced trout lie
    In the quiet reaches;
Taking all her clothes off,   15
    Leda went to swim.

There was not a flag-leaf
    By the river's margin
That might be a shelter
    From a passer-by;   20
And a sudden whiteness
    In the quiet darkness,
Let alone the splashing,
    Was enough to catch an eye.

But the place was lonely,   25
    And her clothes were hidden;
Even cattle walking
    In the ford had gone away;
Every single farm-hand
    Sleeping after dinner,—   30
What's the use of talking?
    There was no one in the way.

In, without a stitch on,
   Peaty water yielded,
Till her head was lifted   35
   With its ropes of hair;
It was more surprising
   Than a lily gilded
Just to see how golden
   Was her body there: 40

Lolling in the water,
   Lazily uplifting
Limbs that on the surface
   Whitened into snow;
Leaning on the water,   45
   Indolently drifting,
Hardly any faster
   Than the foamy bubbles go.

You would say to see her
   Swimming in the lonely   50
Pool, or after, dryer,
   Putting on her clothes:
"O but she is lovely,
   Not a soul to see her,
And how lovely only   55
   Leda's Mother knows!"

Under moving branches
   Leisurely she dresses,
And the leafy sunlight
   Made you wonder were   60
All its woven shadows
   But her golden tresses,
Or a smock of sunlight
   For her body bare.

When on earth great beauty   65
   Goes exempt from danger,
It will be endangered
   From a source on high;
When unearthly stillness
   Falls on leaves, the ranger,   70
In his wood-lore anxious,
   Gazes at the sky.

While her hair was drying,
  Came a gentle languor,
Whether from the bathing   75
  Or the breeze she didn't know.
Anyway she lay there,
  And her Mother's anger
(Worse if she had wet hair)
  Could not make her dress and go.   80

Whitest of all earthly
  Things, the white that's rarest,
Is the snow on mountains
  Standing in the sun;
Next the clouds above them,   85
  Then the down is fairest
On the breast and pinions
  Of a proudly sailing swan.

And she saw him sailing
  On the pool where lately   90
She had stretched unnoticed,
  As she thought, and swum;
And she never wondered
  Why, erect and stately,
Where no river weed was   95
  Such a bird had come.

What was it she called him:
  Goosey-goosey gander?
For she knew no better
  Way to call a swan;   100
And the bird responding
  Seemed to understand her,
For he left his sailing
  For the bank to waddle on.

Apple blossoms under   105
  Hills of Lacedæmon,
With the snow beyond them
  In the still blue air,
To the swan who hid them
  With his wings asunder,   110
Than the breasts of Leda,
  Were not lovelier!

Of the tales that daughters
  Tell their poor old mothers,
Which by all accounts are   115
  Often very odd;
Leda's was a story
  Stranger than all others.
What was there to say but:
  Glory be to God?   120

And she half-believed her,
  For she knew her daughter;
And she saw the swan-down
  Tangled in her hair.
Though she knew how deeply   125
  Runs the stillest water;
How could she protect her
  From the wingèd air?

Why is it effects are   130
  Greater than their causes?
Why should causes often
  Differ from effects?
Why should what is lovely
  Fill the world with harness?   135
And the most deceived be
  She who least suspects?

When the hyacinthine
  Eggs were in the basket,—
Blue as at the whiteness   140
  Where a cloud begins;
Who would dream there lay there
  All that Trojan brightness;
Agamemnon murdered;
  And the mighty Twins?

OLIVER ST. JOHN GOGARTY

Title: Disguised as a swan, Zeus made love to Leda, who, in
the myth, is grown-up, the wife of Tyndareus, king of Sparta.
Eggs (138): From the eggs came Castor and Clytemnestra
(children of Tyndareus) and Pollux and Helen of Troy (children of Zeus). **Agamemnon** (143): killed by his wife Clytemnestra. **Twins** (144): Castor and Pollux.

Leda and the Swan

A sudden blow: the great wings beating still
Above the staggering girl, her thighs caressed
By the dark webs, her nape caught in his bill,
He holds her helpless breast upon his breast.

How can those terrified vague fingers push   5
The feathered glory from her loosening thighs?
And how can body, laid in that white rush,
But feel the strange heart beating where it lies?

A shudder in the loins engenders there
The broken wall, the burning roof and tower   10
And Agamemnon dead.
                              Being so caught up,
So mastered by the brute blood of the air,
Did she put on his knowledge with his power
Before the indifferent beak could let her drop?

WILLIAM BUTLER YEATS

broken wall (10): breached to admit the wooden horse.

Leda

Heart, with what lonely fears you ached,
    How lecherously mused upon
That horror with which Leda quaked
    Under the spread wings of the swan.

Then soon your mad religious smile   5
    Made taut the belly, arched the breast,
And there beneath your god awhile
    You strained and gulped your beastliest.

Pregnant you are, as Leda was,
    Of bawdry, murder and deceit;   10
Perpetuating night because
    The after-languors hang so sweet.

ROBERT GRAVES

GROUP 20

Come In

As I came to the edge of the woods,
Thrush music—hark!
Now if it was dusk outside
Inside it was dark.

Too dark in the woods for a bird   5
By sleight of wing
To better its perch for the night,
Though it still could sing.

The last of the light of the sun
That had died in the west   10
Still lived for one song more
In a thrush's breast.

Far in the pillared dark
Thrush music went—
Almost like a call to come in   15
To the dark and lament.

But no, I was out for stars:
I would not come in.
I meant not even if asked,
And I hadn't been.   20

ROBERT FROST

The Darkling Thrush

I leant upon a coppice gate
   When Frost was spectre-gray,
And Winter's dregs made desolate
   The weakening eye of day.
The tangled bine-stems scored the sky   5
   Like strings of broken lyres,
And all mankind that haunted nigh
   Had sought their household fires.

The land's sharp features seemed to be
   The Century's corpse outleant,   10
His crypt the cloudy canopy,
   The wind his death-lament.
The ancient pulse of germ and birth
   Was shrunken hard and dry,
And every spirit upon earth   15
   Seemed fervourless as I.

At once a voice arose among
   The bleak twigs overhead
In a full-hearted evensong
   Of joy illimited;   20
An aged thrush, frail, gaunt, and small,
   In blast-beruffled plume,
Had chosen thus to fling his soul
   Upon the growing gloom.

So little cause for carolings   25
   Of such ecstatic sound
Was written on terrestrial things
   Afar or nigh around,
That I could think there trembled through
   His happy good-night air   30
Some blessed Hope, whereof he knew
   And I was unaware.

THOMAS HARDY

The Night Is Freezing Fast

The night is freezing fast,
  To-morrow comes December;
  And winterfalls of old
Are with me from the past;
  And chiefly I remember   5
  How Dick would hate the cold.

Fall, winter, fall; for he
  Prompt hand and headpiece clever,
  Has woven a winter robe,
And made of earth and sea   10
  His overcoat for ever,
  And wears the turning globe.

A. E. HOUSMAN

Immortal Helix

Hereunder Jacob Schmidt who, man and bones,
Has been his hundred times around the sun.

His chronicle is endless—the great curve
Inscribed in nothing by a point upon
The spinning surface of a circling sphere.   5

Dead bones roll on.

ARCHIBALD MACLEISH

GROUP 22

Ode on a Grecian Urn

Thou still unravish'd bride of quietness,
    Thou foster-child of silence and slow time,
Sylvan historian, who canst thus express
    A flowery tale more sweetly than our rhyme:
What leaf-fring'd legend haunts about thy shape   5
    Of deities or mortals, or of both,
        In Tempe or the dales of Arcady?
What men or gods are these? What maidens loth?
    What mad pursuit? What struggle to escape?
        What pipes and timbrels? What wild ecstasy?   10

Heard melodies are sweet, but those unheard
    Are sweeter; therefore, ye soft pipes, play on;
Not to the sensual ear, but, more endear'd,
    Pipe to the spirit ditties of no tone:
Fair youth, beneath the trees, thou canst not leave   15
    Thy song, nor ever can those trees be bare;
        Bold Lover, never, never canst thou kiss,
Though winning near the goal—yet, do not grieve;
    She cannot fade, though thou hast not thy bliss,
        For ever wilt thou love, and she be fair!   20

Ah, happy, happy boughs! that cannot shed
    Your leaves, nor ever bid the Spring adieu;
And, happy melodist, unwearied,
    For ever piping songs for ever new;
More happy love! more happy, happy love!   25
    For ever warm and still to be enjoy'd,
        For ever panting, and for ever young;
All breathing human passion far above,
    That leaves a heart high-sorrowful and cloy'd,
        A burning forehead, and a parching tongue.   30

Who are these coming to the sacrifice?
  To what green altar, O mysterious priest,
Lead'st thou that heifer lowing at the skies,
    And all her silken flanks with garlands drest?
What little town by river or sea shore,   35
  Or mountain-built with peaceful citadel,
    Is emptied of this folk, this pious morn?
And, little town, thy streets for evermore
  Will silent be; and not a soul to tell
    Why thou art desolate, can e'er return.   40

O Attic shape! Fair attitude! with brede
  Of marble men and maidens overwrought,
With forest branches and the trodden weed;
    Thou, silent form, dost tease us out of thought
As doth eternity: Cold Pastoral!   45
  When old age shall this generation waste,
    Thou shalt remain, in midst of other woe
Than ours, a friend to man, to whom thou say'st,
  Beauty is truth, truth beauty,—that is all
    Ye know on earth, and all ye need to know.   50

JOHN KEATS

Tempe (7): a beautiful valley in Thessaly praised by the Greek
poets. Arcady (7): Arcadia.

The Progress of Beauty

When first Diana leaves her Bed
Vapors and Steams her Looks disgrace,
A frouzy dirty colour'd red
Sits on her cloudy wrinckled Face.

  But by degrees when mounted high   5
Her artificiall Face appears
Down from her Window in the Sky,
Her Spots are gone, her Visage clears.

'Twixt earthly Femals and the Moon
All Parallells exactly run;   10
If Celia should appear too soon
Alas, the Nymph would be undone.

To see her from her Pillow rise
All reeking in a cloudy Steam,
Crackt Lips, foul Teeth, and gummy Eyes,   15
Poor Strephon, how would he blaspheme!

The Soot or Powder which was wont
To make her Hair look black as Jet,
Falls from her Tresses on her Front
A mingled Mass of Dirt and Sweat.   20

Three Colours, Black, and Red, and White,
So gracefull in their proper Place,
Remove them to a diff'rent Light
They form a frightfull hideous Face,

For instance; when the Lilly slipps   25
Into the Precincts of the Rose,
And takes Possession of the Lips,
Leaving the Purple to the Nose.

So Celia went entire to bed,
All her Complexions safe and sound,   30
But when she rose, the black and red
Though still in Sight, had chang'd their Ground.

The Black, which would not be confin'd
A more inferior Station seeks
Leaving the fiery red behind,   35
And mingles in her muddy Cheeks.

The Paint by Perspiration cracks,
And falls in Rivulets of Sweat,
On either Side you see the Tracks,
While at her Chin the Conflu'ents met.   40

A Skillfull Houswife thus her Thumb
With Spittle while she spins, anoints,
And thus the brown Meanders come
In trickling Streams betwixt her Joynts.

But Celia can with ease reduce   45
By help of Pencil, Paint and Brush
Each Colour to its Place and Use,
And teach her Cheeks again to blush.

She knows her Early self no more,
But fill'd with Admiration, stands,   50
As Other Painters oft adore
The Workmanship of their own Hands.

Thus after four important Hours
Celia's the Wonder of her Sex;
Say, which among the Heav'nly Pow'rs   55
Could cause such wonderfull Effects.

Venus, indulgent to her Kind
Gave Women all their Hearts could wish
When first she taught them where to find
White lead, and Lusitanian Dish.   60

Love with White lead cements his Wings,
White lead was sent us to repair
Two brightest, brittlest earthly Things
A Lady's Face, and China ware.

She ventures now to lift the Sash,   65
The Window is her proper Sphear;
Ah Lovely Nymph be not too rash,
Nor let the Beaux approach too near.

Take Pattern by your Sister Star,
Delude at once and Bless our Sight,   70
When you are seen, be seen from far,
And chiefly chuse to shine by Night.

In the Pell-mell when passing by,
Keep up the Glasses of your Chair,
Then each transported Fop will cry,   75
G--d d--m me Jack, she's wondrous fair.

But, Art no longer can prevayl
When the Materialls all are gone,
The best Mechanick Hand must fayl
Where Nothing's left to work upon.   80

Matter, as wise Logicians say,
Cannot without a Form subsist,
And Form, say I, as well as They,
Must fayl if Matter brings no Grist.

All this is fair Diana's Case   85
For, all Astrologers maintain
Each Night a Bit drops off her Face
When Mortals say he's in her Wain.

While Partridge wisely shews the **Cause**
Efficient of the Moon's Decay,   90
That Cancer with his pois'nous Claws
Attacks her in the milky Way:

But Gadbury in Art profound
From her pale Cheeks pretends to show
That Swain Endymion is not sound,   95
Or else, that Mercury's her Foe.

But, let the Cause be what it will,
In half a Month she looks so thin
That Flamstead can with all his Skill
See but her Forehead and her Chin.   100

Yet as she wasts, she grows discreet,
Till Midnight never shows her Head;
So rotting Celia stroles the Street
When sober Folks are all a-bed.

For sure if this be Luna's Fate,   105
Poor Celia, but of mortall Race
In vain expects a longer Date
To the Materialls of Her Face.

When Mercury her Tresses mows
To think of Oyl and Soot, is vain,   110
No Painting can restore a Nose,
Nor will her Teeth return again.

Two Balls of Glass may serve for Eyes,
White Lead can plaister up a Cleft,
But these alas, are poor Supplyes   115
If neither Cheeks, nor Lips be left.

Ye Pow'rs who over Love preside,
Since mortal Beautyes drop so soon,
If you would have us well supply'd,
Send us new Nymphs with each new Moon.   120

JONATHAN SWIFT

the Pell-mell (73): Pall Mall. Wain (88): wane. Partridge
(89), Gadbury (93): astrologers. Endymion (95): in Greek
myth, a beautiful sleeping youth kissed by the moon. Mercury
(96): a medicine for venereal disease. Flamstead (99): an as-
tronomer.

GROUP 23

The Ecstasy

Where, like a pillow on a bed,
   A pregnant bank swelled up to rest
The violet's reclining head,
   Sat we two, one another's best.

Our hands were firmly cemented   5
   With a fast balm, which thence did spring;
Our eye-beams twisted, and did thread
   Our eyes upon one double string;

So to entergraft our hands, as yet
   Was all the means to make us one;   10
And pictures in our eyes to get
   Was all our propagation.

As 'twixt two equal armies Fate
   Suspends uncertain victory,
Our souls, which to advance their state   15
   Were gone out, hung 'twixt her and me.

And whilst our souls negotiate there,
   We like sepulchral statues lay;
All day, the same our postures were
   And we said nothing, all the day.   20

If any, so by love refined
   That he soul's language understood,
And by good love were grown all mind,
   Within convenient distance stood,

He, though he knew not which soul spake   25
   Because both meant, both spake the same,
Might thence a new concoction take,
   And part far purer than he came.

This ecstasy doth unperplex,
   We said, and tell us what we love.   30
We see by this it was not sex;
   We see we saw not what did move.

But as all several souls contain
   Mixtures of things, they know not what,
Love these mixed souls doth mix again   35
   And makes both one, each this and that.

A single violet transplant,
   The strength, the color, and the size,
All which before was poor and scant,
   Redoubles still, and multiplies.   40

When love with one another so
   Interinanimates two souls,
That abler soul, which thence doth flow,
   Defects of loneliness controls.

We, then, who are this new soul, know   45
   Of what we are composed and made,
For the atomies of which we grow
   Are souls, whom no change can invade.

But oh, alas, so long, so far,
   Our bodies why do we forbear?   50
They are ours, though they are not we; we are
   The intelligences, they the sphere.

We owe them thanks, because they thus
   Did us to us at first convey,
Yielded their forces, sense, to us,   55
   Nor are dross to us, but allay.

On man heaven's influence works not so
   But that it first imprints the air;
So soul into the soul may flow,
   Though it to body first repair.   60

As our blood labors to beget
   Spirits as like souls as it can,
Because such fingers need to knit
   That subtle knot which makes us man,

So must pure lovers' souls descend   65
   To affections and to faculties
Which sense may reach and apprehend:
   Else a great prince in prison lies.

To our bodies turn we then, that so
  Weak men on love revealed may look;   70
Love's mysteries in souls do grow,
  But yet the body is his book.

And if some lover, such as we,
  Have heard this dialogue of one,
Let him still mark us; he shall see   75
  Small change when we're to bodies gone.

                                    JOHN DONNE

eye-beams (7): thought to be actual streams of images coming from the eyes to an object. **entergraft** (9): graft together. **get** (11): beget. **concoction** (27): a mixture purified by an alchemical process. **saw** (32): that is, before the experience took place. **several** (33): individual. **mixtures** (34): because man is part spiritual, part animal. **Interinanimates** (42): gives life mutually to. **intelligences** (52): in Ptolemaic astronomy, the powers that move the heavenly spheres. **allay** (56): a necessary ingredient in a metallurgical process. **air** (58): the medium through which heavenly bodies affect man. **spirits** (62): subtle vapors manufactured by the blood that link body and soul together.

Youth's Spring-Tribute

On this sweet bank your head thrice sweet and dear
  I lay, and spread your hair on either side,
  And see the newborn woodflowers bashful-eyed
Look through the golden tresses here and there.
On these debateable borders of the year   5
  Spring's foot half falters; scarce she yet may know
  The leafless blackthorn-blossom from the snow;
And through her bowers the wind's way still is clear.
But April's sun strikes down the glades to-day;
  So shut your eyes upturned, and feel my kiss   10
Creep, as the Spring now thrills through every spray,
  Up your warm throat to your warm lips: for this
  Is even the hour of Love's sworn suitservice,
With whom cold hearts are counted castaway.

                        DANTE GABRIEL ROSSETTI
                          (from *The House of Life*)

GROUP 24

Elegy Written in a Country Church-Yard

The Curfew tolls the knell of parting day,
The lowing herd wind slowly o'er the lea,
The plowman homeward plods his weary way,
And leaves the world to darkness and to me.

Now fades the glimmering landscape on the sight,   5
And all the air a solemn stillness holds,
Save where the beetle wheels his droning flight,
And drowsy tinklings lull the distant folds;

Save that from yonder ivy-mantled tow'r
The mopeing owl does to the moon complain   10
Of such, as wand'ring near her secret bow'r,
Molest her ancient solitary reign.

Beneath those rugged elms, that yew-tree's shade,
Where heaves the turf in many a mould'ring heap,
Each in his narrow cell for ever laid,   15
The rude Forefathers of the hamlet sleep.

The breezy call of incense-breathing Morn,
The shallow twitt'ring from the straw-built shed,
The cock's shrill clarion, or the echoing horn,
No more shall rouse them from their lowly bed.   20

For them no more the blazing hearth shall burn,
Or busy housewife ply her evening care:
No children run to lisp their sire's return,
Or climb his knees the envied kiss to share.

Oft did the harvest to their sickle yield,   25
Their furrow oft the stubborn glebe has broke;
How jocund did they drive their team afield!
How bow'd the woods beneath their sturdy stroke!

Let not Ambition mock their useful toil,
Their homely joys, and destiny obscure;   30
Nor Grandeur hear with a disdainful smile,
The short and simple annals of the poor.

The boast of heraldry, the pomp of pow'r,
And all that beauty, all that wealth e'er gave,
Awaits alike th' inevitable hour.   35
The paths of glory lead but to the grave.

Nor you, ye Proud, impute to These the fault,
If Mem'ry o'er their Tomb no Trophies raise,
Where thro' the long-drawn isle and fretted vault
The pealing anthem swells the note of praise.   40

Can storied urn or animated bust
Back to its mansion call the fleeting breath?
Can Honour's voice provoke the silent dust,
Or Flatt'ry sooth the dull cold ear of Death?

Perhaps in this neglected spot is laid   45
Some heart once pregnant with celestial fire;
Hands, that the rod of empire might have sway'd,
Or wak'd to extasy the living lyre.

But Knowledge to their eyes her ample page
Rich with the spoils of time did ne'er unroll;   50
Chill Penury repress'd their noble rage,
And froze the genial current of the soul.

Full many a gem of purest ray serene,
The dark unfathom'd caves of ocean bear:
Full many a flower is born to blush unseen,   55
And waste its sweetness on the desert air.

Some village-Hampden, that with dauntless breast
The little Tyrant of his fields withstood;
Some mute inglorious Milton here may rest,
Some Cromwell guiltless of his country's blood.   60

Th' applause of list'ning senates to command,
The threats of pain and ruin to despise,
To scatter plenty o'er a smiling land,
And read their hist'ry in a nation's eyes,

Their lot forbad: nor circumscrib'd alone   65
Their growing virtues, but their crimes confin'd;
Forbad to wade through slaughter to a throne,
And shut the gates of mercy on mankind,

The struggling pangs of conscious truth to hide,
To quench the blushes of ingenuous shame,   70
Or heap the shrine of Luxury and Pride
With incense kindled at the Muse's flame.

Far from the madding crowd's ignoble strife,
Their sober wishes never learn'd to stray;
Along the cool sequester'd vale of life   75
They kept the noiseless tenor of their way.

Yet ev'n these bones from insult to protect
Some frail memorial still erected nigh,
With uncouth rhimes and shapeless sculpture deck'd,
Implores the passing tribute of a sigh.   80

Their name, their years, spelt by th' unletter'd muse,
The place of fame and elegy supply:
And many a holy text around she strews,
That teach the rustic moralist to die.

For who to dumb Forgetfulness a prey,   85
This pleasing anxious being e'er resign'd,
Left the warm precincts of the chearful day,
Nor cast one longing ling'ring look behind?

On some fond breast the parting soul relies,
Some pious drops the closing eye requires;   90
Ev'n from the tomb the voice of Nature cries,
Ev'n in our Ashes live their wonted Fires.

For thee, who mindful of th' unhonour'd Dead
Dost in these lines their artless tale relate;
If chance, by lonely contemplation led,   95
Some kindred Spirit shall inquire thy fate,

Haply some hoary-headed Swain may say,
"Oft have we seen him at the peep of dawn
Brushing with hasty steps the dews away
To meet the sun upon the upland lawn.   100

There at the foot of yonder nodding beech
That wreathes its old fantastic roots so high,
His listless length at noontide would he stretch,
And pore upon the brook that babbles by.

Hard by yon wood, now smiling as in scorn,   105
Mutt'ring his wayward fancies he would rove,
Now drooping, woeful wan, like one forlorn,
Or craz'd with care, or cross'd in hopeless love.

One morn I miss'd him on the custom'd hill,
Along the heath and near his fav'rite tree;   110
Another came; nor yet beside the rill,
Nor up the lawn, nor at the wood was he;

The next with dirges due in sad array
Slow thro' the church-way path we saw him born.
Approach and read (for thou can'st read) the lay,   115
Grav'd on the stone beneath yon aged thorn."

The Epitaph.

Here rests his head upon the lap of Earth
A Youth to Fortune and to Fame unknown.
Fair Science frown'd not on his humble birth,
And Melancholy mark'd him for her own.   120

Large was his bounty, and his soul sincere,
Heav'n did a recompence as largely send:
He gave to Mis'ry all he had, a tear,
He gain'd from Heav'n ('twas all he wish'd) a friend.

No farther seek his merits to disclose,   125
Or draw his frailties from their dread abode,
(There they alike in trembling hope repose,)
The bosom of his Father and his God.

                                THOMAS GRAY

Lycidas

*In this monody the author bewails a learned
friend, unfortunately drowned in his passage
from Chester on the Irish Seas, 1637. And by
occasion foretells the ruin of our corrupted
clergy then in their height.*

Yet once more, O ye laurels, and once more
Ye myrtles brown, with ivy never sere,
I come to pluck your berries harsh and crude,
And with forced fingers rude,
Shatter your leaves before the mellowing year.   5
Bitter constraint, and sad occasion dear,
Compels me to disturb your season due:
For Lycidas is dead, dead ere his prime,
Young Lycidas, and hath not left his peer.
Who would not sing for Lycidas? He knew   10
Himself to sing, and build the lofty rhyme.
He must not float upon his watery bier
Unwept, and welter to the parching wind,
Without the meed of some melodious tear.
     Begin then, sisters of the sacred well,   15
That from beneath the seat of Jove doth spring,
Begin, and somewhat loudly sweep the string.
Hence with denial vain and coy excuse;
So may some gentle muse
With lucky words favor my destined urn,   20
And as he passes turn,
And bid fair peace be to my sable shroud.
For we were nursed upon the self-same hill,
Fed the same flock, by fountain, shade, and rill.
     Together both, ere the high lawns appeared   25
Under the opening eyelids of the morn,
We drove afield, and both together heard
What time the gray-fly winds her sultry horn,
Battening our flocks with the fresh dews of night,
Oft till the star that rose, at evening, bright,   30
Toward heaven's descent had sloped his westering wheel.
Meanwhile the rural ditties were not mute,
Tempered to the oaten flute,
Rough satyrs danced, and fauns with cloven heel,

From the glad sound would not be absent long,   35
And old Damaetas loved to hear our song.
   But O the heavy change, now thou art gone,
Now thou art gone, and never must return!
Thee, shepherd, thee the woods and desert caves,
With wild thyme and the gadding vine o'ergrown,   40
And all their echoes mourn.
The willows and the hazel copses green
Shall now no more be seen,
Fanning their joyous leaves to thy soft lays.
As killing as the canker to the rose,   45
Or taint-worm to the weanling herds that graze,
Or frost to flowers, that their gay wardrobe wear,
When first the white-thorn blows:
Such, Lycidas, thy loss to shepherd's ear.
   Where were ye, nymphs, when the remorseless deep   50
Closed o'er the head of your loved Lycidas?
For neither were ye playing on the steep,
Where your old bards, the famous druids, lie,
Nor on the shaggy top of Mona high,
Nor yet where Deva spreads her wizard stream: 55
Ay me, I fondly dream!
"Had ye been there"—for what could that have done?
What could the Muse herself that Orpheus bore,
The Muse herself for her enchanting son
Whom universal nature did lament,   60
When by the rout that made the hideous roar,
His gory visage down the stream was sent,
Down the swift Hebrus to the Lesbian shore?
   Alas! What boots it with uncessant care
To tend the homely slighted shepherd's trade,   65
And strictly meditate the thankless Muse?
Were it not better done, as others use,
To sport with Amaryllis in the shade,
Or with the tangles of Neaera's hair?
Fame is the spur that the clear spirit doth raise   70
(That last infirmity of noble mind)
To scorn delights, and live laborious days;
But the fair guerdon when we hope to find,
And think to burst out into sudden blaze,
Comes the blind Fury with the abhorrèd shears,   75
And slits the thin-spun life. "But not the praise,"

Phoebus replied, and touched my trembling ears:
"Fame is no plant that grows on mortal soil,
Nor in the glistering foil
Set off to the world, nor in broad rumor lies,   80
But lives and spreads aloft by those pure eyes
And perfect witness of all-judging Jove;
As he pronounces lastly on each deed,
Of so much fame in heaven expect thy meed."
    O fountain Arethuse, and thou honored flood,   85
Smooth-sliding Mincius, crowned with vocal reeds,
That strain I heard was of a higher mood.
But now my oat proceeds,
And listens to the herald of the sea,
That came in Neptune's plea.   90
He asked the waves and asked the felon-winds,
What hard mishap hath doomed this gentle swain,
And questioned every gust of rugged wings
That blows from off each beakèd promontory.
They knew not of his story,   95
And sage Hippotades their answer brings:
That not a blast was from his dungeon strayed;
The air was calm, and on the level brine,
Sleek Panopë with all her sisters played.
It was that fatal and perfidious bark   100
Built in the eclipse, and rigged with curses dark,
That sunk so low that sacred head of thine.
    Next Camus, reverend sire, went footing slow,
His mantle hairy, and his bonnet sedge,
Inwrought with figures dim, and on the edge   105
Like to that sanguine flower inscribed with woe.
"Ah, who hath reft," quoth he, "my dearest pledge?"
Last came, and last did go,
The pilot of the Galilean Lake;
Two massy keys he bore of metals twain   110
(The golden opes, the iron shuts amain).
He shook his mitered locks, and stern bespake:
"How well could I have spared for thee, young swain,
Enow of such as for their bellies' sake
Creep, and intrude, and climb into the fold!   115
Of other care they little reckoning make,
Than how to scramble at the shearers' feast,
And shove away the worthy bidden guest.

Blind mouths, that scarce themselves know how to hold
A sheep hook, or have learned aught else the least   120
That to the faithful herdman's art belongs!
What recks it them? What need they? They are sped,
And when they list, their lean and flashy songs
Grate on their scrannel pipes of wretched straw.
The hungry sheep look up and are not fed,   125
But swollen with wind, and the rank mist they draw,
Rot inwardly, and foul contagion spread;
Besides what the grim wolf with privy paw
Daily devours apace, and nothing said;
But that two-handed engine at the door   130
Stands ready to smite once, and smite no more."
    Return, Alpheus, the dread voice is past,
That shrunk thy streams; return, Sicilian Muse,
And call the vales, and bid them hither cast
Their bells and flowerets of a thousand hues.   135
Ye valleys low, where the mild whispers use
Of shades and wanton winds and gushing brooks,
On whose fresh lap the swart star sparely looks,
Throw hither all your quaint enameled eyes,
That on the green turf suck the honeyed showers,   140
And purple all the ground with vernal flowers.
Bring the rathe primrose that forsaken dies,
The tufted crow-toe, and pale jessamine,
The white pink, and the pansy freaked with jet,
The glowing violet,   145
The musk-rose, and the well-attired woodbine,
With cowslips wan that hang the pensive head,
And every flower that sad embroidery wears.
Bid amaranthus all his beauty shed,
And daffodillies fill their cups with tears,   150
To strew the laureate hearse where Lycid lies.
For so to interpose a little ease,
Let our frail thoughts dally with false surmise.
Ay me! Whilst thee the shores and sounding seas
Wash far away, where'er thy bones are hurled,   155
Whether beyond the stormy Hebrides,
Where thou perhaps under the whelming tide
Visitest the bottom of the monstrous world;
Or whether thou to our moist vows denied,
Sleepest by the fable of Bellerus old,   160

Where the great vision of the guarded mount
Looks toward Namancos and Bayona's hold;
Look homeward, Angel, now, and melt with ruth.
And, O ye dolphins, waft the hapless youth.
   Weep no more, woeful shepherds, weep no more,   165
For Lycidas your sorrow is not dead,
Sunk though he be beneath the watery floor,
So sinks the day-star in the ocean bed,
And yet anon repairs his drooping head,
And tricks his beams, and with new-spangled ore   170
Flames in the forehead of the morning sky:
So Lycidas sunk low, but mounted high,
Through the dear might of him that walked the waves
Where, other groves and other streams along,
With nectar pure his oozy locks he laves,   175
And hears the unexpressive nuptial song,
In the blest kingdoms meek of joy and love.
There entertain him all the saints above
In solemn troops and sweet societies
That sing, and singing in their glory move,   180
And wipe the tears forever from his eyes.
Now, Lycidas, the shepherds weep no more;
Henceforth thou art the genius of the shore,
In thy large recompense, and shalt be good
To all that wander in that perilous flood.   185
   Thus sang the uncouth swain to the oaks and rills,
While the still morn went out with sandals gray;
He touched the tender stops of various quills,
With eager thought warbling his Doric lay.
And now the sun had stretched out all the hills,   190
And now was dropped into the western bay.
At last he rose, and twitched his mantle blue:
Tomorrow to fresh woods, and pastures new.

JOHN MILTON

Title: a lute-player and shepherd in ancient pastorals whose
name Milton gives to his dead fellow-student at Cambridge,
Edward King. **dear** (6): dire. **sisters** (15): Muses. **Damaetas**
(36): conventional pastoral name, perhaps designating someone
at Cambridge. **taint-worm** (46): parasitic worm. **white-thorn**
(48): hawthorn. **Mona** (54): Anglesey, and **Deva** (55): the
River Dee—both areas near where King was drowned. **Muse**
(59): Calliope, mother of Orpheus. **rout** (61): Thracian women

who tore Orpheus to pieces. The Hebrus River carried his head down to the sea, which washed it up on Lesbos. **use** (67): do. **Amaryllis** (68) and **Neaera** (69): any pretty girl. **Fury** (75): a Fate. **shears** (75): for cutting life's thread. **Phoebus** (77): The god of poetry interrupts the speaker. **Arethuse** (85) and **Mincius** (86): Water from these sources, a fountain and a river, inspired pastoral poets in antiquity. **strain** (87): Phoebus's interruption. **herald** (89): Triton. **Hippotades** (96): Aeolus. **Panopë** (99): a sea nymph. **eclipse** (101): an unlucky omen. **Camus** (103): spirit of the River Cam and symbol of Cambridge University. **flower** (106): the hyancinth, whose markings supposedly resemble a Greek word meaning "alas." **pilot** (109): St. Peter, originally a fisherman on the Sea of Galilee; traditionally first Bishop of Rome. **keys** (110): See Matthew xvi:19. **engine** (130): variously explained as the sword of divine justice, the English Parliament, the common people. **Alpheus** (132): Sicilian river-god, symbolizing pastoral poetry. **star** (138): the dog star. **fable of Bellerus** (160): Land's End, Cornwall; Latin *Bellerium,* after the giant Bellerus. **mount** (161): Mount St. Michael, Cornwall. **Namancos** and **Bayona** (162): on the Spanish coast. **Angel** (163): St. Michael. **daystar** (168) sun. **him** (173): Christ. **unexpressive nuptial song** (176): in expressible heavenly music, celebrating the soul's union with God. **Doric** (189): pastoral.

GROUP 25

Ulysses

It little profits that an idle king,
By this still hearth, among these barren crags,
Match'd with an aged wife, I mete and dole
Unequal laws unto a savage race,
That hoard, and sleep, and feed, and know not me.   5
I cannot rest from travel: I will drink
Life to the lees: all times I have enjoy'd
Greatly, have suffer'd greatly, both with those
That loved me, and alone; on shore, and when
Thro' scudding drifts the rainy Hyades   10
Vext the dim sea: I am become a name;
For always roaming with a hungry heart
Much have I seen and known; cities of men
And manners, climates, councils, governments,
Myself not least, but honour'd of them all;   15
And drunk delight of battle with my peers,
Far on the ringing plains of windy Troy.
I am a part of all that I have met;
Yet all experience is an arch wherethro'
Gleams that untravell'd world, whose margin fades   20
For ever and for ever when I move.
How dull it is to pause, to make an end,
To rust unburnish'd, not to shine in use!
As tho' to breathe were life. Life piled on life
Were all too little, and of one to me   25
Little remains: but every hour is saved
From that eternal silence, something more,
A bringer of new things; and vile it were
For some three suns to store and hoard myself,
And this gray spirit yearning in desire   30
To follow knowlege like a sinking star,
Beyond the utmost bound of human thought.

   This is my son, mine own Telemachus,
To whom I leave the sceptre and the isle—
Well-loved of me, discerning to fulfil   35

This labour, by slow prudence to make mild
A rugged people, and thro' soft degrees
Subdue them to the useful and the good.
Most blameless is he, centred in the sphere
Of common duties, decent not to fail   40
In offices of tenderness, and pay
Meet adoration to my household gods,
When I am gone. He works his work, I mine.

    There lies the port; the vessel puffs her sail:
There gloom the dark broad seas. My mariners,   45
Souls that have toil'd, and wrought, and thought with me—
That ever with a frolic welcome took
The thunder and the sunshine, and opposed
Free hearts, free foreheads—you and I are old;
Old age hath yet his honour and his toil;   50
Death closes all: but something ere the end,
Some work of noble note, may yet be done,
Not unbecoming men that strove with Gods.
The lights begin to twinkle from the rocks:
The long day wanes: the slow moon climbs: the deep   55
Moans round with many voices. Come, my friends,
'Tis not too late to seek a newer world.
Push off, and sitting well in order smite
The sounding furrows; for my purpose holds
To sail beyond the sunset, and the baths   60
Of all the western stars, until I die.
It may be that the gulfs will wash us down:
It may be we shall touch the Happy Isles,
And see the great Achilles, whom we knew.
Tho' much is taken, much abides; and tho'   65
We are not now that strength which in old days
Moved earth and heaven; that which we are, we are;
One equal temper of heroic hearts,
Made weak by time and fate, but strong in will
To strive, to seek, to find, and not to yield.   70

                          ALFRED, LORD TENNYSON

race (4): the people of Ithaca, to whom King Ulysses has returned after ten years' wandering. Happy Isles (63): Elysium.

Gerontion

Thou hast nor youth nor age
But as it were an after dinner sleep
Dreaming of both.

Here I am, an old man in a dry month,
Being read to by a boy, waiting for rain.
I was neither at the hot gates
Nor fought in the warm rain
Nor knee deep in the salt marsh, heaving a cutlass,   5
Bitten by flies, fought.
My house is a decayed house,
And the jew squats on the window sill, the owner,
Spawned in some estaminet of Antwerp,
Blistered in Brussels, patched and peeled in London.   10
The goat coughs at night in the field overhead;
Rocks, moss, stonecrop, iron, merds.
The woman keeps the kitchen, makes tea,
Sneezes at evening, poking the peevish gutter.
        I an old man,   15
A dull head among windy spaces.

Signs are taken for wonders. "We would see a sign!"
The word within a word, unable to speak a word,
Swaddled with darkness. In the juvescence of the year
Came Christ the tiger   20
In depraved May, dogwood and chestnut, flowering judas,
To be eaten, to be divided, to be drunk
Among whispers; by Mr. Silvero
With caressing hands, at Limoges
Who walked all night in the next room;   25

By Hakagawa, bowing among the Titians;
By Madame de Tornquist, in the dark room
Shifting the candles; Fräulein von Kulp
Who turned in the hall, one hand on the door.
        Vacant shuttles   30
Weave the wind. I have no ghosts,
An old man in a draughty house
Under a windy knob.

After such knowledge, what forgiveness? Think now
History has many cunning passages, contrived corridors   35
And issues, deceives with whispering ambitions,
Guides us by vanities. Think now
She gives when our attention is distracted
And what she gives, gives with such supple confusions
That the giving famishes the craving. Gives too late   40
What's not believed in, or if still believed,
In memory only, reconsidered passion. Gives too soon
Into weak hands, what's thought can be dispensed with
Till the refusal propagates a fear. Think
Neither fear nor courage saves us. Unnatural vices   45
Are fathered by our heroism. Virtues
Are forced upon us by our impudent crimes.
These tears are shaken from the wrath-bearing tree.

The tiger springs in the new year. Us he devours.
    Think at last   50
We have not reached conclusion, when I
Stiffen in a rented house. Think at last
I have not made this show purposelessly
And it is not by any concitation
Of the backward devils   55
I would meet you upon this honestly.
I that was near your heart was removed therefrom
To lose beauty in terror, terror in inquisition.
I have lost my passion: why should I need to keep it
Since what is kept must be adulterated?   60
I have lost my sight, smell, hearing, taste and touch:
How should I use them for your closer contact?
These with a thousand small deliberations
Protract the profit of their chilled delirium,
Excite the membrane, when the sense has cooled,   65
With pungent sauces, multiply variety
In a wilderness of mirrors. What will the spider do,
Suspend its operations, will the weevil
Delay? De Bailhache, Fresca, Mrs. Cammel, whirled
Beyond the circuit of the shuddering Bear   70
In fractured atoms. Gull against the wind, in the windy straits
Of Belle Isle, or running on the Horn,
White feathers in the snow, the Gulf claims,
And an old man driven by the Trades
To a sleepy corner.   75

Tenants of the house,
Thoughts of a dry brain in a dry season.

T. S. ELIOT

Title: "Little Old Man." Epigraph: Shakespeare, *Measure for Measure*, III.i. **hot gates** (3): Thermopylae, a battle in which the Greeks defeated the Persians, 480 B.C. **jew** (8): symbol of homelessness. **merds** (12): dung. **sign** (17): See Matthew xii:38–9. **word** (18): Compare Lancelot Andrewes (1555–1626), a sermon on Luke ii:11: "I add yet farther; what flesh? The flesh of an infant. What, Verbum infans, the Word of an infant? The Word, and not able to speak a word? How evil agreeth this!" **juvescence** (19): juvenescence. **eaten** (22): in Communion. **Silvero** (23), **Hakagawa** (26), **de Tornquist** (27), **von Kulp** (28): invented personages. **Titians** (26): paintings. **tree** (48): the cross (?), the tree of knowledge (?). **concitation** (54): concerted action. **inquisition** (58): introspection. **De Bailhache,** etc. (69): more invented personages. **Bear** (70): the Great Bear. **Horn** (72): Cape Horn. **Gulf** (73): of Mexico (?). **Trades** (74): trade winds.

INDEXES

INDEX OF TERMS

INDEX OF AUTHORS, FIRST LINES, AND TITLES

All titles are listed under their authors, but when a title is identical with the opening words of the first line, only the first line is given a separate entry. An asterisk following a title indicates an excerpt.